THE NEWS UNTOLD

The News Untold

COMMUNITY JOURNALISM AND THE FAILURE TO CONFRONT POVERTY IN APPALACHIA

MICHAEL CLAY CAREY

WEST VIRGINIA UNIVERSITY PRESS • MORGANTOWN 2017

Copyright 2017 West Virginia University Press
All rights reserved
First edition published 2017 by West Virginia University Press
Printed in the United States of America

ISBN:

CL: 978-1-943665-96-9
PB: 978-1-943665-97-6
EPUB: 978-1-943665-98-3
PDF: 978-1-943665-99-0

Library of Congress Cataloging-in-Publication Data is available from the
Library of Congress

Cover design by Than Saffel / WVU Press

For my family

Contents

Acknowledgments

This book would not have been possible were it not for the graciousness of the many men and women in Greenburg, Priorsville, and Deer Creek who participated in interviews, entertained my intrusions, and shared their experiences and ideas. I wish to thank the community journalists in those towns who were so candid and generous with their time. I am also deeply appreciative of local residents who welcomed me into their homes and businesses, introduced me to others in their communities, and spoke so vividly and passionately about the places they call home. I would also like to thank Peter Hille, Dee Davis, William Isom, Peggy Holman, and Margo Miller for their insights.

I am grateful to the outstanding faculty members at Ohio University's E. W. Scripps School of Journalism who provided guidance, questioned my assumptions, and otherwise helped give shape to the pages that follow. I owe Aimee Edmondson a special debt of gratitude for the time and energy she put into several early drafts of this project. I am thankful for the input of Bill Reader, Karen Riggs, and Steve Scanlan, all of whom have influenced this book, and me, in important ways. I am also grateful to Cynthia Anderson, Jatin Srivastava, Nerissa Young, and Michael Sweeney for their guidance and feedback, especially in the early stages of the project. John Hatcher, Linda Steiner, Jeanne Criswell, and Al Cross were of great help in the process of fine-tuning the manuscript, as was the outstanding staff at West Virginia University Press, especially Andrew Berzanskis, Valerie Ahwee, and Derek Krissoff.

Finally, and most importantly, my wife Lisa and my children Michael and Jace are especially deserving of thanks for their support. I could not ask for better companions on my journey through life.

CHAPTER 1

Poverty and Community Media in Rural Appalachia

Downtown Greenburg was once a hub for regional activity. A busy rail line brought people and money in and raw materials for production out. When profits from coal production, salt mining, and manufacturing fueled the local economy, the town was a destination for residents from other communities looking to spend cash and have a good time. It was, a Greenburg native in her eighties told me, a "Saturday-night town" where young people from nearby counties would congregate to drink and socialize.

Today, however, many of the storefronts along the town's main drag, a half-mile stretch lined with taverns and clothing shops in the 1950s and '60s, sit empty. People don't drive *into* Greenburg looking for a good time anymore. Now they drive *out* in search of better jobs and more comfortable lives. The folks who own businesses downtown work hard to create an aura of prosperity in Greenburg's tiny city center—they use grant money to patch sidewalks, and hang baskets of purple petunias from ornate metal lampposts in the spring. They recruit barbecue festivals in the summer and hold business open houses in the winter. Those efforts help make Greenburg a better place to live for some people. But they do not change the fact, many residents say, that the small Central Appalachian town is in decline. Walk past the historic courthouse, just down the road from the statue of a well-known Civil War general, and you will pass boutiques and cafés and payday loan shops and boarded-up storefronts. One spring day, I paused at a bench in front of a three-chair beauty salon a block from the courthouse. The door was propped open, and inside I could hear women talking about how high their electric bills were, and how difficult they would be to pay. Such struggles are not unusual for those who live in Greenburg, or in the sprawling, hilly countryside that surrounds it.

The office of the *Greenburg Star*, the town's small daily newspaper, is right around the corner from that small downtown salon. The *Star* is not unlike many other small daily and weekly community newspapers in Appalachia and across the United States. Readers will find on the pages of those publications announcements of upcoming festivals, local award winners, rosters of the recently arrested, family reunion notices, and other bits of information that may be pieced together to reflect a version of local life. That down-home news—the fish fries, the middle school graduation photos, the Rotary Club meeting announcements—affirms the links among members of those communities, just as it does in towns and neighborhoods all over the United States. It is, as journalism professor and former newspaper publisher Jock Lauterer wrote, news designed "to persuade people their lives are important."[1]

But there are some aspects of community life readers *will not* regularly see in the *Star*, or on the pages of many of its contemporaries. Stories about the struggles of the poor to find and keep jobs, to get adequate health care, or to manage the stigma of accepting local charity or government welfare are rare. So too are the voices of those who live on the economic fringes, getting by for now, but one late paycheck or expensive breakdown away from financial turmoil. When news about poverty does appear in the *Star*, and many other local newspapers, it usually appears in one of journalism's more sterilized forms: press releases about unemployment rates burdened by bureaucratic language or small announcements about clothing giveaways tucked away near the back of the publication.

In Greenburg—one of the most economically distressed communities in the United States—the omission is especially pronounced. The dissonance reflected by that omission is the core subject of this research. This book describes the relationship between newspapers and their audiences. It is a story of action and inaction that describes the ways a ubiquitous community institution can (or could) help or hurt individuals through the provision or withholding of information. It is also a story about intentional and unintentional acts of representation, and the consequences of those acts. The book's main characters are the community journalists and residents of three Appalachian communities, Greenburg, Priorsville, and Deer Creek (all three communities were assigned pseudonyms to protect the identities of research participants). The communities are among the most economically distressed in Appalachia, and the United States, and many of their residents wrestle daily with poverty, unemployment, and associated issues. Print and digital journalists in those communities face those issues too, but sometimes in a different way—they struggle with how to cover economic need in a manner that is constructive for the community, good for their own professional interests, and also sensitive to the needs of local individuals. Because of the magnitude of that struggle, community journalists in the three towns rarely broached the issue of poverty. This book describes the motivation for that omission, as well as its intended and unintended consequences.

By talking about poverty in certain ways—or by not talking about it at all—journalists in Greenburg and other towns create broad social narratives about what it means to be poor in rural Appalachia. Those narratives join others generated through other community institutions like strands in a rope to establish how poverty as an issue, and how the poor as individuals, should be viewed, talked about, and treated. In their 1977 essay on the sociology of Appalachia, David S. Walls and Dwight B. Billings pointed out that "being poor involves a social identity which is learned early and enforced by informal relationships in the local community."[2] Those social identities enable or restrict the accumulation of social capital. They alleviate or accelerate stratification and inequality. Social interactions that take place in schools, workplaces, and government offices establish and enforce these social identities. Those interactions also take place in and through local media, although comparatively little scholarly attention has been paid to the ways such mediated interactions are structured or interpreted by those who take part in them.

This book explains the structural aspects of social life and journalistic practice that limit local news coverage of poverty and related issues. It also examines limits on the poor's ability and/or willingness to engage in local discussions about poverty through local media and the ways their absence contributes to feelings of powerlessness and stratification in rural Appalachian communities. The three communities studied in this book are different in many ways. But in all three, local journalists' approaches to poverty combined with readers' interpretations to reinforce a long-standing, dominant view of Appalachian poverty as a cultural deficiency that exists because destructive values and behavior are passed from generation to generation, creating large groups of people who are ill-equipped to participate in broader social life.[3] Rural sociologist Cynthia Duncan described the "culture of poverty" understanding as the impression that

> individuals are trapped in poverty because poor families pass on bad values and norms of behavior that prevent successful participation in mainstream social institutions. Poor places are condemned to stagnation or deterioration because they do not have the human or natural resources to sustain economic activity, and social institutions are backward.[4]

This view, which is the dominant way poverty is understood by U.S. policy makers and, in many cases, local residents, can be an accurate way to describe the conditions associated with economic need. However, it often leads to victim blaming and social stratification that further separates the poor from opportunities to engage their communities economically or socially. This book shows how the absence of poor voices in news stories is interpreted in ways that reinforce an understanding that the poor remain poor, and are responsible for their own condition, because of their own cultural deficiencies.[5] Some individuals had knowledge, and sometimes a willingness, to add to the public discussion and understanding about what it means to deal with poverty in a rural community, but they felt limited in their ability to express that knowledge because of barriers that restricted (or seemed to restrict) their ability to interact with their local news outlets, contributing to a sense of powerlessness that has been pervasive in Appalachia for decades.[6] Those barriers are not intentionally set by journalists. The attitudes, philosophies, and routines they encounter daily establish a social habitus for journalists, but a habitus can be changed.[7] Journalists in rural Appalachia can alter limitations if they choose to engage the production and dissemination of news in different ways. This book concludes by suggesting some ways that might happen. The newspapers in this book are all located in rural Appalachian communities, but the ideas their stories illustrate are relevant to many rural communities both in and outside the region. In any community, there will be social outsiders. In some ways, the stories of the poorest residents in Greenburg, Priorsville, and Deer Creek are their stories as well.

History shows that local media can work to combat cultures of silence on social problems in Appalachia: Abolitionist newspapers took root in the mountains in the early 1800s, and in the 1960s and 1970s, regional publications such as *Mountain Life and*

Work (published by the activist Council of Southern Mountains) and *Hawkeye* (published by the Highway 979 Community Action Council) challenged the perceptions of (and control by) outsiders, including the companies that operated local mines.[8] More recently, local newspapers such as the weekly *Mountain Eagle* in Whitesburg, Kentucky, have actively campaigned against mountaintop removal mining and other exploitative enterprises.[9] However, research suggests that such efforts are the exception rather than the rule.

Scholars of poverty and inequality in Appalachia have occasionally criticized local newspapers in the region for doing too little to speak up for their readers or to encourage unity and action among community members. In *Power and Powerlessness: Quiescence and Rebellion in an Appalachian Valley*, John Gaventa wrote that local newspapers in the region do little "to encourage people to think about the important issues they face, nor about themselves as actors upon them. . . . The power of the media rests just as much in what is unwritten and unsaid as in what is."[10] Rural sociologist Cynthia Duncan likewise took the local media in Appalachia to task for reinforcing what Gaventa called a "culture of silence"[11]: "The current paper [in the Appalachian community Duncan visited] is in no danger of violating the norms of silence—it consists mostly of advertisements and coverage of some high school sports events," Duncan wrote in *Worlds Apart: Why Poverty Persists in Rural America*.[12] Reflections such as these are fair critiques of many local newspapers in Appalachia and elsewhere. But they are also flyover views of institutions that hold—or may hold—great social influence. Existing scholarship tells us little about why those who manage such news outlets act as they do, and how they might reorient themselves to better address long-standing social problems. This book provides more insight into the routines, pressures, and philosophies that drive their decisions. It is not, however, my intent merely to critique a set of local newspapers. By understanding how they work and recognizing how their work influences those in the communities they serve, we can identify opportunities for news outlets to push for substantive local change.

As it addresses *local* media representations of poverty, this book also considers broader parallels to the ways Appalachia as a *region* is portrayed in news and popular media. The integration of new voices and new perspectives on poverty and other social issues opens the door to a broader, more inclusive depiction of Appalachia. Almost all the individuals who participated in this study said they saw regional and national news reports on Appalachia and popular culture representations of the region as demeaning. Some were upset by those images, but others were not, in large part because they did not feel those negative images represented them personally. They said they had the power to ignore those images and, as a result, saw no need to challenge them. A view of stereotyping as an individual experience rather than a communal one is problematic in the same way that understanding poverty as an individual rather than a social issue is problematic. If local news organizations in Appalachia rededicate themselves to serve as platforms for the lived experiences of *all* residents, including the poor, they also make possible a broader retelling of Appalachia.

News outlets are most effective when they approach their work as a *concerned friend* of the community—what former newspaper publisher Gil Thelen called a "committed observer," candid and interdependent with the needs of the individuals in the communities they serve.[13] As concerned friends of their communities, local media outlets must provide flexible, open forums for the frank discussion of social problems in a community. Local newspapers can contribute to a broader consciousness of the ways the fates of all members of a community—rich or poor—are linked. By addressing the ways their own communities discuss poverty, they may help their readers reconceptualize community need in a way that challenges the traditional understandings of poverty that dominate cultural stereotypes of Appalachia. In the process, local news organizations create an opportunity to address the way poverty is discussed at the regional level, and to contribute to a strong external narrative about Appalachia that may serve as a counter to the often demeaning dominant narrative of Appalachia as a land of Others, separated economically and culturally from civilized America.

Media and the Creation of Culture in Appalachia

To understand those opportunities, it is important to consider local media as not only a means to stay informed, but also as tools individuals use to place others, and themselves, in a community. The inclusion and exclusion of information and sources in narratives about local life and the whitewashing of community problems send signals about what (or who) a community values and what (or who) it does not. Scholars who study social production and reproduction through media have traversed the ground associated with those processes in many different ways, including but not limited to audience studies, gatekeeping research that explain the process by which "news" is identified and produced, and critical analyses of media practices and representations. Those works add value, but they often do so as snapshots of particular stages in the media production process. This book takes a less common approach, offering a holistic view of the full social circuit of media texts, from inception to dissemination to interpretation. In the process, the stories included here help us better understand how a community institution shapes, and is shaped, by the social world around it. Journalists' views of poverty, the poor, and their communities influence the ways they write about social need, but journalists do not operate in social vacuums. Histories, relationships, and cultural views influence the creation, interpretation, and internalization of media messages. In this messy process, ideas are produced and reified not always as broad, explicit judgments of right and wrong, but rather as subtle but no less powerful conceptions of "us" and "them" that influence local attitudes.

The sets of ideas and attitudes broadly referred to as *cultures* are not fixed identities. They are rather in a constant state of flux, being made, maintained, and remade. Media and other forms of communication are key components of that making and remaking in that they provide a forum for the "reading of prevailing behavior" that often determines how individuals in a community will act.[14] The narratives created by media and other forms of local and national storytelling contribute in important ways to the "stream of sociocultural knowledge" that help individuals decide how to act and how to best place themselves and others in a common communal body.[15] Certainly, the development of commonality through patterned interactions and shared social experiences (including experiences mediated by newspapers and other communication outlets) help individuals situate themselves in communities and develop local cultures. Cultural studies scholar Stuart Hall argued that cultural identity also is formed by focusing on and describing what a group is *not*. In the process of that construction, power is wielded through discourse that turns outsiders into "Others" and calls members of the group to adopt certain positions based on cultural understandings.[16] Individuals do have the ability to resist that calling, however, because of the agency they have to construct self-identity. The shaping of media messages that set out dominant understandings of what a community *is* and *is not*, the subsequent interpretations of those messages, and the way those interpretations are integrated into individual and group identity all are influenced by their own sets of fluid social relations.[17] Professional ideologies, tools of production, and journalistic routines are a few of the many factors that weigh on the journalist as she or he translates some aspect of daily life into a "communicative event" we might recognize as news.[18] As a news message makes its way through those social relations, Hall argued, they encode upon that message dominant social codes and structures of meaning that lead to understandings we might broadly define as *common sense*: what is right, what is wrong, and what should be valued. The process of encoding is clearly vital to understanding how "common sense" is created via the news, but dominant media codes in and of themselves wield no social power. It is only when media messages are decoded by audiences that they may be "put to a 'use'" in the ongoing maintenance of culture.[19]

But how much agency do the recipients of media messages *actually have* to make sense of media messages in their own way, and to use that sensemaking process to shape identity? Cultural scholars offer a range of theoretical answers to that question. French theorist Pierre Bourdieu saw the power to shape social/cultural identity as being diffuse and hidden in the daily, often taken-for-granted practices of individuals.[20] Bourdieu argued that cultural transmissions such as media messages largely reinforced the values of dominant classes: Cultural consumption, he wrote, is "predisposed, consciously and deliberately or not, to fulfil a social function of legitimating social differences."[21] Stuart Hall also recognized the power of communication to create and reinforce a dominant social order, but at the same time he acknowledged that individuals who were called to play certain social roles have some say in whether they accept those calls and play the parts.[22] Hall argued that media consumers had the ability to decode messages in an *oppositional* way, rejecting and struggling against inherent ideas of normalcy coded into messages.[23] Dominant cultural notions about the people who rely on welfare from the government, for example, need not define individuals who find themselves in need of that aid. Through the construction of identity, Hall argued, individuals could voice counternarratives that oppose dominant understandings about what it means to be Othered based on race, class, the location of one's home, or other factors.

Bourdieu's British contemporary, sociologist Anthony Giddens, saw more room for individuals to alter the routines that shape their understandings of social life. Giddens's understanding of structure and agency suggests that the reproduction of media discourses by individuals (journalists, other online content producers, and those who consume news) allows those narratives to exist as structures.[24] Those structures in turn enable and restrict individual agency, and through agency, the structures may be modified. Giddens argued that all people were capable of understanding the relationship between their actions and the unintended social consequences of those actions (vis-à-vis the creation of structures that dictate social norms). That ability to understand in turn makes possible significant changes to the social systems we might collectively consider culture.[25] Giddens's understanding of the relationship between structure and agency is of particular importance when one considers the roles journalists and journalistic routines play in the construction of normative ideas of what it means to be poor in a rural community. Journalists and their readers alike possess what sociologist Chris Shilling called "the power to act differently."[26] That power manifests itself specifically in the ability to accept, reject, or alter discursive expressions of what one "is" or "should be." If we are to believe in the power to act differently, we need not deny the fact that much of our daily social lives consists of routine, seemingly invisible actions that reinforce social positions.[27] Hall recognized that it was possible to bring disenfranchised social movements, "through a developing practice of struggle, into an articulation with those forms of politics and ideology which allow them to become historically effective as collective social agents."[28] For that to occur, we must recognize, as Giddens did, that opportunities to diverge from those routines will present themselves, and that individuals are capable of divergence in those moments. This book outlines some ways in which divergence could lead to more robust public discussions about matters related to poverty in rural Appalachian communities.

Engagement through the expression of oppositional media

readings that challenge dominant narratives offer an opportunity for individuals to develop their ability to identify codes that suggest what is "normal," and to challenge the validity of those codes. Such interactions among individuals have the potential to be fruitful in that they allow group members to clearly define what they are, as well as (and just as importantly) what they *are not*. The resulting counternarratives might not in and of themselves alter dominant narratives, but they have the potential to help individuals sustain social identity and challenge dominant narratives more effectively. Unfortunately, as Wheatley and Kellner-Robers noted, questions of "Who are we?" and "What matters?" that challenge dominant social understandings are too often discussed in closed circles of family and friends rather than at the institutional or community level.[29] Literature on economic and social development suggests that, when people who are normally on the outside of conversations about development and community growth are allowed to participate in those discussions in a meaningful way, they develop efficacy and new attitudes about their relationship to community powers. Maxine Waller, a resident of Ivanhoe, Virginia, who became involved in efforts to recruit industry to that town in 1986, recalled her experience this way:

> I used to feel so inferior to these people [economic development professionals]; they had their little suits and they go to the club for lunch, but now I don't feel inferior to them. I feel superior to them. Theirs is an educated ignorance. They are educated to the point that they are ignorant. I can't feel equal to them. I can't be equal to them because I have an open mind. People in Ivanhoe are receptive to new ideas, new thoughts. But these people are not. Is it because they are not cold and hungry? Is it because they have plenty to eat and plenty of money? Is it because we don't have those things, is that why we are grasping and doing so much and

being so receptive to everything and they are not? Because they are comfortable and we are uncomfortable?

They don't have to listen to us because they are not dependent on us and we are dependent on them—or they thought we were. But somewhere along the line, someday they are going to wake up and they are going to find out that this bunch of people here, this core bunch of people in Ivanhoe, are going to be independent.[30]

Media can be used to help level those social playing fields. The founders of the Appalachian Media Institute (AMI) use media to do just that; by teaching documentary film-making skills to young people in Central Appalachia, the institute helps residents address stereotypes and misunderstandings and develop strong ties in their communities. Brittany, one young person who took part in AMI, described a social transformation in an interview with program staff:

First of all, I learned that I am a capable person because I created something [a video documentary] and it's something that I'm proud of and it's something that other people see. I developed an identity as an Appalachian. Before I knew where I was from, but I didn't have any feelings of pride. It wasn't an important part of my identity. It [the video production process] gave me something to identify with and be passionate about. It gave me something to want to fight for and to want to make change for.[31]

Brittany's new Appalachian identity is especially significant given the challenges people in the region face today. Appalachia's history is one of economic trial, environmental degradation, and social Otherness that has lingered for more than 200 years. From a popular culture perspective, Appalachia is a region that, to paraphrase mass communication scholar Walter Lippmann, is understood before it is seen,[32] and that understanding of Appalachia as a place apart has tangible social consequences. The region's position in the national discourse was cemented by the work of journalists who traveled to Appalachia to write local color pieces during the decades following the U.S. Civil War, a period when advances in the publishing industry allowed magazines to become America's first true mass media.[33] Journalists who traveled to Appalachia in search of the next big article easily found compelling story lines in the hills of West Virginia, eastern Kentucky, Tennessee, and elsewhere, historian Ronald Eller wrote:

> Those writers who disliked modernity saw in the region a remnant of frontier life, the reflection of a simpler, less complicated time that ought to be preserved and protected. Those who found advancement in the growth of material production, consumption, and technology decried what they considered the isolation and backwardness of the place and sought to uplift the mountain people through education and industrialization.[34]

Munsey's, Cosmopolitan, and other magazines popular at the dawn of the twentieth century regaled readers with tales of bloody mountain feuds that shattered the peaceful Kentucky forests and rogue whiskey distillers who roamed the hills of north Georgia.[35] After Lyndon Johnson focused the nation's attention on Appalachian poverty in 1964, many magazine and newspaper reporters again trekked to the region in search of images that would reflect the bleakness of the human condition there. They found what they were looking for, as journalists tend to do[36]: "Ignoring the mountain middle class and the mountain rich, they did indeed find sordidness and deprivation. Mountain people—*all* mountain people—were represented as uneducated, poor, and unable to help themselves."[37] In her analysis of national media coverage of Appalachia in the 1970s, Sally Ward Maggard found that the prevailing stereotypes led to victim blaming and a lack of information necessary for "a realistic and informed assessment of persistent problems in Appalachia."[38] The joviality with which Americans generally and the press specifically characterize white trash, hillbillies, and rednecks in the mountains has receded little since then.[39] In January 2014, for example, writer Kevin D. Williamson of the conservative *National Review* drew on as many regional stereotypes as possible in this breathless description of one Appalachian Kentucky community in an article headlined "The White Ghetto":

> Thinking about the future here and its bleak prospects is not much fun at all, so instead of too much black-minded introspection you have the pills and the dope, the morning beers, the endless scratch-off lotto cards, healing meetings up on the hill, the federally funded ritual of trading cases of food-stamp Pepsi for packs of Kentucky's Best cigarettes and good old hard currency, tall piles of gas-station nachos, the occasional blast of meth, Narcotics Anonymous meetings, petty crime, the draw, the recreational making and surgical unmaking of teenaged mothers, and death: Life expectancies are short—the typical man here dies well over a decade earlier than does a man in Fairfax County, Va.—and they are getting shorter, women's life expectancy having declined by nearly 1.1 percent from 1987 to 2007. If people here weren't 98.5 percent white, we'd call it a reservation.[40]

A stereotype is, Lippmann argued, the "fortress of our tradition, and behind its defenses we can continue to feel ourselves safe in the position we occupy."[41] Power permeates that statement—the stereotype is a means by which society establishes normalcy and identifies those who dwell outside of it.[42] Richard Dyer argued that cultural representations determine in large part how social groups are treated, "that poverty, harassment, self-hate and discrimination (in housing, jobs, educational opportunity and so on) are shored up and instituted by representation."[43] Stereotypical depictions, Dyer argued, reinforce images of the natural rightness of certain groups and the "wanting, hence inadequate, inferior, sick or grotesque" images of others.[44] Journalists rely on stereotypes as much as anyone, despite being trained to avoid such overgeneralizations.[45] Herbert Gans suggested in his study of news habits that journalists are often unaware that the use of those stereotypes leads to the spread of certain ideologies.[46] In Appalachia, those representations, even if unintentional, "seem designed to produce confusion, self-doubt, passivity, frustration, [and] anger" among those being represented.[47] At the same time, writer Rebecca R. Scott argued, they illustrate an Otherness so profound that it cannot be the result of exploitation—"mountain culture," the stereotypes suggest, is to blame for Appalachia's problems. Scott noted that "Appalachian difference is naturalized in both popular culture and in academia; hence, the processes of Appalachian marginalization are taken for granted and invisible."[48]

From documentaries such as CBS's *Christmas in Appalachia* and 2009's *The Wild and Wonderful Whites of West Virginia* to popular television shows such as *The Beverly Hillbillies* and *The Andy Griffith Show* and, more recently, *Justified* and *Moonshiners*, media on the region are entrenched in the notion of the poor, simple mountaineer. In the twentieth century, Walter Precourt argued, "the mass media emphasized the very worst economic conditions and, at the same time, it portrayed a picture of the Appalachian as culturally backward, if not actually depraved."[49] The resulting images of the region were "so stereotypically described as 'hillbilly-land' that most Americans, including journalists, are hooked on cartoon images portraying debilitating distinctiveness."[50] In most cases, historian Ronald Lewis argued, such images of the region have not appeared by chance: "'Appalachia' was a willful creation and not merely the product of literary imagination."[51] Katherine Ledford argued that the idea of Appalachians as "adversarial, unnatural, and out of control" became popular at the same time the mountains were commoditized—when "settlers were a potential barrier between the explorers and exploitation of natural resources."[52] As such, the stereotype normalized the wealth experienced by the broader American middle class and justified the exploitation of the region.

The Othering of a region and its people has tangible social consequences, rural sociologist Ann R. Tickamyer wrote: "Regional identities and cultures, such as Southern or Appalachian, often the center of heated academic debate over their meaning and existence . . . are believed to be real and are therefore real in their consequences—consequences that include structures of inequality."[53] Stereotypes ascribed to poor people generally and the rural poor specifically are key components in the development of social class, which enables—and also (if not more often) restricts—access to physical resources and social capital. The "manipulations of symbols"[54] that label individuals in a community as "troublemakers" or "ne'er-do-wells" can suffocate individuals' wills to take part in a discursive process to improve problems in their communities and discourage those who need help from seeking it.[55] Stereotyping of the rural poor makes it even more difficult for them to find work in competitive job markets, resulting in increased competition for limited resources and further social isolation.[56] Precourt argued the negative effects of the poverty label are not limited to individuals: "When a person becomes identified with the label [poverty] the label becomes a stigma having far-reaching emotional, psychological, and social consequences. When the poverty label is attached indiscriminately to an entire region the influence on inhabitants of the region is similar."[57] Ronald Eller suggested that the prevailing focus on Appalachia as a land of welfare cheats, moonshiners, miners, and other "types" distances society "from the political and economic realities of the region, including our own injustices toward those stereotyped." In Appalachia, he wrote, "such images allow the rest of America to keep the region at arm's length, rather than to confront the systemic problems of a dependent economy, environmental decay, and institutional weakness that challenge mountain communities today."[58] The discursive power of those labels makes it important to understand the shaping and manipulation of "social myths, language, and symbols,"[59] to recognize the ways those myths and symbols are legitimated and spread, and ultimately to acknowledge the ways in which they contribute to poverty as a *social* (not merely *financial*) phenomenon.

Academic work on news coverage of poverty as a broader issue has come to similar conclusions, suggesting media have the power to shape public perceptions of welfare policy and poor people, and that the perceptions they create are often negative.[60] Sociologist Gregory Mantsios observed that the poor are largely absent from media coverage. When they do appear, media consumers get a variety of contradictory but overwhelmingly negative perspectives of the poor as faceless entities or community eyesores, as people who are "down on their luck" due to unfortunate circumstances or indigents who are to blame for their own condition.[61] Mantsios's frames were common in Diana Kendall's analysis of the *New York Times*' coverage of poverty; some poor people—particularly children, the elderly, and the ill—received sympathetic media treatment, but even then media messages may "cast them in a negative light without necessarily intending to do so and convey the idea that many poor people are responsible for their own condition."[62]

Media practitioners often contribute to the national discourse on poverty without recognizing the stereotypes they disseminate. Sociologist Patrick Champagne argued that media workers may feel they have been useful when they bring issues of poverty and disenfranchisement "into the light," so to speak, but "such optimism seems at the very least excessive since it does not take into account the symbolic effects which are particularly powerful when exercised over populations that are culturally deprived."[63] Hancock observed that negative imagery of the "welfare queen" was present in media coverage of welfare policy options in 1995 and 1996, and that the trope, "either by intent or neglect, played a role in linking the social construction of the welfare population" that amplified negative attitudes toward poor people generally.[64] Although he questioned whether it was reasonable to ever expect a "socially accurate" portrayal of individuals in poverty, Gilens concluded that media coverage of poverty concentrated on black urban ghettoes, concentrations of poverty "that represent the worst failures of our economic, educational, and social welfare systems."[65] The representations, he argued, distort the nature of American poverty, help advance the stereotype that black men are lazy, and contribute greatly to negative public attitudes and misconceptions about the poor and about welfare policy.

Some Appalachian residents interviewed for this book had experienced the repercussions of those representations firsthand. They told stories about being questioned about incest on dates, teased by strangers at bars, and insulted by classmates at universities. The men and women who took part in this study largely agreed that Appalachia and the broader notion of hillbilly culture carried a lot of negative cultural baggage. There was much more disagreement on whether that baggage did tangible harm to residents or communities in the region. Some expressed great offense; others concluded that Appalachian stereotypes were inconsequential. Either way, residents reported that they felt there was little they could do to push back against negative representations of their communities or the region. Many dismissed the stereotypes as *just the way things are*, an expression of powerlessness also used to explain the inability to combat negative portrayals of the poor in their local news outlets.

Understanding Community and Community Media

Broad critiques of media practices, such as those levied in the previous section, should come with an important caveat: There is no singular, all-encompassing "media." There are, rather, different kinds of media that produce different products and narratives for different reasons and with different impacts. While all media may contribute in some way to the creation of shared beliefs integrated into national and regional culture and individual identity, it is wrong to equate the motives and outcomes of a large media organization such as the *New York Times* or CNN with the small community newspapers and hyperlocal web sites observed in this book. Those weekly newspapers and smaller web sites are different from their larger national counterparts in terms of nearness to their audiences, business structures, and economic conditions of their production,[66] and research has shown that audiences expect different things from them.[67] Often, media researchers recognize "community media" as small news outlets (typically newspapers, but also Internet sites, radio, and television programming) designed for people who live in specific geographic areas[68] or people who share common values, experiences, interests, or backgrounds.[69] The most basic definition of community journalism—media produced for a specific subgroup of people who share common traits (perhaps including, but not limited to, geography)—may not fully express the complex and at times profound influence media outlets can have on social groups. Writing about the *New York Times* specifically, and newspapers in general, sociologists Peter Berger and Thomas Luckmann suggested media reinforce a subjective reality and reaffirm "the widest co-ordinates of the individual's reality," assuring the consumer that he or she "is, indeed, in the most real world possible."[70] Community journalists make those wide coordinates narrower, describing, delineating, and defining individuals' places among others like them.[71]

The social roles of media complicate the simple definition of community journalism as a local news organization for local people. Rather than saying a news outlet *is* or *is not* an example of community journalism based on publication frequency or size, it may be more productive to consider community journalism as a collection of practices in which news outlets may choose to engage.[72] Those practices might include making people aware of spaces and resources that community members share, the creation of networks and connections among readers, and the reinforcement of small-group values, in addition to the journalistic role of informing the public.[73] If journalists leave out a segment of their community or downplay that segment's concerns, either intentionally or unintentionally, then those journalists' abilities to help contribute to a strong sense of togetherness is diminished.[74] When community journalism is viewed through those lenses, it becomes apparent that some local newspapers and niche publications practice it more heartily than others.

But does that desire to build community stand at odds with the clichéd journalistic urge to "comfort the afflicted and afflict the comfortable"? How can media promote conflict and debate on one hand and compromise and conciliation on the other? After all, it is this perceived failure for which Appalachian news media, and community news publications more generally, are most commonly criticized. The answers to those apparent contradictions, media scholar James Curran wrote, stems from the important fact that there is no singular "media": "There should be a division of labor in which different sectors of the media have different roles, practice different forms of journalism, and make different contributions to the functioning of society."[75] Local newspapers in small towns are sometimes faulted for a lack of tenacity and stereotyped as unsophisticated, ineffective publications reduced to "reporting of social items and local news already known by everyone."[76] Such criticism sorely underestimates the power the community press can have to facilitate change in a community.[77] Just as importantly, it typecasts the newspaper in a way that undermines its position in social life. Newspapers and other media can be critical agents in what James W. Carey called the "projection of community ideals."[78] Carey refers here to the information that helps an individual carve out a personal identity and situate herself or himself in a broader collective. Media serve as a vessel for the communicative ritual of sharing ideas and ideals, Carey argued, making possible the "maintenance of society in time."[79] Community building, however, often seems at odds with journalism that questions the status quo and challenges the powerful. Mike Buffington, an editor and co-owner of several local newspapers in Georgia, told a 2015 gathering of the International Society of Weekly Newspaper Editors that it was their job to question the powerful and to advocate for change "forcefully and with clarity." "An aggressive and passionate approach to news doesn't endear us to many people in our small towns. I guess if we wanted to be loved, we would have become nurses or nuns," Buffington said. He later added, "If we're outspoken and fair in equal measure, many will come to understand that we are just doing our job with a passion for the truth."[80]

It is important to note, however, that the roles of community watchdog and community builder are not mutually exclusive. In that same speech, Buffington observed that editors and publishers like himself "don't publish 52 individual newspapers a year. Rather, we are weaving an ongoing narrative about life in our communities—a narrative that is a circle of triumph and tragedy, of folly and fame, of love and loss." Local newspapers serve the important function of cataloging and making visible the daily routine interactions that help us find security in the familiar and navigate difficult moments.[81] In the process, they help facilitate the "social opportunities" that Nobel Prize–winning economist Amartya Sen found so crucial to the pursuit of freedom from poverty. In his book *Development as Freedom*, Sen suggested it was the role of systems of education, health care, and media to "influence the individual's substantive freedom to live better" by facilitating participation in economic, political, and social activities and helping individuals connect with one another.[82] This book strives to examine the ways media work in three Appalachian communities to enable such participation and connection, who benefits from that work, and how those benefits might be more evenly distributed.

A Note About Methodology

The local media ecosystems in three rural Appalachian communities are studied in this book. Each case focuses on a community in central and north-central Appalachian regions. Over six months in 2013 and 2014, I immersed myself in each community's local media, reading newspapers, web sites, and social media for common themes. The bulk of the findings discussed in the chapters that follow were the result of my own personal observations over six months of fieldwork, unstructured interviews with fifty-one local residents, and dozens more informal exchanges that took place in diners, shops, offices, parks, and homes in each community I studied. A more detailed description of the research methodology used may be found in Appendix A.

Interviews conducted for this study attempted to adhere to Pierre Bourdieu's model of the interview as a "spiritual exercise" of "intellectual love."[83] Bourdieu encouraged an open dialogue in which interviewees would feel empowered enough to dominate the discussion. The creation of such an environment reduces the objectification of participants in the research project, instead offering them what can be viewed as a therapeutic opportunity to take their private sphere experiences into the public realm. Such an approach requires the interviewer to engage in *true conversation* with the interviewee and, in the course of that conversation, to give of oneself. Bourdieu likened the interviewer to a midwife who helps the interviewee "deliver up their truth or, rather, to be delivered of it."[84] The purpose of this study is not to "assign blame" for socioeconomic conditions in any particular community or to provide "if/then" typologies. Rather, the aim is to provide insights into the ways local media in three different communities facilitate dialogue, and the barriers that keep community media from engaging in such a dialogue on contentious social issues such as poverty.

In order to protect the privacy of research participants, pseudonyms have been assigned to the communities and individuals discussed in this book, including third parties who were discussed during interviews or featured in news stories. The extension of anonymity to protect the identities of research participants has a long history in social science.[85] It is vital in studies such as this, in which individuals who often find themselves at a social disadvantage are asked to critique the work of newspaper workers who are often among the social elite in small towns. In order to protect the identities of study participants *and* provide the level of detail that is a strength of this study, it was also necessary to use pseudonyms for the communities themselves, as well as important institutions within those communities (including local newspapers and online news organizations). Had actual community names been used in the study, it would have been necessary to limit details about individual participants to sufficiently obscure their identities. For example, if I were to reveal the actual names of the communities described in this book, it would be quite easy for the journalists interviewed for this study to identify regular newspaper sources who were critical of their professional practices. Residents voiced varying levels of concern about the social repercussions of speaking to me: Some talked openly, while others were guarded or uninterested in participating in formal interviews. A few residents specifically said they feared social and/or economic repercussions if their identities were compromised. In two cases, residents discussed things during interviews and later asked me not to include those statements in this study, even though they knew they would be reported using pseudonyms. I complied with those requests.[86]

The histories, media markets, and dominant local perspectives on poverty in each community are described in detail in Chapter 2. Chapter 3 describes the content of local newspapers and news web sites, which provided precious few perspectives on local poverty. Stories that did address the issue were framed in ways that did little to empower poor residents, and they at times reinforced the idea of poverty as a cultural norm, relieving the non-poor of any social responsibility for poverty. Chapter 4 shows how those media messages came to be. Through interviews with community journalists, it examines the factors that influence decisions about how poverty will (or will not) be presented to local news consumers. Journalists generally (but not always) saw economic need around them, but they were often quite reluctant to write about that need. External influences contributed to that reluctance in some cases. But more often, internal pressures and understandings of journalistic conventions were responsible for the relative silence on poverty.

Chapter 5 deals with the ways local news about poverty—and, in many cases, the absence of such news—was interpreted by local residents. Coverage patterns were understood to mean different things by different people, but several important themes emerged. Those themes often culminated with the idea that community members, and especially the poor, had little ability to influence dialogue on poverty or other social issues. Feelings of conflict and powerlessness were also evident when residents talked about demeaning media messages about Appalachia. Although most of the people interviewed acknowledged negative stereotypes about their own communities and Appalachia as a whole, they were divided about whether those stereotypes were worth fighting, or whether such an effort could ever be successful.

The book closes with an argument for the importance of local news in rural communities. The absence of poor voices and poverty news in local coverage sends a series of messages to news consumers that reinforce the notion that poverty is a cultural norm in these rural Appalachian communities. The chapter argues for the importance of print and digital community journalism in the region and contends that community journalists should practice their craft more reflexively. The book concludes with the idea that, as a concerned friend of the community, a news outlet can present poverty and related issues in a way that builds up individuals and the community as a whole.

The three towns described in this study—Greenburg, Priorsville, and Deer Creek—can perhaps be thought of as characters themselves. They have seen booms and busts, successes and heartaches. They have histories, economies, and social structures that are similar to those of many other rural Appalachian communities. They have watched outside companies come in search of coal, timber, oil, and natural gas, and they have seen those companies leave when natural resources dried up. They have seen industries come and go and watched hospitals open and close. But they are home to many optimists—people with energy and drive to make their homes better for everyone. They have their own social and economic idiosyncrasies that make them at the same time difficult and special places. In describing those similarities and differences, the pages that follow can help us see the challenges faced in these three communities—and in many more like them—and the opportunities that are at the same time present.

CHAPTER 2

Greenburg, Priorsville, and Deer Creek: Community Case Studies

The three communities under study in this book share some common traits, but they also are different in important ways. This chapter describes those similarities and differences. The histories of the communities, analyses of their media markets, and descriptions of local attitudes toward poverty all shed important light on the roles local media play in discussions on poverty there. To maintain the anonymity of research participants, the names of individuals, communities, newspapers, web sites, and media companies discussed in this study have been replaced with pseudonyms. The historical information in this chapter was compiled through research at local libraries, museums, and community historical societies in each of the three communities. Citations have been withheld to maintain the anonymity of communities, media companies, and individual study participants.

Greenburg

It is likely that the area now known as Greenburg was sparsely populated by early Indians—there is little evidence of widespread Native American settlement, aside from burial mounds likely built by the Hopewell or Adena cultures. While few Native Americans lived in the area, a number of tribes used it for hunting grounds before the Iroquois Confederacy drove them out in the 1650s, claiming the land for themselves. The first lasting European settlement was established in the late 1770s on land inhabited by the Delaware Indians. The Delawares took issue with the fact that white settlers were squatting on their land and brought their concerns to the Continental Congress, which in 1779 ordered that the settlers leave the land and not be allowed to return. However, the federal government found it impossible to enforce the decree given the demands of the Revolutionary War, and the Delaware—who were allied with the government—did not move to evict the white settlers, so they stayed put. In the 1780s a territorial government was established, and the promise of cheap land brought many new settlers to the region. Greenburg's proximity to natural resources and river transportation made it an ideal place to settle.

Agriculture was an important economic force in the developing towns in Green County. On their farms, residents raised cows, sheep, and chickens, and they grew corn, potatoes, sorghum, and other crops. Early settlers were sustenance farmers, but as state taxes made farm production more expensive, they began growing more than they needed and shipped the surplus for sale in New Orleans or St. Louis. However, the extraction of coal and salt quickly came to dominate the local economy and fuel Greenburg's growth. The first coal mine in the region opened in 1805. Thirty years later, the city was home to some of the largest mines in its state, many of them owned by a major coal company headquartered on the East Coast. Coal production in the community peaked between 1860 and 1880, although production remained strong through World War I. Large salt deposits near Greenburg also made the town a major supplier of that resource.

The end of World War I marked the beginning of a major economic contraction in Greenburg. In the 1920s, the Pittsburg Coal Company and other coal operators pooled millions of dollars to break the United Mine Workers of America in the region. Greenburg's mines were among their first targets. One local account, published by the Green County Historical Society, noted: "They broke the union alright, but at a frightful loss of property and lives. There were five big coal tipples burned, besides other acts of sabotage. There was fighting between pickets and non-union miners and two men were shot and killed before it ended." Coal continued to be an important economic force into the 1960s, when two large mines were established in Green County. Large numbers of people were expected to move to Greenburg to work in those mines, but employment numbers failed to reach anticipated marks, and many of those who did work in the mines were locals, not new residents. Greenburg's population declined sharply in the years following World War II. Coal mines in the area were hotbeds of labor strife and conflict, and new salt deposits discovered in other areas drained off that business. A busy railroad line had brought jobs and money to the city, but local train service was discontinued in the early 1950s, leading to a large loss of jobs and a 50 percent drop in population.

In 2012, the estimated population of Green County was roughly 23,000; about 2,000 of those people lived in Greenburg. Eighty-three percent of county residents were high school graduates in 2012 (below the state average), and roughly 11 percent had at least a bachelor's degree (less than half the state average). The poverty rate reported at the time of this study was 21.6 percent, nearly 50 percent higher than the state average, and more than 40 percent of Greenburg families with children under the age of five lived below the federal poverty line. Median home values and per capita income were also significantly lower than the state average. The fields of public education, health care, and social assistance produced 27 percent of the jobs in Green County in 2012, with the fields of retail, construction, and manufacturing also accounting for significant portions of the county's jobs. Once-common mining jobs were rare in 2012—agriculture, forestry, fishing and hunting, and mining work made up less than 3 percent of the county's jobs. There is still coal in the area's mines, some local residents insisted, and a few suggested that they believed mining might make a comeback in the area one day.

The main road through Greenburg, Oak Avenue, is a two-lane street bordered on one side by a river and on the other by storefronts and small lots that house bars and restaurants, shops, banks, a Laundromat, churches, gas stations, and a small park. Some storefronts sit vacant. Others have been converted into apartments. The short stretch of shops and offices represents almost all of Greenburg's commerce—locals who want to shop at big-box retailers drive to one of the bigger towns nearby. Community leaders have emphasized efforts to keep Oak Avenue's businesses afloat in recent years, and that work has been covered prominently in the local newspaper. An ongoing downtown revitalization effort resulted in pots of pink and purple petunias hanging from lampposts along Oak Avenue, new landscaping in public spaces, and tourism promotion efforts by the local chamber of commerce (which partners with the local newspaper to produce visitor's guides and other promotional materials). The efforts speak to the fact that local leaders see tourism as an important part of Greenburg's economic future.

Almost all of the Greenburg residents interviewed for this book said the community's economy was in bad shape. "We're a poor county. There's not a lot of places to work," said Linda, a Greenburg native in her mid-thirties who did clerical work three days a week at a small local history museum. Several longtime residents described a sense of entitlement among young people that did not exist a generation ago. Mary, a social service manager who oversaw a food distribution program in the community, said older members of the baby boomer generation in the community have a sense that nothing is free. Some younger people, on the other hand, have "a huge sense of entitlement," which manifests itself as an expectation that they will be taken care of. "When you grow up in an area like this, you deal with a lot of apathy," Mary said. "It is hard to reeducate people" to get them to want to work. Other local residents pointed out that there were few jobs in Greenburg, and little to help young people and low-wage earners adjust to compete in a global economy. Theresa, who operated a local news web site, pointed out that the local school system does little to "prepare our kids for the culture shock of leaving the area" and, as a result, many who do leave for better jobs or education end up coming back without either. Low-wage earners said that higher-paying jobs are hard to come by, in part because people who have those jobs tend to hold on to them. "Pretty much all we need is jobs. That's all anybody needs, is a job," said Jenn, a single mother of two in her late teens who was unemployed and drawing welfare benefits. Clint, a middle-school teacher in his late forties and lifelong Greenburg resident, made a similar point:

> There are stores, but there's no real business. So there is no real chance that anybody's going to go out and make a lot of money. There's just not, until somebody comes in and thinks of an industry that they can put in this area. Even my children talk about it all the time. As we're driving through town they'll see an empty lot and they'll say, "Boy, it'd be nice if there was something there." People around here get excited if they put in a Taco Bell. That just gives a few people a few minimum-wage jobs. That's not industry and it's not helping our economic status at all. We're not ever sending a product out into the rest of the world.

Those lacks of opportunity, coupled with stigma, make it difficult in some cases to motivate people to believe they *can* succeed. Floyd, a local nonprofit manager in his late fifties, said the community makes too many assumptions about its poorest residents: "We're so judgmental. We judge people first and condemn 'em, when they may be the nicest people." That persistent judgment, he said, makes it hard for young people to try to find the fortitude to pull themselves out of bad situations. "They've been told all their lives that you're welfare trash, or trailer trash, or whatever you want to call it. So there's no self-worth."

Some people—mostly local journalists and businesspeople—did point out some reason for optimism about the local economy. In the 1990s and early 2000s, Greenburg established several festivals focusing on local history and cooking competitions, among other things, that drew tourists from the region, and the community had embarked on the beautification effort to make the downtown commercial area more attractive to potential businesses and customers. Although coal mining had not been an important part of the local economy for two decades, some residents suggested that fossil fuel extraction or power plants would be good for the future of Greenburg. Theresa said a coal-fired power plant that was proposed for the area in the 2000s but never built "would have transformed everything" in a positive way. Others said they held out hope that new mines or power plants could boost the town's economy one day.

Despite the economic hardships and other social problems they experienced there, most of the Greenburg residents inter-viewed for this book said they had no interest in moving else-where. Many pointed out that they liked the close ties that they had developed with others in the community and the willingness of neighbors to help those in need. Others said family relation-ships in the area were important and that leaving Greenburg would represent a sacrifice of ties that they were not willing to make. Those expressions of security available in a tightknit social setting were common among people of all incomes, and they were mentioned by residents in Priorsville and Deer Creek as well.

Greenburg was served by one local newspaper, the *Greenburg Star*. The *Star* published five days a week, with a circulation of roughly 3,500. It was owned by Henderson Media, a large media chain with several other newspaper holdings in the region.

Henderson owned a larger daily newspaper near Greenburg; a managing editor at that newspaper had editorial oversight over both publications. The *Star* had a small editorial staff consisting of an editor/general manager, a news reporter, and a sports writer who also wrote for the other Henderson newspaper. When fieldwork for this book began, the Henderson editor who oversaw the *Star* and other newspapers in the region was Nancy, a Green County native in her late thirties who sometimes pitched in to write stories for the *Star*.[1] She said she liked her job because "I really enjoyed being able to speak on behalf of a community that largely doesn't have a voice, I guess." As a teenager, she said, she wanted to leave Greenburg. Like many youth in the town, she said, she saw few career opportunities. But she did not want to live in a large city, so she attended a small regional college and earned a bachelor's degree in communication, and when a local newspaper job became available, she took it. "There's a lot of need here. There's no shortage of things to write about. There's no shortage of issues that need [to be] addressed in this region. I liked being one of the ones that didn't run away from that and that stayed put to try to address some of those issues," Nancy said. She frequently referred to the service element of journalism, once describing its importance this way:

> I think some of that just goes back to just the kind of person you were born to be. I think that some people just automatically from a young age lean toward being more empathetic about other people's problems and try to be more considerate of other people, and then there are other people who don't [pause], that's not what's in their head. Maybe they feel that the people they're most responsible to might be their immediate family, and they feel like successfully doing that means bringing home a great big paycheck, which pushes them out of the region, possibly. I guess I never looked at it quite like that. In my mind, I've

never really been hung up on material things. So I think
that I am more interested in being able to look at myself in
the mirror, and being able to sleep at night. And I feel a
certain sense of pride in serving the area that I grew up in,
and not only that but the area that my parents grew up in.

For the most part, two people produce the *Star*'s editorial
content: Sandra, the editor and general manager, and Susan, a
reporter. Sandra, who grew up in a neighboring town and was in
her early eighties, first started working at the *Star* as society
editor in the late 1960s. Back then, she said, Greenburg was "a
Saturday-night town" with a bustling downtown full of shops
and taverns. Nearly fifty years later, she said, Greenburg is "certainly not what I'd call 'thriving,'" although she believed local
efforts to attract more businesses, most notably the local business
association's downtown revitalization effort, were moving the
economy in the right direction. "We're never going to be what we
were thirty years ago, but I think we are showing some improve-
ment," she said. Sandra saw herself as a part of that momentum.
She said on several occasions that, as the town's newspaper
editor, it was her job to advocate for business growth. As fieldwork for this study began, Sandra was finishing the *Green
County Visitor's Guide*, a magazine the newspaper produces
every year in partnership with the local chamber of commerce.
Henderson Media profits financially from the *Visitor's Guide*,
which is supported by advertisements. Sandra also said she gets
a great deal of personal satisfaction from her role in putting the
guide together, and that she spent a great deal of her personal
time working to make it as visually appealing and interesting as
possible.

Sandra wrote mostly about local schools and social organizations, and Susan covered government meetings and crime-related
stories and handled all the newspaper's social media. Stories and
photos were shipped off to a design center in another state every

night, where Henderson Media employees placed stories and photos on pages that were then sent to the printer. Sandra said she disliked that arrangement because it resulted in uncreative page designs. Susan, the *Star*'s reporter, was a recent college graduate in her late twenties who grew up in Green County and got her first job as a sportswriter at a nearby Henderson Media newspaper. Susan was a single mother; she said she enjoyed working at the newspaper, but found it difficult to raise her young child on the salary she received there (Nancy said young reporters like Susan generally started at $9 an hour). She said she hoped to parlay her position at the *Star* into a better job, perhaps as a reporter at a larger newspaper or, more likely, as a manager at one of Henderson Media's other area publications. "I think this [position] is a stepping stone for a lot of people," Susan explained, although she was conflicted about the possibility of leaving her hometown, even if it meant higher pay.

Theresa, the Green County native mentioned earlier, launched an online competitor, GreenburgToday.com, after losing her reporting job at a nearby newspaper during a round of layoffs in the early 2010s. Theresa wrote local news stories for the site, and it also published large amounts of submitted material, such as news releases and obituaries. Theresa, a college graduate in her late thirties, said she launched GreenburgToday in part because of what she saw as negative and inaccurate reporting on Greenburg that appeared in regional news media. She also said she believed the local newspaper had done too little to address corruption in local government. She criticized the *Star* for being too close to local officials, but said she believed the presence of a competing news source had forced the *Star* to publish more complete accounts of government activities. Theresa said in February 2014 that GreenburgToday.com had not yet turned a profit, but she was building an advertising base. Advertisers included some local radio stations (one of which she partnered with to produce local news segments), a church, and some local businesses in Greenburg. A local bank held the largest advertising spot (the bank was also one of the *Star*'s major advertisers). Nine of the 13 non-journalists interviewed in Greenburg said they read GreenburgToday with some regularity, although most said they saw little significant difference between its coverage of local issues and the *Star*'s.

Priorsville

Priorsville's remote location and the fact that there are no river lanes in and out of the area meant that early settlements grew much more slowly than other communities in the region. No tribes laid permanent claim to the land, although the Cherokees, Shawnees, Chickasaws, and Choctaws used it as a hunting ground. The first white settlers—mostly Scots-Irish—laid down roots in what is now Priorsville in the early 1800s. Early settlers in Priorsville found life challenging. Mountain trails made accessing the land difficult, and the soil was hard to farm. Land speculators in other states sometimes worked with local residents to fleece newcomers with fraudulent property titles, promising them fertile river bottom lands that were, in reality, often rocky ledges. Still, the region's first residents managed to make lives for themselves as subsistence farmers, and they raised large families—it was not uncommon for couples to have ten or fifteen children.

Timber was the dominant force behind Priorsville's economy in the nineteenth and early twentieth centuries. Hardwood flooring companies and mills set up shop to process the poplar, maple, chestnut, and oak trees that were abundant on local hillsides. Much of the county's virgin timber was gone by the 1950s, but logging continues to be a source of income in the area. Commercial coal mining took hold in Prior County in the early 1880s after railroads were built in the region, allowing coal to be shipped out. A Cincinnati businessman opened the first mines in the community and recruited people from Wales and England (and later black Americans) to work in them. Miners' wages, meager as they were, still were desirable to local residents who had lived largely off the farm products they could produce on their land. By the late 1800s, the biggest mine in the area was producing 350 tons of coal a day. During that period, Prior County developed a reputation for drunkenness and debauchery. Liquor flowed freely from local saloons, and local lore suggests that, at one point, it was rumored that a killing happened in Prior County every day.

Like many nearby communities, Priorsville residents supported the Union during the U.S. Civil War. There was little support for slavery there, in part because so few white residents could afford them—one local historical account suggests that only five families in the county owned slaves at the start of the Civil War. Large numbers of African Americans came to work in the community's coal mines in the late 1800s—blacks made up half the workforce at the community's largest mine. People of different races lived separate but largely conflict-free lives until the high-profile murder of a popular local shopkeeper in the first decade of the twentieth century. The clerk, who was white, was killed by a black man, and the crime brought to a boil racial tensions that local historians suggest had been simmering for some time. After the murder, Priorsville's white residents put their black neighbors on notice—leave now or face the threat of violence. Signs were posted at the county line warning blacks to stay away. By 1910, the community's black population had fallen from more than 300 to just sixteen, according to U.S. Census records. The signs are distant history, but the county is still overwhelmingly white (98.3 percent in 2012, well above the state average, according to the U.S. Census Bureau).

By the mid-1950s, Priorsville's economy was booming. A short-line railroad terminated there, allowing locals to export lumber, coal, and livestock. Several factories were producing doors, flooring, and other wood products; four automobile dealerships were in business; and one newspaper account from the era noted that there was over $6 million in construction going on around town. That growth slowed significantly in the 1990s and early 2000s. Aside from the two-room local library, a large church, and a few other government offices, Priorsville's old downtown district, which built up around the railroad terminal, was largely vacant in 2014. Many of the town's businesses migrated to the highway that runs into town from the north, joining Walmart and several fast-food restaurants. Priorsville seemed more economically vibrant than Greenburg and Deer Creek, but much of the town's commerce took place at discount retailers such as Walmart and fast-food restaurants, which typically create low-wage jobs. Following the closure of a large manufacturing plant that made flooring in 2010, unemployment in Prior County rose as high as 23 percent. The county held its state's highest unemployment rate fairly consistently in the years that followed; in 2012, the county's 16 percent unemployment rate was the highest in its state.

The estimated population in Prior County in 2013 was roughly 22,000. About 4,000 of the county's residents lived in Priorsville, the largest incorporated town in the county. Seventy-five percent of the county's residents were high school graduates in 2012 (below the state average), and roughly 11 percent had a college degree (less than half the state average). The poverty rate reported in 2012 was roughly 26 percent, eight percentage points higher than the state average, and a third of the families with children under the age of five lived below the federal poverty line. The remote community is surrounded by forests and recreation areas. The state government bought thousands of acres of surrounding forest land in the 1980s and 1990s, and many study participants pointed to parks and natural resources as the primary amenity that set Prior County apart from its neighbors. At the time of this study, local officials were discussing growth in the ecotourism industry in Prior County as a means to create new jobs. Almost all of the people interviewed for this project were familiar with those discussions, and most were generally supportive of ecotourism development, although some doubted its ability to substantially improve economic conditions in the community.

Local residents said unemployment was Priorsville's most pressing economic/social problem. The cause of the county's high unemployment rate, however, was a source of at times contentious debate in the community. Two building-material factories that served as the community's largest employers closed in the early 2000s. A few years later, another large building-material plant laid off more than 250 workers, and local residents said that the town's workforce never recovered. Several people noted that local jobs are hard to find, and it takes more than an hour and a half to commute to the nearest major city. Ed, the owner of the *Priorsville Record*, one of Priorsville's two newspapers, suggested that local leaders do little to bring in new businesses because they are resistant to change: "They don't want to mess Mayberry up," said Ed, who is in his late forties. Nick, the editor of the other local newspaper, the *Priorsville Post-Examiner*, said a lack of jobs is the primary problem, but "the other side of it is an unwillingness to work."

Some local residents blamed that unwillingness to work on government aid programs that they saw as too generous. Bill, the publisher and owner of the *Priorsville Post-Examiner*, said he believed the expansion of welfare benefits was "a detriment" to the needy, because it only encouraged them not to work. Scott, a local resident in his late sixties who owned a company that provided in-home health care in Prior County, expressed a concern that "our government doesn't seem to realize that work ought to be worth more than not working." Scott's company employed about 150 people, most of whom made minimum wage or slightly more. "I just pay what I can. I don't put my company in jeopardy by guaranteeing something I don't know if I'm going to be able to meet," he said. At the time of our interview, he said he had fifteen open positions he could not fill. Others said more jobs would help matters significantly. "Jobs do away with a lot of poverty," said Micah, a former coal company executive in his early sixties who opened a textile plant in Priorsville after the local mines closed. While some people are not motivated to leave behind unemployment benefits ("There are always people who want to be on the wagon—some people push and some people want to ride," Micah explained), he said he believed many Priorsville residents would return to the workforce if there were more, and better, opportunities.

Priorsville's first newspaper was founded in 1887 and published just a few issues before closing. It was replaced by a Republican newspaper that published until 1915. When that paper closed, a local businessman established the *Priorsville Record*, which is still in publication today. The newspaper had been owned by the same family for five decades at the time of this research. The *Record*'s owner, Ed, bought the newspaper from his stepmother, who had owned it for more than forty years, when she decided to retire in 2011. Ed, who grew up in Priorsville, was not a journalist by trade—he had worked stints as a policeman, a truck driver, a welder, and a barber. For two years before he bought the newspaper, Ed worked in the circulation department at the *Record*, delivering newspapers. I interviewed Ed in the spring of 2014 at his barber shop in Priorsville; he worked at the newspaper on Mondays, Tuesdays, and Wednesdays, and cuts men's hair on Thursdays, Fridays, and Saturdays. As he spoke in the small one-room shop on a Friday afternoon, a John Wayne movie played on the television in the corner and a small stream of customers trickled in and out. Many were regulars, so well-known to Ed that he didn't have to ask them how they wanted him to cut their hair. Ed said people in town know him more as "Ed the Barber" than "Ed the Newspaper Publisher." He emphasized several times that he did not consider himself a journalist, and that he never planned to own a newspaper before buying the *Record*. When asked why he bought the newspaper from his stepmother, he hesitated for a moment. "It was there," he replied. "I was getting a good deal on it." Ed made some editorial decisions and sold ads, but never wrote stories for the *Record*. The *Record* was edited by Jim, a retired government employee in his early sixties who worked at the newspaper three days a week and wrote many of the newspaper's stories.[2] Jim had lived all over the United States. He moved to Priorsville in the mid-2000s to be close to his wife's family. Priorsville has "got its plusses and minuses," Jim said. He said he was not sure he would recommend people move there, in large part because of the economy and the number of people who are "on the draw." He got the editor's job at the *Record* through a temp agency, and Ed convinced him to stay on. Both Ed and Jim said they believed the fact that Jim was not from Priorsville helped him be a good local journalist because he could see community issues from a fresh perspective.

Priorsville has a second weekly newspaper, the *Priorsville Post-Examiner* (known locally as the *PPE*). Four local men founded the *PPE* in the mid-1970s, when Priorsville's economy was still growing. Bill, one of the four founders, was the newspaper's editor and publisher for nearly thirty years. A soft-spoken Vietnam War veteran whose family moved to Priorsville when he was four, Bill worked out of a room in the back of the *PPE*'s office where old issues of the paper were stored, a workspace where he could smoke Marlboro Reds and pull historical articles for quick reference. He and his fellow investors founded the newspaper at the same time the government was establishing a large recreational area just outside Priorsville. "I thought we were going to bloom. And we did, we had some good years. But we had a lot of bad years," he said. During his first interview, he told stories about selling *Grit* magazine to make money as a nine-year-old, about covering cock-fights ("that sold a lot of papers"), about the time he was physically attacked (by one of the subjects of the cockfighting story), and about taking on crooked cops.

Nick, a Priorsville native in his mid-thirties who had covered sports for the newspaper, was hired to be the *PPE*'s editor in the mid-2000s. Bill, who was in his mid-sixties, said he was "burning out" because of the workload and needed someone younger to take over editorial duties. He still acted as the newspaper's publisher and occasionally wrote articles and commentary. Nick noted that he originally went to college with plans to be a teacher, but chose to pursue journalism instead because he liked to write: "I decided I would rather do something else—teaching wasn't for me. I always liked to cover sports, so it seemed natural. That is what spurred my interest—covering sports." As editor, he still covered sports, and he wrote most of the newspaper's news copy as well. Nick was also actively involved with the Priorsville chamber of commerce, serving on its thirty-member board of directors. Nick and Sharon, the chamber's director, both said that Nick's ability to "get the word out" about chamber efforts through the *PPE* was one of the main strengths he brought to the organization. Nick said he had no trouble separating his duties as the newspaper editor from his chamber of commerce responsibilities, and that he saw his chamber involvement as a natural extension of his role as a community journalist.

The *PPE*'s weekly circulation was about 5,000 in the spring of 2014. Most local residents who said they read a local newspaper mentioned the *PPE*, and many said they consider it a superior product to the *Record*. Local residents who liked the *PPE* often attributed its success to Nick, whom they saw as a force for positive change. "Nick's really digging into the roots" of local issues, said Sharon, the director of the Priorsville chamber of commerce. Nick was born in Priorsville and graduated from the local high school, and he said he enjoyed working in his hometown and the outdoor opportunities there. However, Bill noted that he worried about whether he'd be able to keep his young editor around—he knew Nick had turned down job offers from other, larger newspapers recently.

When Priorsville resident Micah fought in the Vietnam War in the early 1970s, he had the *Priorsville Record* mailed to him. He shared this recollection:

> The *Priorsville Record*, rolled up, is the size of your pinky finger. The guys that I was in the service with was getting the *New York Times* and the *Chicago Herald*, from all over. They'd get daily papers that, rolled up, were two inches in diameter. And I'm getting the *Priorsville Record* once a week, and there come this little bitty paper rolled up—this is the truth, this is funny. The *Priorsville Record* would have all local stuff: So-and-so visited so-and-so, somebody killed a rattlesnake or a deer, this happened. And those guys would line up to get the *Priorsville Record*, and they would read every word [laughs]. It was their entertainment for the week.

When asked why he thought they liked it, he recalled the "personal" stories that appeared in the local paper: "It was about this family and that family. It was stuff that the [metropolitan] newspapers did not, could not cover. The big papers didn't care who killed that rattlesnake, or who got their first deer, or whatever." Micah still subscribed to a local newspaper in 2014, but he had switched to the competing *Priorsville Post-Examiner*. Like many residents, Micah said he found the *PPE* more interesting than the *Record*. The owners of both newspapers had for years questioned how long the small town's advertising and subscriber bases would be able to support two local newspapers. Bill and Ed both said there had been discussions about merging the two papers, but those never materialized into an actual business plan. Both publications were losing subscribers as older readers died and younger people chose not pick up the newspaper. To try to attract a younger audience, the *PPE* published an e-edition, which allowed paid subscribers to view its content online. The *Record* also launched a paid e-edition in 2013, but owner and publisher

Ed said it was scrapped after a few months because of a lack of subscribers.[3] Ed said he valued the business because of its place in the community's history, but he found it increasingly difficult to sell enough ads to make the *Record* profitable. Most of the roughly 4,900 newspapers sold weekly were purchased at racks and businesses. The newspaper's subscriber list had fallen to 600 in spring of 2014, and some weeks the cost of mailing out the newspaper consumed all of its profits. "I'd hate to give it up, just for the heritage side of it," Ed said.

Deer Creek

Deer Creek is the smallest and most remote of the three communities described in this book. Compared to Priorsville and Greenburg, there is little locally produced history of the community, which sits in a wide spot in the valley carved out by the waterway that gives the town its name. The creek was once a transportation lifeline for the community, but years of erosion runoff, illegal dumping, and falling trees have made it unnavigable for boats larger than canoes. The first white settlers established themselves in what is now Deer Creek in the first decade of the 1800s. They came slowly—Deer County did not have enough people to organize until the mid-1800s. Agriculture was an important part of the community's early economy. Tobacco was grown, harvested, and packed into barrels known as hogsheads, and floated down Deer Creek for larger waterways and eventual shipment to Europe. Potatoes, oats, hay, sheep, and cattle were also important agricultural products. Farms still dot the landscape around Deer Creek, although the sheep, cattle, and tobacco that were once so important to local markets are becoming less common. Timber was (and still is) an important industry, although the rich virgin stands of white oak, yellow poplar, and black walnut, the most valuable trees in the area, were largely gone by the late 1940s.

Since the 1870s, oil and natural gas have driven the local economy in Deer Creek. The first oil well in the county was drilled in 1875, and after that, small wells were scattered all around the area. Systematic drilling began in the early 1900s, and there was an oil boom in 1917. In the early 1920s, one local historical account reported, a Deer Creek man told of a well that produced 17 million cubic feet of oil (about $1,000 worth) a day. "Dozens of communities in particular and the entire county in general was changed forever by the population increases and greater prosperity brought by the discovery of oil," that historian wrote. Many Deer Creek residents described jobs with local oil and gas companies as the best employment opportunities in the community. The availability of those jobs waxed and waned based on the price of oil and gas. When prices were up, oil companies were busy and jobs were available. When prices were down, companies idled their drilling crews. When people discussed the economic elite, they almost always referred to the men who owned those companies. A few local operators had achieved millionaire status. Their names were on local bridges, athletic facilities, and academic buildings at the small local college, and they often came up in conversations with residents.

There were roughly 8,700 residents in Deer County, with 1,500 of them living in the town of Deer Creek. The county was more racially diverse than the other communities included in this study—84 percent of the residents of Deer County were white. Despite the presence of a small local college, the number of residents in Deer Creek with a college degree was below the state average. The community's 27 percent poverty rate from 2008 to 2012 was the second highest in its state. Deer County's per capita income in 2012, about $16,000, was well below the state average. However, the 7.4 percent unemployment rate in Deer Creek was below the state, regional, and national average. Some local residents said the college acted as a stabilizing force for the local economy. The college is Deer County's second largest employer. The largest is a medium-security prison built a few miles outside of town in the early 2000s. The prison, tucked away in a valley off a two-lane highway, was billed as the community's employment savior. Many locals suggested it actually produced relatively few jobs for people in Deer Creek, and that most of its employees lived elsewhere and commuted to the prison. A few residents suggested that unemployment was low because locals who were unemployed dropped out of the workforce once their unemployment benefits ran out, living off Social Security or disability payments. About 59 percent of Deer County residents over the age of 16 were not part of the workforce in 2012, according to the U.S. Census Bureau.

Deer Creek's old downtown district is built up around a single stoplight near the creek. The downtown area was home to three restaurants, a bank, a small hotel, two churches, and a few storefronts that housed real estate agents, insurance companies, a small grocery, a florist, and other businesses. Another small commercial district, which included a chain auto parts shop and a fast food restaurant, was about a mile down the highway. Local residents observed a great deal of business turnover in Deer Creek, in large part because there was little support for local entrepreneurs. There was no local chamber of commerce, and most people traveled an hour or more to larger towns to get anything more than the basic necessities.

Although the poverty rate in Deer Creek was higher than either Greenburg's or Priorsville's at the time this study was conducted, residents in Deer Creek discussed it with less uniform concern than those in other towns. Juanita, a librarian in her early sixties, said the economy in Deer Creek was "not real good, but it's not as bad as people think it is." Those who worked in oil and gas, at the university, or with the local prison made decent wages, she said. Those who did not work in those fields made far less, but were able to get by because the cost of living in Deer Creek was low. Rick, a retiree in his mid-seventies, said the economy "is pretty good in some respects"—tax appraisals were up, for example. "I think looking around, we have pretty good roads, things have been improved over the years," he said. Quinn, a secretary in her early forties who once worked as a reporter at the *Deer Creek Chronicle*, said that, while she had often heard about how poverty-stricken the area is, she had always been able to find a job and support her family. She continued:

> I think there's work out there, you know, if people want to look for it. It is slow, there's not good jobs to be had, really. A lot of people are on welfare, food stamps, but you know, that's all over the country. You know, it's not growing. It's shrinking, the population is shrinking, people are taking their families and moving when they grow up, and they're not moving to this area. It's stagnant, at best.

Quinn's ambivalence about the local economy is reflective of the attitudes of many of the men and women interviewed for this study: She saw and understood the difficulties others faced to make a living wage, but at the same time suggested that there were jobs to be had. Other residents were more concerned about the state of Deer Creek's economy. "I think all of us are struggling, more so than we would like to admit," said Stacy, a single mother in her mid-thirties who worked as a clerk at a struggling retail shop in Deer Creek. A few residents specifically mentioned the challenges in finding affordable housing, and nonprofit directors I interviewed said homelessness was an issue locally.

The *Deer Creek Chronicle*, Deer Creek's local newspaper, has been in circulation since the first decade of the 1900s. Gregory bought the newspaper in the early 1990s. He was introduced to journalism at a young age—his father worked in the editorial department of a metropolitan newspaper in the Southeast for nearly fifty years—but newspapers were his second career. He had a PhD in history from a large state university in the Southeast and had training as a museum curator and historic preservationist. As a museum director in the early 1970s, he found himself doing a great deal of writing in a public relations capacity, so he decided to get into journalism in the mid-1970s, taking a job as the publisher of a small local newspaper. "I essentially learned to be a publisher and editor on the job," and through training he received through his state press association, Gregory recalled. He said his advanced schooling has helped him as a journalist—he was able to integrate his knowledge of economics, political science, and history into his reporting, leading to a style of writing he described as "kind of academic." He worked at several newspapers in Appalachia and the Midwest (he mentioned somewhat proudly that he'd been fired from two different publisher's jobs for refusing to bend to the demands of corporate owners) before buying the Deer Creek newspaper to be closer to his adult children, who lived nearby. Gregory often wrote about his private life in the *Deer Creek Chronicle* in personal columns that sometimes filled half a page. In the six months' worth of newspapers reviewed for this project, he discussed, among other things, his allergies, his travels, and the person chosen to be the president of his state's flagship university (which is in another part of the state). In one issue, he published a photo of himself at the state capital, standing beside a state politician who was considering a campaign for the U.S. Senate. In another, he published an entire page of photos from a vacation he took with his two sons.

In the spring of 2014, Gregory was in his early seventies and suffered from a recent back injury, but he still did a great deal of the front-page reporting, wrote a weekly column, edited submitted copy, and designed news pages. In the absence of a local chamber of commerce, he also organized a monthly meeting for local businesspeople, which he used to promote advertisers to others in the community (he also wrote about those events in his newspaper). The *Chronicle*'s weekly circulation was about 3,500. Gregory said advertising revenue had suffered in recent years, but he noted that the *Chronicle* still ended 2013 with a profit in excess of $70,000. Gregory said he occasionally thought about retiring, but had no immediate plans to do so. Gregory's son Eric worked with him as general manager of the newspaper, handling managerial duties, keeping computers operating properly, and occasionally writing stories. "I hesitate sometimes to call myself a journalist because journalism implies that I've got the funny hat on with the little press sticker and I go around and I do stories all the time. Which I don't really," Eric once joked. Eric, who was in his mid-forties, had spent much of his adult life working at various newspapers. Gregory suggested Eric might take over the newspaper when the time came for him to retire, but Eric was noncommittal about his interest when asked. "The newspaper business is just something I've always done, and it's something I'm doing automatically now. It's not really a challenge," Eric said. His passion was helping people with their computers—he had left an IT job in another state about two years earlier to help his father at the newspaper following Gregory's back injury.

High-speed Internet was available in Deer Creek, but was hard to come by in much of the rest of the county. Several web sites covering Deer Creek news had come and gone in recent years. Most interview participants in the community said they took what they read on those sites with a grain of salt—many of them were run by people with political agendas, and some published claims that seemed outlandish (shortly before fieldwork for this book began, one site published a photo of a topless woman it claimed was the daughter of a prominent local businessman). One site, the Deer Creek Advocate, seemed to provide a more even-keeled analysis of local events, and several residents said they read it to find out what was going on around town. Lance, a computer company executive who founded the site, chose not to participate in interviews for this book.

Gregory said he believed his newspaper was well-liked in the

community. However, many residents were not shy about expressing their disdain for the *Chronicle* and its owner. Crystal, a local
resident in her early sixties who wrote a column for the newspaper
under its previous ownership, called Gregory "incompetent." "I've
written up stories and handed them in. He will change names and
things, just because he's the editor." The result was inaccuracy.
"He's always so apologetic, so surprised," she said sarcastically.
But still, the problems happened. Crystal said she believed the
newspaper presented too much positive news and kowtowed to its
advertisers. "There's not any real reporting going on. It's really just
a journal for out-of-town people," she said, referring to the large
numbers of photos from school events published in the newspaper
weekly. She said she did not believe Gregory really cared about the
newspaper: "It's just a business. It's about his ego and his legacy for
his children. It's not about helping the community."

Rebecca, an executive at a local social service agency, shared
similar opinions about the *Chronicle*. She said Gregory once interviewed her for a story, taking notes on the back of a business card.[4]
"The article turned out horrible," riddled with inaccuracies, she
said. She had also had problems with mistakes in advertisements
and, as a result, she had become reluctant to submit stories or ads
to the newspaper. "It could be such a good newspaper, and years
ago it was," Rebecca said. The previous editor had reporters who
covered local stories. Now, "it's almost like they're trying to fit
photos of everybody's kids in it to get news." She continued:

> It [the newspaper] is only about a few businesses, a few
> people and their families. It doesn't benefit the community
> as a whole. I would subscribe again if there was something
> to see, not just them [the newspaper] trying to build up the
> higher-ups, the people who have millions of dollars. I don't
> have millions of dollars—what I do, they may not notice.
> They need to actually get the news, not cater to certain
> employers or the college. Make it a people's newspaper.

As Rebecca, Crystal, and others who will be introduced later in this study illustrate, there are sometimes disconnects between the view journalists have of their work and the view their readers take. One of the main goals of this book is to examine those disconnects—to show how journalists view their work on poverty, to explain what influences that work, and to show how their readers interpret the final product. Before discussing the social inputs that influence coverage (the *encoding* of media messages) and the way stories are interpreted by readers (the *decoding* process), it is important to show exactly *what kind* of poverty coverage the news organizations under study were providing. The next chapter will describe how much coverage of poverty local news consumers in Greenburg, Priorsville, and Deer Creek receive, and exactly what that coverage looks like.

CHAPTER 3

Dominant Frames in Local Poverty Coverage

In spring of 2014, *Priorsville Post-Examiner* editor Nick visited a small nonprofit thrift store on the edge of town to interview Sally, the nonprofit's founder. Sally, a lively grandmother in her mid-fifties, moved to Appalachia from a large Midwestern city in the late 1980s with her husband, who had family ties nearby. After commuting to and from a large city an hour and a half away for about ten years, her religious faith moved her to quit her job in the late 1990s to try to help those in need in Priorsville. For several years, she ran a local women's shelter where she helped women escape abusive relationships and try to overcome addiction. Then, in the early 2000s, Sally's son, who was in his early twenties, was killed in a car crash in rural Prior County. His death devastated Sally and her family. At his funeral, people gave her cash rather than flowers. Sally said she was overcome with grief and had no idea what to do with the money. A year later, she used the money to open the thrift shop, which she operated as a vehicle to raise money to help people who needed a few dollars to make their rent, buy groceries, or keep their electricity on that month.

Nick's article, which appeared on a back page of the newspaper set aside for business profiles, shared Sally's story with her community. She described the grief and uncertainty she experienced following her son's death. Not one to hold back her opinions, Sally also spoke in strong terms in the article about living conditions for Priorsville's poorest residents, using words like "oppression" to describe the lives of those in need. She discussed meeting single mothers who could not buy clothes for their children and families unable to afford groceries from week to week. In one quote from the article, Sally told Nick, "We have a community with a lot of issues right now. . . . There is lots of unemployment, there are a lot of families that can't seem to make ends meet. [The nonprofit thrift shop] is a Band-Aid."

But Sally's profile was not a story of a woman to be pitied, or about a withering community unable to help itself. It was, rather, a caring call for compassion, told in a way that she found unexpectedly positive and constructive. A few weeks after the article's publication, she told me she had been "shocked" by the positive way she spoke of Priorsville when Nick interviewed her, despite the suffering she's seen some of its residents endure. "I love this community, and I love these people with my whole heart," she said. "And they are worth fighting for. It's who we are."

When the *PPE* article about her came out, "I was a superstar for about a week," Sally laughingly said. "People came up to me in Walmart and hugged me. There was a lot of good reaction." One particularly memorable exchange took place at a local gas station. One of the men who worked at the station, someone Sally had known casually for a few years, remarked that he had seen her photo in the newspaper, and had read her story. Sally recalled the conversation that followed this way:

> He says, "You never know what people have gone through in their life." He didn't know, he had no idea, you know, about me losing a child, why [the nonprofit] was there. He said, "I liked you before. I like you better now."

After her story was published, donations to her nonprofit organization increased. "I think people, they read it and they heard my heart," she said. "They didn't know, you know. I assumed people knew."

The story of Sally's life and passion for the less fortunate in Priorsville, and how the broader community came to know of it, offers a small demonstration of the power local media can have to shape views among their readers. There are people in communities all over the world fighting to change minds and challenge status quos. But people like Sally, who are outspoken and at times critical of community institutions in place to address social issues locally, often have a difficult time making their voices heard. In Sally's case, appearing in the newspaper elevated the credibility of someone who was viewed as a community outsider because she moved in from somewhere else and vocally challenged those who thought Priorsville did not need to change. But who gets the opportunity to talk to newspaper audiences about matters such as poverty, and how are those stories framed? This chapter is primarily concerned with those questions. As journalists go about the business of recording information and relaying events to their audiences, they make a myriad of decisions, selecting which sources to interview, which facts to highlight, and which scenes to describe. Those decisions to highlight or suppress some aspects of an issue, its causes, and its remedies generate media frames for a topic.[1] Consumers of news and other media subsequently use those embedded frames to make sense of new information.[2] News about poverty and issues that residents directly tied to poverty, such as unemployment and homelessness, was largely absent from the columns of local newspapers, the pages of local news web sites, and their social media feeds. Quantitative analyses of samples of the four newspapers published in the fall and winter of 2013 and the spring of 2014 showed that the percentage of front-page stories that addressed poverty or economic need in the community ranged from 10 percent in the *Priorsville Record* to 4.4 percent in the *Deer Creek Chronicle.*

That absence has visible consequences that will be discussed later in this book. Before discussing what *was not* written, however, this chapter will examine what *did appear* in the four newspapers and in two popular local news web sites in Greenburg and Deer Creek, which were cited by residents as important alternatives to local newspapers. When news about poverty was present in local media in Greenburg, Priorsville, and Deer Creek, it typically took the form of one of three dominant frames:

- *Hard facts*, usually in the form of statistics about economic issues in the community and often presented in the newspapers with little or no context. These stories were almost always based on the release of statistics (in most cases, unemployment rates) from a state government. The news outlets did not include many stories utilizing the hard-facts frame, but those stories that did appear tended to be featured prominently. The fact that hard-facts stories tended to make it to the front page (four front-page stories in the *Record* featured the hard-facts frame, and the *Star* and the *PPE* each published three front-page stories using the frame), coupled with the seriousness of unemployment and poverty in the three communities under study, make the hard-facts frame important, despite its relative infrequency.

- *Community responses* to poverty that show readers what others in the community are doing to help their less fortunate neighbors. To borrow a phrase from newspaper lingo, this frame often appeared as "grip-and-grin" coverage: a photo of one person or group handing over a check or donated goods to the representative of a nonprofit organization over a smile and a handshake. Community response stories sometimes appeared as nothing more than a small photo and a caption describing a one-time gift buried deep in the newspaper. At other times, they took the form of news stories with bylines on the front page about local church efforts or charities. Many community response stories have a congratulatory tone. They show that individuals in the community care about those who are less fortunate and are able to mobilize resources to help them. Often, community response news is less about those who use services and more about those who provide them.

- *Resources* for those who need help with emergency housing, food, clothing, and other matters. In some newspapers, recurring announcements about permanent resources for the needy such as food banks and clothing drives were published in almost every issue. In other cases, news about community resources came more sporadically, as deadlines for aid applications approached. Unlike stories about hard facts or community responses, information about resources for the needy rarely took the form of a fully reported news story. More often, it appeared as a paragraph or two tucked away inside the newspaper.

The local newspapers in Greenburg, Priorsville, and Deer Creek—three of the most economically distressed communities in the United States—provided little information about those in their communities who were struggling. Why weren't their stories "newsworthy"? It was not because ordinary individuals were not newsworthy or important: The sample of 804 front-page newspaper stories considered in this study included stories about many "regular people" who made it into the newspaper for acts as simple as walking a dog through town (this man was profiled on the front page of the *Deer Creek Chronicle* after the editor met him and struck up a conversation) or feeding bread crumbs to the ducks at a local pond when the weather turned cold (in a short profile on the front page of the *Greenburg Star*). It was not because advertisers did not want to see those stories: Local businesspeople who advertised in each of the three communities said they wished their newspapers would cover poverty more aggressively. The reasons the stories of low-income people are rarely told is often much more complicated but nonetheless problematic. The dominant local news frames described in this chapter largely relate to (and, in most cases, reinforce) established understandings of poverty in Appalachia as a cultural phenomenon, in which the poor are responsible for their own condition. They also exclude the voices of the poor and hinder their ability to engage in meaningful discussion of local need.

Greenburg: "We're Moving Forward"

During the study period, the *Greenburg Star*'s front pages were most often dominated by stories about government acts or local crimes. Those story types accounted for 21 percent and 16 percent of the front-page news items in the *Star* between November 2013 and February 2014. Sandra, the *Star*'s editor, explained that the remote pagination center that designs the newspaper used a formulaic approach to layout and, as a result, front pages often tended to look alike. Most front pages reviewed for this study included a lead story running all the way across the top of the page. That lead story was almost always about crime, local government, or local politics.

Of the 406 stories that appeared on the front page of the *Star* between November 1, 2013, and February 28, 2014, thirty-seven (9 percent) referenced poverty in some way. Twenty-three of those news items (which included photos as well as stories) were about philanthropic efforts in the community or events honoring volunteers that fell neatly into the *community response* frame. The sample included three front-page stories about unemployment that were consistent with the *hard-facts* frame (no other front-page stories used statistics about poverty or unemployment). Seven of the stories referenced *resources* for locals in need.[3] Nonprofit agency directors or spokespeople were quoted in seventeen of those stories, government officials were quoted in three stories, and a local resident (a business owner who organized a food drive) was quoted in one. Seventeen of the stories that referenced poverty, including the three unemployment stories, did so without attributing comments to any source. At no time were any sources identified as low-income residents quoted in stories.

Twenty-four of the thirty-seven news items that referenced poverty included a photo. Some of those were "stand-alone" photos—pictures published with a caption but not accompanied by a story. As was the case with story sources, nonprofit organizers and spokespeople were featured heavily in those photos. Only two of the twenty-four photos appeared to picture individuals who were receiving services for economically distressed people. One of those photos was a wide-angle shot of people at a food bank in which few faces are clearly visible. The other was a photo of police officers shopping with children at a "Shop with a Cop" event. In that photo, which showed readers how the local police force accompanied young children to a local retailer and bought them Christmas toys using money donated by others in the community, the faces of service recipients were clearly visible. Their names were not included in the photo caption—they were identified only as people who benefited from the program.

The "Shop with a Cop" story, versions of which also appeared in newspapers in Priorsville and Deer Creek at about the same time, is an example of a story that reflects the *community response* frame. The frame highlighted the work individuals in Greenburg were doing to address the needs in their community. Of the three frames described in this study, the community response frame was the most common, especially around the Thanksgiving and Christmas holidays. In a front-page story published under the headline "Signup Time for Christmas Toys and Food Boxes," Sandra wrote:

> GREENBURG—For many years the [local faith-based non-profit organization] has given out special holiday food boxes to disadvantaged Green County families. In addition, the [organization] has provided toys to assure that no child

wakes up on Christmas morning to find there are no gifts under the tree.

Churches, community organizations and many individuals have contributed generously to both the food and the gifts for children programs over the years. However, as jobs have disappeared and money has become tight for many families, the contributions have decreased just as the need increased.

Recognizing the plight of many community residents, the [local social club] which earlier carried out a program of providing gifts for children, joined the [organization] in its toys for kids of parents who qualified to participate in other programs offered at the [organization] [sic].

The headline suggests that the main thrust of the story will be about signing up for the services, but only the last three paragraphs speak to what individuals need to do to benefit from the services. The rest of the story is about the volunteers who organized the efforts, as are the two photos published alongside it (one of members of the faith-based organization, the other of members of the social club). The story does little to encourage people to relate to those who are in need or foster discussion about ways to change their situations. Rather, it focuses attention on other individuals who are providing the gifts—an admirable act, but one that does little to encourage the community to reconsider its attitudes toward the poor.

Although community responses to poverty were sometimes reported under bylines on the front page, much of the coverage attributed to that frame appeared in the forms of photos of groups donating food, clothing, or a check to a local charity, or as announcements about opportunities to engage in such donations. Churches, civic groups, and nonprofits often submitted news items such as this one, which ran on an inside page in November:

> [Local community organization] will hold their fall food
> drive on [date] at the Dollar General Parking lot in [com-
> munity] from 8 a.m. to 1 p.m. We will be collecting canned
> food, non perishable [sic] food items, paper product,
> personal hygiene products, and monetary donations. All
> items collected will be donated to [local nonprofit] and will
> be distributed at Christmas time. For information, contact
> [organizer name and telephone number].

Although it was by no means common, the *Greenburg Star*
utilized the community resource frame far more often than the
other newspapers considered in this study. Those resources took
many forms: advertisements for housing vouchers for low-income
residents (better known as Section 8 housing), notes about
one-time free clothing giveaways, and brief informative pieces
about standing opportunities to get assistance. The following
announcement often appeared at the end of a church calendar
published in the *Star*:

> The [local faith-based nonprofit organization] hosts a
> variety of events and service projects available throughout
> the week at [community center]. Some of those are as
> follows,
>
> • Meals at [community center]—11:30 a.m.–1 p.m.,
>   Tuesday and Thursday.
> • [Organization] shop [a thrift store]—9 a.m.–3 p.m.,
>   Monday–Friday and 9 a.m.–1 p.m., Saturday.
> • Comfort Club—9 a.m.–noon, Wednesday.
> • Food Pantry—9–11 a.m., Tuesday–Friday.
> • Celebrate Recovery—7–9 p.m., Monday.
> • Shape-up—9–11 a.m. and 5–7 p.m., Tuesday and
>   Thursday.
> • Zumba—6:30 p.m., Tuesday.

The announcement provides dates and times of events at this nonprofit, one of the larger charitable organizations in Greenburg and the recipient of quite a bit of coverage in the *Star* (often in the form of a photo of an organization volunteer accepting a check). However, resource information oriented more toward people who need help is fairly uncommon (the infrequency of the resource frame was even more pronounced in the other three newspapers studied). The Greenburg man who managed the faith-based nonprofit mentioned in the announcement above said the coverage the *Star* does provide, while appreciated, often does little to offer real help to its readers or community activists who want to address poverty.

The voices of those who struggle with financial uncertainty were so rare across the four newspapers studied for this book that they were not assigned a frame. However, they were present in some ways in the *Star*, albeit in ways that did little to tie the issue of poverty directly to Greenburg. The *Star* occasionally published a column by a woman in another part of the state who wrote about parenting children with special needs. In one column, that writer spoke to the experiences of those who live with need:

> But the true pain felt by the special needs community during these festive months is financial. Often on fixed incomes or one-income households due to needing one parent constantly available for care, medical appointments and therapy, the added expenses of the colder months when the heat is usually turned on, additional groceries for the holiday dinner, buying unnecessary presents for too many people based on society's expectations, and all the while truly needing to purchase warm winter clothing/boots/hats in this year's sizes for their loved one. Or a new therapy item. Or to fill a small corner with sensory items recommended by the therapist.

I know that feeling. Our family applied for food bank help a week or so ago only to find it closed for the next two weeks. In addition, many families like ours have difficulty receiving help from food banks due to dietary restrictions which are wide-spread in our demographic. I don't qualify for medical or dental help since my divorce isn't final. My children have been making due [sic] in summer clothes far too long, and the looks on their faces when they put it on and intentionally don't complain lances my heart in horrible pain. We've stretched groceries farther than I ever thought they could be. None of us ever want to see beans and rice again, a wish I'm quite sure won't come true. I'd give anything to have the funds to get the iTouch devices and behavioral apps that the therapist recommended as they make real progress when they have help dealing with not only the autism and bipolarism but especially ADD/ADHD. Instead, I will pray I can get her new socks, underwear, gloves, and a hat for this winter already forecast to be harsh and snowy. My budget for groceries, medical copays and medication next week is so small that I cried when I saw it in print.

In this piece, the writer offered her readers a glimpse into what it's like to live with need and uncertainty—a perspective many in Greenburg know well. Although it published very few locally produced editorials and columns, the *Star* often published nationally syndicated opinion columns about matters ranging from national politics to which electronic tablet would make the perfect Christmas present this year (even if it is a gift that would be too expensive for many local residents). Several of those columns published in late 2013 and early 2014 expressed support for efforts to increase the minimum wage. The *Star* also published eight different syndicated editorial cartoons that addressed social inequality, often from a political perspective and usually about the minimum wage. While that syndicated editorial content was present, it did not have a local angle and did not seem to resonate with local readers in Greenburg. Most Greenburg residents interviewed for this study suggested the *Star* rarely wrote about poverty; none of them mentioned the syndicated content that appeared on the editorial page of their local newspaper.

Under her *Star* byline, editor Sandra often was quick to point out the economic positives in the community. The first two paragraphs of a front-page November story she wrote provided a typical example:

> GREENBURG—"Lots of customers, busier than usual," was the general consensus of merchants in downtown Greenburg about the traditional holiday open house held Monday night as a kickoff to the Christmas shopping season.
>
> Shelves in the downtown stores were filled with holiday decorations and gift items for holiday giving and customers were in the mood to begin their shopping.

In another article the same month (and using the same general lead construct), Sandra again expressed optimism about the community, and particularly its efforts to put a good face forward, as she wrote about a local marketing effort:

> GREENBURG — "We're moving forward."
>
> That was the response from two business people when asked last week about the [community marketing] project being carried out in collaboration with [large state university in the region].

The images of a thriving downtown Greenburg business scene were particularly off-putting to some individuals who had less cash for Christmas goods. Their interpretation of stories like the ones above is discussed in Chapter 5.

At GreenburgToday.com, the community's new hyperlocal

news site, editor and founder Theresa suggested readers could expect to see a news product that was markedly different from the *Star*. While she prided herself on her willingness to cover political arguments and challenges to local government that did not make it into the *Star*, Theresa said her primary motivation for founding the site was to provide positive news about Greenburg. During the time period analyzed for this book (November 1, 2013–February 28, 2014), Theresa typically posted four to six new news items every weekday. Some were reported stories that carried her byline. Most were news releases or short announcements. She published many press releases from state government offices, a small regional university not far from Greenburg, and corporations with a regional interest (including a health care chain that owns several hospitals in the area). Many of those news releases had no clear local connection, although most had regional or state relevance. Articles with bylines were most often stories about drug busts (frequently involving methamphetamines) or coverage of city council meetings in Greenburg. She also published many obituaries (with each obit warranting its own separate post) and announcements about upcoming events in Greenburg.

GreenburgToday maintained an active Facebook account, where Theresa posted links to stories and announcements about breaking news such as winter school closings and traffic accidents that, in most cases, were later integrated into posts on GreenburgToday. com. Readers rarely commented on GreenburgToday's Facebook posts.[4] However, locally produced copy on the web site, such as submitted sets of photos, time-sensitive local announcements, and stories about local arrests and fires, occasionally took on a social media life of their own. Some of those stories were "shared" on Facebook one hundred times or more. Most press releases published on the site were not shared on Facebook by GreenburgToday's readers.

As was the case with the *Star*, GreenburgToday rarely addressed local need in the community. Of the 197 articles posted on the site between November 1, 2013, and February 28, 2014, only eight addressed local need, with four of those fitting into the community response frame. The web site posted stories about a local fraternal organization donating coats for local children, deer hunters giving venison to area food banks (a statewide story with no local angle), and a bank-sponsored fund-raiser for a local food pantry. Although it did not provide standing information about community resources as the *Star* did, GreenburgToday did publish two resource-related stories. One was about a local job fair. The other, posted during a period of extreme cold in early January 2014, told readers that a local church had opened its doors to provide a warm space for local residents who did not have heat in their homes, or had no place warm to go that week. The reaction to that story on social media shows the impact that such information, rare as it may be, can have in Greenburg. The story about the local church warming station was shared on Facebook 315 times. Only one GreenburgToday.com story, a report about a sizable snowstorm in the county, got more exposure on that social network in the fall and winter of 2013–14.

Priorsville: Discouraging Numbers, Optimistic Stories

The *Priorsville Post-Examiner* and the *Priorsville Record* were run by different sets of men with different professional backgrounds and, as the next chapter will show, somewhat different views of their newspapers' roles in the community and their own jobs as editors and publishers. However, they both covered a fairly small number of groups that were active in local affairs, so there was some overlap in the information they provided about social life, and it was not unusual to see some of the same stories and photos published in both newspapers in the same week.

The *Priorsville Record* published 117 front-page stories between

October 3, 2013, and March 27, 2014. Of those stories, twelve (10 percent) directly referenced economic hardship in the community. Four stories reported state unemployment figures, providing numbers in stories that were only a few paragraphs long, and a fifth referenced local government layoffs. Five front-page stories addressed philanthropic efforts in the community (the community response frame). One front-page story, about free medical clinics for rural individuals, fit into the community resources frame. Only two of the stories directly quoted sources speaking to need in the community (one nonprofit spokesperson and one local resident who described the reasons she donated to charity).

Of the ninety-nine stories that appeared on the *PPE*'s front page between October 2013 and March 2014, nine (9 percent) addressed economic hardship directly. Although the percentages were similar, the nature of the *PPE*'s front-page writing on poverty was different from its crosstown competitor, the *Record*, and the *Greenburg Star*, which is produced by journalists similar to those at the *PPE* in terms of education, background, and experience. The *PPE* did not publish check presentations to nonprofits on its front pages. In fact, it did not publish any stories about philanthropic efforts related to poverty on the front page during the study period.[5] The region's economic status instead was referenced in stories about local elections, crime, education, and agriculture. The *PPE* called upon a slightly larger and more diverse set of sources in those stories: politicians, a police officer, the chamber of commerce director, and a nonprofit agency manager.

The *Record* relied on reader submissions for much of its content. Several residents interviewed for this book had submitted information to the newspaper for publication; many said their submissions appeared in the newspaper pretty much as they had written them, with minimal editing or cuts for length. The *PPE* also published a great deal of submitted content, but it was more likely than the *Record* to edit content for length. Many of those submitted news items illustrated this study's community response frame. Shortly before Christmas 2013, the *Record* ran a six-paragraph story at the top of the front page about a toy giveaway at a local community center. The story, which included three photos and took up much of the top of the front page, led with this paragraph:

> When help is needed, people do come through. For the Saturday night and Sunday afternoon Toy Event at [location], a total of 137 volunteers showed up ready to do whatever was necessary to provide each parent with two toys per child for Christmas. That was twice the volunteers we had last year—and the committee is so very grateful.

The story went on to note out-of-town groups that came to help with the distribution, to tell readers how many children "were served" by the event (1,984 from 432 families), and to compare that number to the previous year. From there, however, the *Record*'s submitter provided a rare glimpse into the life of one of the recipients of the toy giveaway:

> A personal story from [event volunteer]—Jane Doe had waited in the long line outside the [location] on Sunday morning. Jane was somewhere around #200 in line. She told the lady waiting in line behind her that she was praying for a bicycle for one of her two children. They prayed together. In years past, bicycles were distributed first come first served. However, a new system was implemented this year hoping to make distribution of the limited number of bicycles fairer. The parents standing in line had no idea of the change. When it was Jane's turn at the registration table, she was asked if she could use a bicycle for her 6 year old. Her eyes filled with tears.

One of the three photos accompanying the story is of Jane, standing with the woman who relayed the anecdote, another event volunteer, and the purple bicycle with white wheels. The *PPE* also ran the photo of Jane Doe, but did so without the lengthy press release and anecdote; only the photo and a caption were published, and they appeared near the back of the newspaper.

The story of Jane Doe's Christmas gift is a typical example of the community response frame to poverty coverage. It shows that the work put forth by community volunteers (who, the reader may presume, are not in need of the program's services) is making the desired impact. It is atypical in that it includes information about an individual who was on the receiving end of the effort. In most cases, those who were donating their time, food, clothes, or money were featured in stories and photos. Those who *used* such donations were rarely seen or heard. Inside the same copy of the *Record* that highlighted Jane Doe's story, the newspaper featured a group of local vocational school students who were giving to the needy. The article, in its entirety, read:

> 1,924 food items were collected during this year's [vocational training program] food drive sponsored by [student organization]. Thanks to everyone who contributed. The food items will be donated to our students who have a need during the Thanksgiving and Christmas holidays. Any remaining food will be donated to the [local nonprofit]. [Local nonprofit] collects food throughout the year to help needy families who have a need in [neighboring county] and Prior County.

The article about the food collection was accompanied by two photos, featuring the individuals who were responsible for collecting the food items standing in front of cardboard boxes filled with canned goods. The *PPE* also published the photos and accompanying information. The food donation story is a much more typical example of a community response story in that it praised the efforts of the non-poor to help the poor, who remained largely faceless.

The *Record*'s first issue of 2014 featured eleven color photos taken during a program that paired low-income children with police officers at a "Shop with a Cop" event, where police officers took children to the local Walmart to pick out a toy that was purchased with money donated for the event. Photos from the event tended to focus more on the volunteer police officers than on the children and families who were taking part: Officers were the prominent subjects in eight of the eleven photos (two of the remaining three were group shots, and the last was a line of police cars driving to the store). Children or families with children—groups that are perhaps easier for middle- and upper-class readers to feel sympathy for—were often noted as the recipients of community support in community response stories. Interestingly, the program that received more coverage in both Priorsville newspapers than any other single effort was a community response effort designed to collect clothing and other goods to be delivered to children in other countries.

The *Record* also published many (mostly short) news items and stories using the resources frame for those in need. A typical example, from the *Record*: "[State agency] will be distributing USDA Commodities on Thursday, [date], at [local church], from 8:30am–1:00pm, weather permitting. Please bring your own bags or boxes, and you may pick up for 3 households only." Another example, from a spring edition of the *Record*, read, in its entirety: "[Local church] has free clothing giveaway every Thursday and Friday 11 a.m.–2:30 p.m. Prom dress ministry Thursdays at church, speak to Joan." Announcements about resources for the needy in the *Record* sometimes told readers about opportunities that were a county or two away, and they occasionally appeared months in advance of actual events. Community organizations that were in need of donations that would be used to aid low-income individuals also received attention in the *Priorsville Record*, often through short (one to four paragraphs) announcements published inside the newspaper. Those announcements frequently ran on multiple days. For example, a call for Salvation Army bell ringers appeared in most issues in November and December 2013. Occasionally, larger stories about agencies experiencing need were published, such as an article about a local children's center published in late 2013. The article, which was about 700 words long, also included a six-column-wide color photo presumed to be of the center's board of directors (the photo was not accompanied by a caption). The article profiled the various programs executed by the center, with frequent calls for donations in the form of quotes from its director. The article concluded with this paragraph:

> [The center director] ended with these words, "Our needs are many and our funding is few. We really just have to look at the community for support. If you can give and you do we appreciate it and thank you so much, but if you can't then we understand just [*sic*] keep the Children's Center and the children that we serve in your prayers."

Programs to help *individuals* often received coverage over several issues of the *Record*, but in most cases, that coverage consisted of a paragraph or two tucked away inside the newspaper. Campaigns to help *organizations* such as the children's center, on the other hand, received much larger spreads, with long stories and photos. It is likely that the difference is the product of the *Record*'s tendency to rely on submitted content. In the *Record*, organizations that have the resources and wherewithal to produce photos and long write-ups will get more attention than those that do not. Such an arrangement favors the larger nonprofit groups, which already dominated much of the poverty coverage in the four local newspapers described in this book.

Both newspapers in Priorsville published hard-facts stories about the county's unemployment rate every month between October 2013 and March 2014. No quotes appeared in any of the stories about local unemployment in the Priorsville newspapers.

The *PPE* told its readers on two occasions that it had asked the state agency that compiles and releases unemployment numbers for clarification on unexplained fluctuations in the numbers. The newspaper did not receive answers to its questions, the stories noted. Stories about unemployment rate increases and decreases were reported monthly in the *PPE*, the *Priorsville Record*, and the *Greenburg Star*, and they constitute the only stories in this study's sample to use the hard-facts frame. None of the three newspapers quoted a local source (only the *PPE* reached out to any source to speak to local numbers), instead relying only on government statistics to tell the story of community joblessness.[6] *Record* stories about unemployment appeared on the front page of the newspaper four times in the six months' worth of papers reviewed for this study. The stories tended to be short and to the point, often using phrases from the state government announcements verbatim. The *PPE* often provided more context. For example, the first five paragraphs from the *PPE*'s February 2014 story about the unemployment rate read:

> Prior County's unemployment rate was 15.4 percent in December, unchanged from November's jobless rate, according to data released last week by the [state agency].
>
> The state's data showed that unemployed persons declined to a five-year low, but employment and the estimated local work force also tumbled, the state said.
>
> Total unemployment in December was 1,200 in Prior County, according to the state's data, the lowest since it stood at 1,130 in October 2008 amid a still-young and deepening economic recession.
>
> But the total number of employed workers in Prior County dropped from 6,590 in November to 6,480 in December, the same data showed. That number of employed workers is the lowest in Prior County since July 1993.

The estimated local work force also stood at a 20-year low, according to the state, falling from 7,810 in November to 7,680 in December.

The separation of hard facts from stories about resources or community responses dehumanizes issues such as poverty and unemployment. Unemployment is a critical news issue that impacts many people in Priorsville and Greenburg (which, in the early 2010s, also had occasionally held its state's highest unemployment rate). However, the three newspapers in those towns covered the issue of unemployment in formulaic ways, sometimes using the same language to describe the issue month after month. For example, the following passage appeared in a front-page *Greenburg Star* story written by Susan about unemployment in early December (reporting September's unemployment numbers):

> When it comes to unemployment rates—in terms of rankings, it's a good thing when a county's number rises with the higher the ranking, the lower the unemployment.
> Counties with an unemployment rate above 10 percent (in addition to Green and [other county]) were [other county] at 11.6 percent, [other county] at 11.2 percent, [other county] at 10.3 percent.

Later in December, Susan wrote another front-page story about more recent unemployment rates, in which she included this very similar passage:

> When it comes to unemployment rates—in terms of rankings, it's a good thing when a county's number rises with the higher the ranking, the lower the unemployment.
> Counties with an unemployment rate above 10 percent (in addition to [other county], Green and [other county]) were [other county] at 11.2 percent, [other county] at 11.1,

[other county] at 10.7, [other county] at 10.4 percent and [other county] and [other county] at 10.1.

The same language (with different numbers) appeared in a February story, again by Susan:

> When it comes to unemployment rates—in terms of rankings, it's a good thing when a county's number rises with the higher the ranking, the lower the unemployment.
>
> Counties with an unemployment rate above 10 percent (in addition to [other county], [other county], [other county], [other county] and Green) were [other county] at 10.8 percent, [other county] at 10.8, and [other county] at 10.5.

Journalists in Greenburg and Priorsville described perceived obligations to publish unemployment data once the state released it—it *is* news, they would say. However, they often passed the numbers along with little attempt at interpretation or local context.

Record and *PPE* coverage of Priorsville's economy and local needs were different in other important ways. Many of those differences stemmed from differences in writing and production practices at the two newspapers. With no full-time editorial employees, the *Record* relied heavily on community members to write and submit editorial content. At the *PPE*, editor Nick and publisher Bill, both of whom had journalism degrees and experience in the industry, produced content that was more in line with journalistic norms. For example, *PPE* stories used quotes from community sources (quotes were often absent from *Record* stories) and included the bylines of the authors (the *Record* rarely used bylines). Editors and publishers at the two newspapers also had different views of their roles in the community. Those factors contributed to a key difference in the two newspapers: While the

Record was often content to let others in the community (normally government officials or business leaders) set the public agenda as it appeared on their pages, the *PPE* was more likely to stake out its own position on public matters and to attempt to present more community views on local issues.

As noted in Chapter 2, Nick, the *PPE*'s editor, was also a member of the Priorsville chamber of commerce's board of directors, and he had taken an active role in promoting business development in the community. That effort included a regular "Business Spotlight" page featuring a single advertisement (paid for by the chamber of commerce) and a long story (typically accompanied by one or more photos) about a successful Priorsville business. The story about Sally described at the beginning of this chapter was a Business Spotlight story. The spotlights sometimes alluded to the area's difficult economy, pointing out that, through endurance and hard work, the businesspeople profiled had been able to succeed despite the economic hardships they had faced in Priorsville. For example, Nick wrote the following passage about Derek, the son of a local coal miner who opened his own auto repair shop:

> Like virtually every other business, [business name] has been forced to weather the storm of economic hardships that have struck Prior County over the past six years. While retail isn't a primary part of Derek's business, he says that declining household income due to shrinking paychecks or layoffs still has an impact.
>
> "People will carry higher deductibles that they can't afford (to keep their insurance premiums lower), they'll drive damaged cars because they don't have the money to repair them, and they'll drive with only liability insurance, which doesn't pay to repair your car if you slide into a ditch," he said.
>
> But, he adds, there is light at the end of the tunnel.

"The working people of Prior County are tough," he said. "We didn't get into this overnight and we aren't gonna get out of it overnight. We're seeing some job growth in our county, our jobless rate is shrinking, and the return of the hospital is exciting because it gives us hope for tomorrow that new and better jobs are coming back.

"The opportunities are there if we'll just work at them and work with each other to grow this county," he adds. "We're not in it alone. We're in it together, and it takes all of us—businesses, consumers, retailers, all of us—working together and keeping our money in Prior County in order for the county to thrive. And I see that. People are trying to shop at home, they're trying to keep their dollars in Prior County. It's exciting to see the potential and opportunity that is there."

In another profile, which coincidentally featured Harold, another auto mechanic, Nick pointed out the businessman's simple beginnings and early struggles, suggesting that those who may be dealing with economic hardships in their own businesses need not give up: "From its humble beginnings in 2010 with a single employee —'we just started with nothing and tried to keep the rent paid,' Harold says—Franklin Automotive recently celebrated its third anniversary with five trained and certified mechanics or technicians."

The profiles acknowledged the difficult economic realities people in Priorsville faced. However, they also suggested that those problems could be overcome.[7] Optimism about the future also came through in other stories in the *PPE*. A story without a byline that appeared as part of a year-end review of local news in early January noted that while the county had held its state's highest unemployment rate for nearly four years, "there has been a sense of cautious optimism that things might be improving." Later in that story, the newspaper quoted the local chamber of commerce director, who said the community is "continuously being looked at by retail and restaurants and we have several interested parties. It's nothing but positive, assuming our current employers holds steady" [*sic*].

In the *PPE*, success—for individuals, for businesses, and for the community as a whole—seemed to hinge on the ability to keep pushing ahead despite economic and social hardships. Success was shown to be in reach for those who have the gumption to persevere, but local news coverage did little to reflect the lives of the large number of people who *could not* get ahead. The notion that perseverance, resolve, and positive thinking are the key to economic and social achievement may sound great to those who have already attained both, but they also place a great deal of the impetus for change on individuals. That approach is a hallmark of the "culture of poverty" argument—considering success as first and foremost an individual trait can be seen to have the same effect as viewing poverty as such. Anthropologist Arjun Appadurai argued that even aspirations to succeed are "never simply individual (as the language of wants and choices inclines us to think). They are always formed in interaction and in the thick of social life."[8] The "capacity to aspire" toward success is not evenly distributed; the more tools you have in your "cultural toolkit,"[9] Appadurai argued, the more likely you are to be aware of the articulation of norms and axioms that help people get what they want.[10] But how are we to equalize the aspirational playing field among poor populations? Appadurai's recommendations were crafted for planning organizations such as the World Bank, but most of them easily fit into this study of local news organizations. He recommended a close examination of the rituals that produce consensus among the poor, and between poor communities and more powerful groups; educational efforts to help disenfranchised people "navigate the cultural map in which aspirations are located"; and efforts to help poor individuals develop a voice.[11]

Deer Creek: "Shining Stars"

During his first interview for this book, *Deer Creek Chronicle* owner and senior editor Gregory said readers would find little news about poverty and related issues in his newspaper. He was right: Of the 182 stories published on the *Chronicle*'s front page between November 2013 and April 2014, only eight (4.4 percent) referenced poverty or local economic need, fewer than any other newspaper in this study.[12] Most weeks, the front page was dominated by human interest stories, and the newspaper's cover always included at least one photo under the header "Shining Stars," a weekly feature that recognized individuals for good deeds in the community. Shining Stars were recognized for a variety of things, from assisting motorists involved in car accidents to thawing out pipes during cold weather to serving as elected officials. Only one of the "Shining Stars" packages published over the twenty-five issues studied featured someone who was identified as struggling financially. That item was about a benefit dinner for a local government worker who was struggling to pay his son's high medical bills following a series of surgeries. That feature and a series of identical news briefs promoting the dinner beforehand accounted for four of the eight front-page references to poverty and economic need in the *Chronicle*. Inside pages of the newspaper contained a mix of local sports, community news columns, opinion pieces by Gregory and others, and photos and news releases submitted by local groups and state agencies. As was the case with the front page, few stories inside the newspaper described local poverty, its causes, or its consequences.

Most of the articles that mentioned poverty or charity described efforts to raise money or collect donations, signifying a community response to need. For example, the newspaper published a pre-Christmas letter to the editor from a nonprofit volunteer who encouraged residents to donate to a program that shipped gifts to children overseas, and in April, the newspaper published an announcement about a food drive to help stock the shelves of a local food pantry. Other community response articles included a December brief telling readers about a food and clothing giveaway, a New Year's resolution piece in which a local woman said she resolved to give more because "there's a lot of people who have a lot less," and the four news items about the local government worker who was struggling financially due to the illness of his adult son. A brief article published three consecutive weeks in December noted that "the hospital bills and days off of work have put a big financial strain on his family." In early January, a few days after the benefit dinner, the newspaper published a photo from the event and a four-paragraph story detailing the medical condition of the government worker's son and relaying his father's gratitude for the community's charity.

The story of the government worker's son illustrated a response to a financial struggle caused by a specific event. A few other *Chronicle* writers submitted articles to the newspaper describing their personal emotional responses to the systemic economic distress they witnessed, a reaction that is different from most other community response stories but, in a sense, produces a similar result. Poverty was addressed on two occasions by a freelance writer who frequently submitted personal columns for publication. In the fall of 2013, the writer (who graduated from the college in Deer Creek but never wrote specifically about the town) authored a piece about a trip to the grocery store that included this passage:

> I walked to the checkout line with my bread and cans of soup. I was looking forward to a warm lunch when I noticed the food pantry bin near the wall. It wasn't empty, but it wasn't full either. I thought for a second of all the loving Moms in the area with no cans of soup to give to their own children. I glanced upward and thought of my own Mom

smiling down on me. Then I paid for my food, grabbed my bag full of soup cans and placed it in the collection bin.

As I walked outside, the cold air did its best to bite into me, but it couldn't chill the God-given warmth I felt inside. I drove home with a heart full of love happily remembering the words "I was hungry and you gave me food; I was thirsty and you have [sic] me drink; I was a stranger and you welcomed me; I was naked and you gave me clothing; I was sick and you took care of me." May all your days here be warm ones full of love, giving and God.

A week before Christmas, the same freelance writer wrote a similar piece about feelings he experienced when he saw a homeless woman while out shopping for gifts. He wrote that he initially drove past the woman, whom he described as "an older woman in worn, dirty clothes with an incredible sadness in her eyes." Feeling guilty about driving by without stopping, he wrote, he later drove back to the interstate interchange where he saw the woman and gave her some money and snacks. Concluding the piece, he wrote:

> I found myself praying to God for the sad eyed lady without a home. I asked him [sic] to wrap his loving arms around her, to send her the help she needed and to be with her always. In the end, I trusted that he would in his infinite love see her home again.
>
> I remembered that Jesus was born in a manger not a mansion, that he too often had no place to lay his head and that he asked us all to love each other as he loved us. And that is what I will continue to strive to do at Christmas time and always.

The edition that carried the freelance writer's story about his encounter with a homeless woman also gave readers a submitted piece by a man whose son, a police officer, had volunteered for a "Shop with a Cop" program (the article did not specify where its writer or his son lived). In that article, the writer's son was helping a child who wanted to use his gift money to buy a coat for his sister. The officer was so moved by the boy's generosity that he pulled money out of his own pocket to buy the boy a coat as well.

In all three of those emotional narratives, the economically disadvantaged people—the young boy shopping for his sister, the homeless woman on the side of the road, and the abstract mom who cannot afford food—serve not as main characters to be known and understood. Instead, the narratives revolve around the writer himself (in the case of the first two stories) and the writer's son (in the third), people so moved by the plight of others that they decided to do something to help. While their charity is admirable, it does little to challenge the perspective that poor people are helpless and merely awaiting a handout. The view of poverty in such stories comes from a distinctively middle-class perspective—the stories are often *really about* those who help, not those who need help.

Three articles published in the *Chronicle* provided a comparatively progressive look at poverty and suggested solutions, a rarity among the newspapers reviewed for this study. In late January 2014, Gregory wrote a personal column in which he discussed presidents John F. Kennedy and Lyndon Johnson and the fiftieth anniversary of Johnson's declaration of a "War on Poverty." The column was largely a historical account of the federal programs installed in the region at that time. However, late in the piece Gregory wrote:

On this 50th Anniversary of the War on Poverty, we editors[13] would hope that President Barack Obama will, once more, take up, advocate and give new life to this important national goal and to run with it. Stressing the need to end joblessness would be a good start.

Obamacare is a good start to help the 40 percent of medically uninsured and uninsurable Americans, but a little old-fashioned creative thinking, like President Kennedy did, could lead to programs for improving the lives of the chronically poor. In part, a little "couponing education"[14] and tech training might be helpful, too!

The call to action in Gregory's column, as vague in places as it may be, was rare across the four newspapers and two news web sites studied for this book. Although mention of poverty was uncommon in the *Deer Creek Chronicle*, the newspaper occasionally provided content that not only described a community need, but also suggested social changes that might address that need. In November 2013, the *Chronicle* published an article under the headline "Growing Up Poor Can Impact Adult Brain Function." The story, produced by a state news service and distributed to local newspapers, described a study produced by a team of researchers in another state. The short news article, which ran near the back of the newspaper, noted that "the research suggests that there needs to be more attention given to low-income children, perhaps through screenings at school or at their pediatrician, to look for indicators of stress." One of the researchers quoted in the story pointed out that children living in poverty were a "particularly vulnerable population." Later that month, a second story from the state news service described evidence that parents who have insurance are more likely to raise healthy children. The article included information about how low-income parents could sign up for Medicaid. Unlike most of the other stories published in the four newspapers examined here, these three pieces suggested broader social responsibilities associated with addressing poverty. They also connected the issue of economic distress with matters such as poor health and poor performance in school, which are often exacerbated by poverty.

The Deer Creek Advocate, the local news web site mentioned by residents as a source for credible (albeit sometimes biased, in their views) local news, provided a wide variety of content. The volume of information on the site was somewhat overwhelming— editor Lance often updated the web site twenty or more times a day, publishing information about local events, obituaries, movie reviews, state government press releases, business announcements, political cartoons, yard sales, and winning lottery numbers, along with a litany of other topics. Although Lance worked in computers, technological aspects of the web site seemed to limit the reach of the Advocate: Animated GIFs and large numbers of high-resolution photos often made pages load slowly, even over broadband connections. Deer County residents who did not live in the town said they had limited access to high-speed Internet connections. They either did not read the Advocate, or they only skimmed it on work computers. The quantity of daily posts and technical limitations made it impractical to draw a sample from the Advocate using publication dates. Instead, a sample of stories was drawn for this secondary qualitative analysis using keywords that were likely to produce stories relating to (or at least mention-ing) poverty. The sample is described in more detail in Appendix A. Because this alternative sampling method was used, frequen-cies were not recorded.

The Advocate did publish some hard-facts articles (mostly gleaned from government data), community response pieces (mainly announcements about upcoming philanthropic events), and community resource information. However, the content of both news articles and reader comments on the Advocate reflected a tone that was quite different from the other news organizations studied for this project. Poverty was addressed more often, and its causes and impacts were described using more emotionally charged language. For example, one passage that appeared in a post about state intervention in the struggling local school system echoed an understanding of powerlessness in the region discussed at length in sociological literature about Appalachia:

> Any wonder that the State has caused too many citizens in the County to believe that their personal participation in decision-making processes with the State is a sham? Accept it or not [state capital] officials, fear lurks in the County too of speaking out freely at meetings because of potential for reprisals. That exercise of personal caution to waive freedom of speech and opinion rights is driven by instincts for economic survival. This behavior is typical in poverty stricken areas similar to Deer county [*sic*] where jobs and other opportunities are scarce under the strict control of a powerful few.

The Advocate also published a column about income inequality on college campuses by American historian Lawrence Wittner, and a separate piece by a peace activist from Massachusetts about Martin Luther King Jr.'s views of poverty and efforts to eradicate it. The columns, and comments such as the one quoted above, begin to shift the tone in discussions of poverty. In those pieces, the Advocate provided an outlet for writers to express their views of the causes of poverty in a way that empowered writers (such as the anonymous commenter) and offered views of social responsibility and inequality that diverged from the "culture of poverty" mindset reflected in much of the community response coverage observed in the other news outlets described here.

Comments on the local stories posted on the Deer Creek Advocate were mentioned by some local residents as particularly salacious, gossipy, and unbelievable, and some of those reviewed for this study lent credence to those concerns. A few commenters, using names such as "No Name Please," "Concerned," and "Also Concerned," lobbed charges of cronyism, government ineptitude, and bias at local government officials, businesspeople, and the town's newspaper (and Gregory specifically). Other comments, written by anonymous posters as well as some who used names, led to civil discussions about community matters. Poverty was mentioned in some comments, and was often discussed from the standpoint of those who experienced significant economic need. For example, one reader, using the screen name "Reality," made this comment at the end of a post recognizing high school graduates: "Great job to all! I can't give you high enough praise for working so hard!!! My concern is that you will have to leave Deer County to get a decent waged job." On a story about school consolidation, another commenter made the following observation:

> Our biggest problem with our economic problem is politics and greed. These two elements are the biggest threats to our poverty and democracy. Seems to me some of us still have the pre-civil war egos. Can it be changed? The greedy and politicians brainwash the people to be patriots. As a result, we volunteer to do their dirty work with inadequate compensation, go to wars we don't have to and put up with their continuous brainwashing that we have democracy. Bullsh**! Are we idiots? Why do we do this? Why do we always watch the media sources with all their lies catering their financial supporters, spreading their garbage? Why do we support their agenda knowing the only beneficiaries are them and not us? We need to use our god given brain and stand up. We thought our boe [board of education] would improve with new members. Are we? Heck No! All we hear on the street from them is nothing and nothing but political agendas rather than education. Teachers and students are just the pawns in their game.

One reader of a story about population losses in rural counties posted this comment, using the screen name "just saying":

People moving out?
Poor job market. Jobs simply disappearing.
Poor business climate. State median income low.
Poverty level high. Getting higher every year.
Younger generation doesn't stand a chance.
[State] educates them and they leave. No choice.
Fifty years ago [former governor] and others talked about
the [state] "brain drain".
Nothing has changed. Or has it? Got worse?

Again, the comments and post passages described here suggest a narrative about poverty and inequality that differs from those that appear in the newspaper. One Deer Creek man interviewed suggested that the Advocate could facilitate and take part in this counternarrative about rural Appalachian poverty because, unlike the newspaper, the Advocate's success was judged by page views rather than advertising revenue. At the time of this study, it was unclear exactly how important the Deer Creek Advocate's financial success was to Lance, its founder. There was only one advertising spot on the Advocate's web site, and Lance said in an e-mail that the site was "not all I do" professionally. A close reading of the site suggests Lance's motives have less to do with turning a profit and more to do with creating a forum for the public to voice its concerns.

Agency and the Framing of Local Poverty

On the whole, local news coverage exemplified by the three frames discussed in this chapter do little to encourage economically disadvantaged individuals to take part in social, economic, or political activities that could lead to the opportunities economist Amartya Sen found so important to the alleviation of poverty. To the contrary, the agentic action possessed by the poor is stripped out of those news articles. The nature of the community response frame also may have the consequence of reinforcing the stereo-typical trope of the unmotivated mountain resident with his or her hand out. Very rarely are the poor *doing for themselves* in those news articles. Rather, they are *being done for* by other parties in the community: nonprofit organizations, churches, or the government. Those organizations benefit from stories about special programs and check presentations, and they seek out that type of coverage. However, community response stories may create false expectations for economically distressed residents and advance the idea that they are merely waiting for a handout.[15] There are low-income individuals in the three communities I studied who are doing for themselves and others, despite the economic and social barriers they face. News about their struggles and successes would tell a story about need and success that differs greatly from the narrative of clothing giveaways and faceless unemployment statistics. Sally, the Priorsville thrift shop manager introduced at the beginning of the chapter, benefited socially from the exposure she received from the *PPE*. Dan, a janitor in Greenburg, also saw his social standing change after a story about him appeared in the *Greenburg Star* in the late 1990s.

Dan had worked as a coal miner when mining was seen as a good job in Green County. He dug for coal for twenty years, until Green County's coal mines closed in the late 1990s. As coal production wound down, Dan, who was in his mid-forties at the time, found part-time work as a custodian at a local public school. When the mine closed for good, his janitorial position became a full-time job. During the first year of his new career, Dan got a visit from a *Star* reporter, a popular local figure who often wrote stories about the lives of ordinary residents. The reporter took Dan's photo and published it along with a story in the *Star*.[16] In the article, Dan described his old job in the mine, and how he adjusted when that work was no longer available. After the story was published, Dan said, he started getting attention from co-workers whom he often saw but rarely spoke with. The school superintendent, he recalled, sought him out and hugged him after she read the article. "It really got to her," Dan said. "This person, she hardly ever talked personally to me, other than business, and it [the news story] got to her, because there was some good stuff in there." Dan said he was surprised by how much his neighbors and co-workers cared about the story of a man who might not have seemed so newsworthy. "I think a lot of them, they don't know you. They don't know what you've done and what you've survived," Dan said. "They think, 'Wow, this guy's just like me. He puts his clothes on just like me.' I got a lot of response from that [story]. That touched me." Stories like those shared by Dan and Sally illustrate the practical impacts journalistic accounts of individuals' lived experiences may have.

At the theoretical level, the three frames, and in particular the community response frame, subtly reinforce a key understanding associated with the long-held notion of an Appalachian "culture of poverty"—that the poor are individually responsible for their conditions. That understanding of poverty largely absolves the non-poor from any social responsibility for poverty, instead encouraging them to act when it makes them feel good or gives them the opportunity to build social capital. The dominance and nature of the community response frame suggests that dropping money into the Salvation Army jar or delivering canned beans to the local food pantry represent the lion's share of the community's responsibility to the poor. The sample drawn for this study was purposively selected to include the Thanksgiving and Christmas holidays—times when public (and media) attention are especially focused on giving. Stories about the poor during that period revolved around children's opportunities to have a Merry Christmas, or their parents' ability to provide the means (i.e., toys and gifts) for that to happen. After Christmas, coverage of poverty became less prevalent in all four newspapers. That coverage pattern, coupled with the fact that issues such as a lack of rural transportation, health care, affordable housing, or jobs were largely absent from local news coverage, reflect a broader emphasis on what individuals *have* as opposed to what they *have the opportunity to do*.[17] Editors, publishers, and reporters in the three communities understood the impact of the latter, but that understanding often was not evident in their stories or photos. The coverage patterns in the news outlets described here mirror broader media narratives that prop up a number of illusions about poverty in the United States. On these media platforms, the poor are faceless numbers, doomed by culture or merely temporarily "down on their luck," as writer Gregory Mantsios aptly noted.[18] Those frames can obfuscate the systemic nature of poverty, making it appear to be a natural part of community life.

The news frames associated with stories about poverty in Deer Creek, Priorsville, and Greenburg are vital to a deeper understanding of the ways media contribute to the overall view of local need in those communities. The overall lack of poverty coverage provides insight that is just as important, if not more so. As Chapter 5 will show, regular and sporadic local news consumers recognized the fact that the economic hardships faced by many members of their communities were rarely reflected in the pages of their newspapers, and they read certain meanings into that absence. Before explaining those interpretations, however, it is important to note that the absence of poverty coverage was not a mere oversight on the parts of the men and women whose work filled those news pages. Journalists from the three communities had philosophies, outlooks, and life experiences that shaped the content of their newspapers, determining what facts got in and— just as importantly—what (and who) got left out. The factors that influenced those decisions are the subject of the next chapter.

CHAPTER 4

Pressures, Philosophies, and the Encoding of Media Messages

In early 2014, Gregory wrote a column for the *Deer Creek Chronicle* in which he criticized his state's open-carry gun laws, which had just been amended to allow permit holders to carry firearms into school events. During a casual conversation in his office, a small side room in a converted home that looked over downtown Deer Creek, talk quickly turned to the fallout from that column: three fairly pointed letters to the editor he's published that week. Those letters led him to reminisce about other columns and stories he'd written that moved people to voice their (typically oppositional) views of the subjects at hand. Gregory viewed critical letters to the editor, like the three taking him to task over the gun column, as good for the community and good for business: If people were talking about what was in the newspaper, he reasoned, then the newspaper was relevant and would continue to be profitable. When asked if he could remember specific stories about poverty-related issues that stirred local passions, Gregory recalled a profile he'd written roughly fifteen years earlier about a homeless man named Albert Hodgekins. In the mid-1990s, he explained, "a couple of homeless people" could sometimes be seen downtown: "You would find them maybe sleeping inside the post office on cold winter nights, that sort of thing." Hodgekins, the subject of Gregory's story, was one of those people. Gregory described Hodgekins this way:

> He was essentially, he had many disorders, he was probably partially a mental case. He was a beggar, he would go down the street and go into businesses and, you know, ask for money to go out and buy a sandwich or whatever, and then he would of course head into the nearest bar [laughs]. And, you know, he was a man about town. To me, it was a story. And I wrote his story, and people just didn't think that that fit the, uh, persona of Deer Creek, the nice little college town that is progressive. We shouldn't have these type[s] of people living here. Eventually, the sheriff, who was his power of attorney, had him placed in a halfway house, assisted living farm, for people that have varying degrees of mental problems and homelessness.

After the article was published, Gregory said, three or four people in town criticized him for writing it. So did Albert Hodgekins. "He read the article, and he didn't like it. He told me that," Gregory recalled. "He said it was, uh, it made him look too bad [laughs]. Yes, he yelled out a few curses at me."

When asked what he had hoped to accomplish by writing the article, Gregory answered this way:

> Well, you know, you've got a homeless person, or two homeless people. And it's just like the current issue of stray dogs and stray cats. Is the community just going to turn its back on the stray dogs and stray cats, or is it going to start a bona fide humane society and have a no-kill shelter, and try to adopt them out? We've taken the stand over the last 19, 20 years, "well, we'll let other counties, shelters, take care of our dogs and cats." And that's, to me, a vital service.

And so we [the newspaper] would promote anybody who goes out there and says, "let's form the humane society and get a shelter here." I've heard, at county government commissions, about killing dogs and all of this. It's really pretty grisly, to hear the sheriff report what they do to the dogs after a certain number of days. Dogs are man's best friend, I know that. But, when it comes to homelessness, it's the same thing: Do we as a community just let it happen? "Sure, it's alright for these people to walk around town and get a couple bucks here and a couple bucks there and go and get drunk and go out in the street and yell at people, you know, and do all kinds of foolish things." Or should we take some kind of responsibility for them and say, look, these people need help? Where is that help going to come from? Are we going to just turn our backs? So that was my, the reason for writing the article was that I thought there was something that could be done to actually help Albert Hodgekins. But I don't have that expertise, I'll tell you that right now.

Gregory said he was unsure what happened to Albert Hodgekins after he left Deer Creek. Eric, Gregory's son and the general manager of the newspaper, said in a separate discussion he believed Albert Hodgekins had died several years after the article was published. Later, Gregory was asked if the criticism he received from the community following the publication of the Albert Hodgekins profile changed the way he thought about the issue of poverty, or the way he wrote about it in the newspaper. He said it did not. Those who were angered by the story, he reasoned, would never change their minds. He hoped that the piece would inspire "some good people out there who see that some fix has to be made for the homeless people here." He believed the opening of the prison just outside Deer Creek created the economic impact that provided that fix: "Since the prison came, I have not seen any homeless people here at all. And I get around. Now I'm not saying they're not there. Because, you know, well, [Gregory described a book he read that suggested that "some people just want to be homeless"].

Gregory did "get around," as he noted in the last passage. He attended government meetings, hosted business socials, and presided over meetings of the Deer Creek Historical Society. However, the company he kept—local business owners, politicians, and well-to-dos in the community—isolated him from those who made Deer Creek's 27 percent poverty rate a reality. He understood homelessness in a stereotypical way that was so foreign to him that he was comfortable comparing homeless people to stray dogs. Because he no longer saw that specific stereotype in Deer Creek, he believed the problem was no longer relevant. Two social service agents who worked with different organizations just blocks from the *Chronicle*'s office described a different Deer Creek, one in which many people without homes were staying on their neighbors' couches or living with a dozen other people in small mobile homes. Gregory's attempt to "actually help Albert Hodgekins" by profiling him as "a man about town" appeared to have had the opposite effect—neither Albert nor Deer Creek seemed to have benefited from the story.

This chapter explores the factors that influence journalists at local newspapers as they decide what their communities' news, particularly news about poverty, will look like. The interview approach used to explore the factors that influence local journalists as they cover poverty is reminiscent of the one used by George Donohue, Clarice Olien, and Phillip Tichenor in their important 1989 study on gatekeeping at local newspapers, although it is certainly executed on a smaller scale. Their work argued that media outlets in smaller, more homogenous communities tended to focus more on maintaining consensus than their larger metropolitan counterparts. That approach can be the result of economic pressures (editors may be wary of angering large advertisers or casting negative lights in ways that could affect the local economy and, thus, local advertising) or personal relationships (in small communities, media workers may be more likely to have social relationships with sources who have stakes in social harmony). Small staffs and minimal professional specialization may similarly constrain local newspapers.[1]

The modern media landscape is vastly different from the one Donohue, Olien, and Tichenor saw when they first explained the effects of structural pluralism and gatekeeping on community journalists in Minnesota in the 1970s and 1980s. Internet and mobile technologies have put information in the hands of many more people and allowed non-journalists to become news publishers, challenging the core economic model of the traditional newspaper company. At the same time, rural communities in many parts of the country are being left behind by regional newspapers that once covered them but, due to financial pressures and the desire to reach wealthy urban and suburban markets, no longer report on (or, in many cases, circulate in) their country hinterlands.[2] Despite the dramatic differences in the industry, many of the core factors that influenced community journalists in structural pluralism and gatekeeping studies of the 1970s and 1980s remain relevant today. Coverage of poverty, unemployment, and related issues in Priorsville, Deer Creek, and Greenburg was influenced by reporters' relationships with others in their communities, by the limited parameters of news production, and by a desire to make their communities look good for the sake of social cohesion and business recruitment. Other important and perhaps more personal factors, such as class isolation, the desire to push for substantive change in their communities, and philosophies about what journalists generally and community journalists specifically should strive to accomplish also heavily influenced the presence and tone of social issue coverage in the three communities studied here. The internal pressures that influenced editorial decisions in Deer Creek, Greenburg, and Priorsville determined to a great degree what information did and did not make it into public discussions of poverty. Cultural studies scholar Stuart Hall would have recognized those internal influences as the "discursive aspects" of news production that dictate the dominant meanings encoded in media messages, and in Deer Creek, Greenburg, and Priorsville, they are just as powerful as the external pressures described in previous media gatekeeping studies.

Greenburg: Servants and Advocates

The current and former *Greenburg Star* journalists interviewed for this book interpreted their social roles in somewhat different but at the same time overlapping ways. Sandra, who had worked with the *Star* for more than forty years, described herself first and foremost as a promoter of the community. "I think that when people think of me, the first thing, they think of me as the newspaper person. I hope they see me as a contributor, as an asset," she said during one conversation. When asked if she thought her work made a difference in Greenburg, she answered that she hoped it did, adding, "I do the best I can do to promote and to work with the [local] organizations." Susan, the newspaper's reporter, more often spoke of herself as a helper *within* the community rather than representative *of* the community. When asked about the responsibilities of working for a local newspaper, Susan said, "It feels like you're actually making a difference because you're doing things that can benefit the community, getting the word out or just different stories about things that are going on that can help people." Nancy, who was the managing editor in charge of Henderson Media's newspapers, including the *Star*, at the beginning of fieldwork for this project, emphasized both the advocacy and public service aspects of journalism more directly:

It became clear to me early on [in college] that the role of advocating for a community and for my family, my neighbors, the people I know and love, and the area in general, is something that we can't do too much of. And I think that journalism has this wonderful yet frustrating model of being a private sector position, but also sort of being a hybrid into the public sector because there's a service element of it.

Trying to keep Greenburg involved in discussions about state government spending was an important part of that advocacy, Nancy explained. Because Greenburg is in a rural area, she said, "I think we have to scratch and claw for that a little more than the urban areas, in part because of our population, and I'm sure there's a million other reasons." She said she believed the *Star* and similar newspapers could aid in the scratching and clawing necessary to ensure that small towns receive the attention they need. If local newspapers, some of which had been in business for more than one hundred years would not advocate for their communities, she said, who would? She added, "So I think I would argue they should advocate for their communities, but I think that needs to be done with great journalistic integrity."

The notion of speaking for someone else is inherent in the ideas of "advocacy" or "promotion." When Nancy, who left journalism for a career in public relations, spoke of advocacy, she did so in a broad sense. Statements like the one above suggest that the newspaper advocates for the community as a whole, with the best interests of all its residents at heart. For Sandra, promoting the community largely seemed to mean promoting local businesses. When Sandra spoke about poverty and the local economy, the conversation often turned to Greenburg's downtown business district. Improvements to Oak Avenue's infrastructure and general aesthetic, such as sidewalk repairs, water line replacements, and the baskets of petunias hanging from downtown lampposts were all indicators that Greenburg's economy was improving, she said. "The emphasis is on getting the downtown looking right," Sandra said. "Beautification is a big thing." Through the newspaper, Sandra heavily promoted the Oak Avenue business district, with the thinking that economic success there would trickle down to the rest of the community. As the next chapter will show, some local residents were skeptical.

When asked what circumstances made poverty newsworthy, Nancy answered that the actions of agencies or organizations gave it news value. For example, press releases from social service agencies were news. Families who found themselves in need due to fires or other crises were news. Meetings of the government or other organizations that might discuss local need were news. Deadlines to apply for assistance were news. Community-driven events to discuss issues tied to poverty, such as drug abuse, were news. "It [news about poverty] isn't constant," Nancy said. "You see things like that pop up at certain times of the year, or randomly."

Speaking about coverage of poverty specifically, Susan said, "I think we inform people that there is the issue, but we also provide them with the information of places that can help them." She described a story written in early 2014 about a school program that sent food home with students who needed it:

> I think us getting the word out has brought them quite a bit of donations, and I know they're very appreciative of it. And it seems like once the story ran, the community jumped on it. They've got enough at this point [early March] to get them through this year and maybe start on next year.

Both Sandra and Susan said the *Star*'s poverty coverage focused mainly on the agencies that attempted to help disadvantaged people in Greenburg, observations that were consistent with analysis of the newspaper's content in late 2013 and early 2014. Sandra, the editor, said regular newspaper readers would find many stories about the work of the community's largest faith-based nonprofit organization and the local senior citizens center, and articles about free lunch programs and summer activities at local public schools. "I think we do a great job on presenting not only the problems in the community and the story of the disadvantaged, but of the other good things that are happening in the community," Sandra said. The emphasis on coverage of agencies that help the town's disadvantaged population extended to sourcing as well. When Susan and Sandra were asked who they would feel most comfortable turning to for information about poverty in Greenburg, they provided an almost identical set of names: the town's economic development director, the mayor, executives at nonprofit aid organizations, and church groups. All three *Star* journalists viewed poverty coverage as a *reactive* exercise: A story about Greenburg's economically disadvantaged population appeared after something happened (i.e., the donation of a check, the loss of a home in a fire, the announcement of unemployment numbers). The reliance on planned or spontaneous events for news coverage is hardly a new phenomenon; scholars have observed for decades that events are more likely than broad issues to spark media coverage.[3] Columns and editorials about poverty would only be appropriate, Nancy explained, if they were a response to a present, organized community effort; that is what she meant earlier when she said stories should be "done with great journalistic integrity." "I guess what keeps popping into my mind as we talk is the difference between a news story and an editorial," she elaborated. Editorial page advocacy on matters such as changes to government aid programs would be appropriate, Nancy said, only "if it was written in the context of an editorial that maybe was pointing back to something that has happened, you know. Because usually editorials come as a response to something that has happened, not just some random thought."

In a different conversation, Sandra, the *Star*'s longtime editor, said her newspaper and others like it have a social responsibility to try to address matters such as poverty, but that doing so required a great deal of care for those who were dealing with poverty first-hand: "I think we have to do it in a way that doesn't make those who are disadvantaged, which we don't use the word 'poor,' but those who are disadvantaged, feel comfortable about seeing that in the paper." When asked why she prefers "disadvantaged" to "poor," she answered, "I just think they're disadvantaged. [pause] I think you have to be careful about putting people in a bloc. I think it requires some tact in how you address those issues." Sandra said she was very mindful of how a reader would feel if she or he was in the situation the story described, in part because she sometimes knew folks who were using the services provided by the nonprofit groups that her newspaper covered. "I think you have to be tactful and not make them feel bad," Sandra explained. Although she was concerned about making disadvantaged people in Greenburg "feel bad" about taking charity, Sandra said she didn't believe there was a strong stigma associated with taking public assistance in the community, a sentiment echoed by Susan and Nancy, and others in the community. Nancy observed that a stigma "exists to a point, but I think that Green County, for whatever reason, it seems to be a little more friendly, for lack of a better term." Susan suggested that the prevalence of government aid contributed to the lack of a stigma associated with taking charity: "I think there's just so much of it here that it's probably the majority instead of the minority." Sandra recalled one experience at a food distribution event in which she participated as a volunteer:

> It was just amazing the number of those people who would walk up to me. I knew they were there to get food. They would just walk up to me and say, "Hello, I haven't seen you in a long time." They knew that I knew they were there getting food. They weren't embarrassed to come up to me and make conversation. And I think that's important, you know.

Sandra's concern about isolating the economically disadvantaged people in her community was expressed by other journalists interviewed for this study. It is ironic that the most common safeguard against socially isolating the poor is to wholly exclude them from coverage of local poverty.[4] That exclusion does nothing to change their stature in the community. It largely abdicates journalists from thinking about how they themselves view their economically disadvantaged neighbors (and, sometimes, co-workers). It also relieves them of any duty to challenge notions in the community about what poverty "looks like." Other sources, such as representatives of nonprofit groups or economic development directors, stand in for the poor in stories about local need. That approach shifts the attention away from those who live with poverty and to others in the community who, in many cases, already benefit from the local standing and social capital associated with being the pastor of a big church or the president of a local civic club.

The *Greenburg Star* was the only newspaper in this study that was not locally owned, and its corporate ownership dictated what kind of news was produced, and who produced it, in both obvious and subtle ways. Nancy, who was once part of Henderson Media's larger company hierarchy, said corporate influence rarely took the form of direct mandates from above. Rather, the biggest corporate constraint on news content came in the form of resource limitations. Henderson Media ran its newspapers in such a way, she said, that larger projects and in-depth pieces had to take a back seat to the never-ending stream of what she called "lesser stories" needed to fill five newspapers every week. "Staffing can't be ignored in terms of what messages go out and to where and exactly how that takes place," Nancy observed. On several occasions, Sandra noted that the *Star* did the best it could with what it had: one editor/general manager and one reporter.

Love for the area is the only real incentive for many small-town reporters to stay at their jobs. Nancy said she knew a local reporter in a village near Greenburg who had been with her newspaper for ten years and still made only $11.25 an hour. Because of the low pay and long hours—Susan said she often works fourteen-hour days on Mondays[5]—staff burnout was a concern at the *Star* and other Henderson newspapers in the area. Nancy said it was one of her biggest managerial concerns, because once reporters and editors started to burn out, they cared less and less about the product they were producing. Low pay also leads to staff turnover, which Sandra and Nancy both noted results in a loss of institutional knowledge that made news coverage more difficult. In the case of the *Greenburg Star*, Sandra acknowledged, pay was one of the primary reasons reporters have decided to move on. Both Sandra and Nancy also noted that it was difficult to find qualified reporters who would stay at the newspaper for what Henderson was willing to pay.

Susan, who had been a Henderson reporter for four and a half years at the time of our interview, said she lived "paycheck to paycheck." Although she wrote about need much less often than Sandra, Susan said her economic position helped her to relate to those in poverty when she was called upon to interact with them:

> I think I can associate more with the situation, so that helps with the compassion and care to report on things like that. Because I think if you don't understand where people are coming from, it makes it a lot harder to report on the situation. I think you have to be able to put yourself in the other person's shoes. And if you're from the big city and have always lived in a million-dollar house, a maid, good money, then you're not going to be able to associate. You have to be able to connect with your person—with your reader and with the subject of your story.

In the sample of newspapers reviewed for this study, Susan's stories rarely reflected those connections, in large part because of the conditions under which they were produced. Sandra and Susan both said that stories about social service activities that account for much of the newspaper's poverty coverage largely fell to Sandra. Young reporters like Susan, Sandra said, tend to be more interested in covering "exciting" stories involving law enforcement. "As you move along [in your journalism career]," Sandra explained, "you change your perspective somewhat. And you let the younger reporters who can get excited about this stuff [crime] do it. I don't want to do it [laughs]."

Susan said she saw the links between poverty and the law enforcement issues she covered. For example, she said, the use of heroin was becoming more problematic in Greenburg in large part because heroin was an affordable alternative to illegally obtained prescription drugs. "Then you also hear it brought up in court: Do people have the money to pay their attorneys? Do they not? And a lot of people will say that the money situation has led to their [legal] problems," she explained. But addressing those links often takes time, and time is in short supply for the *Star*'s small editorial staff.

Henderson Media's remote pagination plant also limits the newspaper in some ways. Sandra and Susan determine what content gets into the newspaper, the editor said, but "we sometimes don't have the say-so on *how* it goes in there." Sandra said readers sometimes notice the lack of creativity and occasional design hiccups (headlines and stories that don't match up, for example), but few complain. One *Star* reader interviewed for this book said she once submitted materials for publication in the Star, and that the layout artist cut off part of her submission. That experience, the reader said, made her less confident in the *Star* and less willing to contribute information for publication.

Greenburg Today: "That's Not All We Are"

Theresa, editor of the hyperlocal news web site GreenburgToday. com, said that when she covered the news, "I see people, not stories." She said she was constantly mindful of the impacts of news coverage on local people's lives. For example, she often covered car crashes but did not take photos of crash scenes in which injured people were visible, because she would not want images of her loved ones to be on the Internet in that situation. "I'm not out to make money off somebody else's misfortune," she said. Theresa conceived of GreenburgToday.com in response to community image problems—problems, she explained, that were caused by Greenburg's negative image in the region, the inattentiveness and irresponsibility of local leaders ("what you had was an old guard that didn't want to create opportunities"), and the laissez-faire attitude the *Greenburg Star* had toward those matters. "I wanted, when people Google Green County, I wanted them to see something positive come up," she said. Theresa grew up in Green County, received a bachelor's degree in communications from a small regional college nearby, and recalled a generally negative mindset about local problems such as coal mine closures. "I see it [that negative mindset] changing," Theresa said over lunch at a Greenburg restaurant. "Just because we live in a depressed area doesn't mean we have to act like it."

She was particularly bothered by television news coverage of the region, which she said often depicted Greenburg negatively. To her, for the most part, local TV news coverage that came from a major city about fifty miles away "perpetuates the poverty mindset, especially in Green County" by focusing on that negativity. "When they talk about meth busts and things like that, it's like that's all we are. That's not all we are," she said. Even positive stories on television news could be problematic, she said, because they suggested Greenburg residents, and the region as a whole, were somehow abnormal. She recalled one television news segment about a local volunteer program (she was one of the volunteers) that provided an after-school program for local children. The program had struggled financially, she said, and "the finished [TV news] product is like we're all bums and our kids are running around wild in the streets."

Although she was bothered by the way government in Greenburg operated and the lack of local job opportunities, Theresa said, "I made a conscious choice to be positive [on the web site]. That's who I am. That's what I hope for out of this area. My faith plays a role in that.... I'm not trying to shine a light here. I'm looking to reflect the light we already have." In doing so, she said she hoped she could contribute to what she called a "generational change" in the pessimism about economic opportunities in Greenburg, although she acknowledged that such a change would not come easily. Theresa was critical of what she called the "Appalachian attitude," which she saw as a belief that the best years of one's life come during high school. Theresa said she believed the Internet could change that mindset by allowing people to connect with one another, exchange stories and ideas, and see new opportunities. "Technology changes everything," she added.

Theresa was more concerned about outside perception of her community than any other journalist interviewed for this project. Her effort to counter that image demonstrates the ways an individual can use the Internet to create a counternarrative about her community. It was not clear based on this study that GreenburgToday was causing people to rethink social issues in the town, but the site was relatively new (it had only been online for about four months at the time of this study). Theresa also operated another hyperlocal news web site in a neighboring town. Both sites were supported by advertisers and between the two, Theresa said, she made a modest living. GreenburgToday.com did not have the same reach and status that the *Star* enjoyed in Greenburg, but many people in Greenburg said they read it.

Priorsville: Trained Journalists and Circumstantial Newspapermen

In Priorsville, local residents had two weekly newspapers to choose from: the *Priorsville Record* and the *Priorsville Post-Examiner*

(*PPE*). While some of the news in both papers was similar, the styles of the publications and the life experiences and journalistic philosophies of those who produced them were quite different. *PPE* publisher Bill and editor Nick were both Priorsville natives who had lived in the community for most of their lives. Both studied journalism at the same regional college about two hours west of Priorsville, and they had ideas about news values and journalistic philosophies that, for the most part, aligned. Ed, the publisher of the *Record*, also grew up in Priorsville, but *Record* editor Jim moved to the area from the western United States with plans to retire. Neither Jim nor Ed had formal journalism training, and both men came to the newspaper from other fields (Jim was a retired government employee, and Ed had held several other jobs). The differences in the training and backgrounds of the two staffs was the primary reason the two newspapers are so visibly different. Nick was skilled with computers and used contemporary newspaper design principles to lay out the pages of the *PPE*, and the newspaper included many bylined stories written by Nick, Bill, or others who submitted material to the paper. The *Record* relied more heavily on submitted materials for its front page, rarely used bylines to indicate that stories were written by someone on the newspaper's staff, and assembled the newspaper column by column using the manual "cut-and-paste" method of newspaper production that had been replaced at many newspapers (including the *PPE*) by computer design. Most importantly, the two staffs also had distinct philosophies about the purpose of a local newspaper and attitudes toward local poverty that shaped their coverage in important ways.

The *Priorsville Record*: "You've Got to Watch What You Say"

Jim, editor of the *Priorsville Record*, said he viewed "local coverage" as his newspaper's primary job. People bought the *Record* to see slices of Priorsville life, such as photos of their children and grandchildren winning school awards or playing sports, he said. "They can get all the other news they want from TV or the [metropolitan newspaper that circulates in the area] or whatever. They'd rather see the local paper stick to local events and things," he continued. When Ed, the *Record*'s publisher, was asked how he defined news, he struggled to formulate an answer. This is perhaps unsurprising, given the fact that he fell into journalism somewhat unexpectedly and did not consider himself a "journalist." Heritage and local traditions are important, he explained. Beyond that, if people care enough to read a story, then it is news: "The newspaper's job is to keep up with the community." When it came to deciding what was published in the *Record*, however, Ed indicated he ultimately relies on two of the traits journalism students are commonly taught to look for in news: impact and novelty. Ed said he made decisions about what will go on the front page based on how many people he believed the information would affect and on how interested he thought people would be. Arrest records appeared on the front pages of all twenty-five issues of the *Record* reviewed for this study, and other stories about crimes were common. Ed said he viewed the prominent publication of those records as a public service. "We've got a bad drug problem in this county," he said. If a Priorsville resident found out through the newspaper that someone he or she knew was arrested on drug charges, Ed reasoned, then the innocent person could distance himself or herself from the offender. Jim, the newspaper's editor, offered this more cynical explanation for the popularity of crime stories: "It generates a lot of buzz because a lot of the drug users are wanting to know who they can't go to anymore."

Ed's role in the production of the *Record* was fairly simple. The process began on Mondays: "I'll look over the stack and see what's in there," he said, referring to the stacks of materials that have been submitted for possible publication. If he approved of what was in the stack, which he usually did, it was cleared for publication. "If I see something in there I don't like, I'll have 'em pull it," he explained.

Ed gave Jim most of the authority to determine what went on the front page in 2013. "Ed has some input" but rarely intervened, Jim said. "He knows people around here, and sometimes there's a particular story he'd like to see on the front [page]." Jim said stories about crime and county government generally tended to draw the most reader interest. When he wrote about those things, Jim said, he made a conscious effort to stick to the facts and to avoid publishing a great deal of background. "I basically say so-and-so is coming up for trial, and maybe give some basic information and not rehash everything way back," Jim said. This approach may reduce the likelihood that connections will be made between poverty and local problems such as health care issues, drug abuse, or teenage pregnancy. There are strong latent ties between poverty and those issues, but if a newspaper actively strives to avoid deep context, then those ties are unlikely to be reported.

Ed was always mindful of how people would react to the information he printed, and he was reluctant to publish anything that might appear controversial. He compared his journalistic life to his barbershop—he said he had seen men come in for haircuts and insult other members of the community while they waited, not knowing that the person in the next chair was the cousin of the person being insulted. "You've got to watch what you say because you never know how it's going to affect people," he said, referring both to idle chatter in the barbershop and front-page news in the paper. Ed said he was especially sensitive to "bad news," such as car accidents and fires. "I wish I didn't have to put any tragedy in my paper," he said, because he did not want the people involved to have to relive those tragedies when they saw images of them in print. Later in that conversation, Ed volunteered that "we try to be a Christian newspaper." When asked what that meant, he said that "we try to have dignity in our news. With things I am totally against in terms of religious views, I try not to put that in the paper." He said he'd never had to deal with such a conflict, although he had thought about situations where he might, and what he might do. For example, he said he would refuse to publish a marriage announcement for a gay couple. If someone (presumably a judge) told him he had to print it, he said, he would run it very small, a decision that would likely result in poor photo quality. He said he would tell the engaged couple that the announcement was published, but that he had little control over the poor quality. "Sometimes printers make mistakes," he said sarcastically.

Poverty certainly fell into the category of topics Ed would cover with care. When it came to writing about people who deal with extreme economic need firsthand, Ed said, "I would never put nothing in there about a poverty family. I wouldn't put their names in there because I don't want to embarrass them." If someone came to him and asked for their names and story to be published, he said, he would probably agree to do it. But he said he would not approach an individual or family and ask them to do such a thing for fear that the story subject would be ostracized because of the attention. Jim, the *Record*'s editor, said poverty was rarely a story topic, although monthly unemployment numbers would get press when they were released by the state. Jim said he took the same approach to unemployment that he took to court cases: Let the facts speak for themselves. Unemployment numbers, the editor explained, were "basically published with a little bit of a local [slant]. It comes out of the state pretty generic, so we direct it toward Prior County: The rate is this, and it went down or it went up, that type of thing." Beyond that, the newspaper did not seek out stories about the negative consequences of poverty. When asked why, Jim answered, "I guess probably a lot of my thought process is people don't want to be reminded. You don't need to tell people they're living in poverty. They know they are. They want solutions to poverty." The newspaper's managers did not see themselves, or the *Record*, as a generator of those solutions. Both Jim and Ed said they believed the duty of addressing local poverty fell primarily to local government, an attitude local journalists said was common in Priorsville. "The poverty situation, you basically have to go through the county commission because it's the leaders of the community who are responsible for helping people with their poverty," Ed said.

Ed at times seemed largely unsure of how news decisions should be made—he knew news when he saw it, and he knew what he liked. His interest largely seemed to be in selling newspapers and printing a publication that fit his personal tastes, and he believed in the formula he had. The *Record*'s approach to social issues was basically "do no harm," and Ed and Jim executed that approach by leaving the public discussion of those issues to other people. Ed and Jim did not want to hurt individuals' feelings or the community as a whole, but they expressed no thoughts or plans on how to help matters either. Ed in particular saw that as the government's job, not the newspaper's. Ed and Jim seemed to have no real social agenda for the newspaper they produced every week. They saw the newspaper largely as a bulletin board where the previous week's happenings could be preserved, either for posterity (in the case of news about achievements) or as a warning (in the case of crime news). A local newspaper can, and should, do those things. However, the "stick to the facts" coverage Ed and Jim provided was reactive by design—they did not proactively seek out alternative opinions on poverty, or any other topic, for fear of disturbing their readers' sensibilities. Such an approach may be a safe way to publish a newspaper (albeit one that struggles to break even financially some weeks), but it does little to foster meaningful community dialogue about matters such as poverty that are sometimes difficult for communities to address head-on without leadership.

The *Priorsville Post-Examiner*: Trying to Get People Riled Up

In Priorsville, people (usually influential people in the community) would sometimes tell me that there *were* jobs in their town, which sat in the county with its state's highest unemployment rate. People can *get work*, I was told, but employers could not get people *to work*. Nick, the *PPE*'s editor, heard those same stories all the time. So he decided to make something of it in the newspaper:

> I kept hearing community leaders say, "There's jobs. People won't take them, but there's jobs." So I did a story where we identified the top 10 employers, by number [of positions], and I called every one of them and said, "are you hiring," and surprisingly found out that eight of them were hiring at the time. And most of them said, "We just can't find people who, number one, are willing to work, and number two, can pass a drug test."

Most of the positions were low-paying jobs—"I mean, we're talking $8 an hour," Nick explained. But still, they were *jobs*. When the story about the positions available with the community's top ten employers was published in 2013, Nick said, the response was "all negative." Many readers did not want to believe jobs were available. One even accused him of fabricating the numbers. The story illustrates not only Nick's willingness to write about local issues in a way that may ruffle feathers, but also a somewhat conflicted view of poverty shared by many in Priorsville. When asked what caused poverty in Priorsville, Nick said that a lack of jobs in general, and good jobs in particular, were to blame. Then, he added,

> The other side of it is an unwillingness to work. We've got a generation, actually we're on the second generation now, of people who have developed this mindset of, I don't know the right way to put it, but basically a welfare generation for lack of a better way to put it.

He'd heard the argument about the welfare generation before, he said. His wife taught elementary school and came home with stories of young boys and girls whose primary aspiration was to get on government assistance. But the news story about how many local jobs were available was "an eye-opener," he recalled, that influenced the way he thought about—and covered—the issue of joblessness.

Unemployment and the poverty that accompanied it were big problems in Prior County. "It's pretty bad . . . as bad as you can imagine it being," said Nick. "Longer term, even before this recession started, poverty was a problem here. . . . When you picture poverty in Appalachia, poverty in rural middle America, I mean we're pretty much top of mind." When people in the community were asked what types of stories were most likely to get Prior County on the evening news or in the region's metropolitan newspaper, most said unemployment or poverty, a fact that troubled many of them, including Nick. "I expect it [regional news about Priorsville] to be negative. Cringe—that's my first reaction. Cringe," Nick said. He continued:

> The story line about Prior County's highest unemployment rate in the state has been absolutely beat to death. I mean, it's not something you sweep under the rug and it's not something you try to cover up or anything. But I mean, there's only so many angles you can hit it from. And it seems like everything, even positive things that happen here where people are trying to make a difference, the [regional metropolitan] media will come up and portray it as, "well, poor old Prior County again." Sometimes it's alright to look at the positive side of things.

The regional media's mention of unemployment in a story about a cultural festival hosted by the chamber of commerce about six months prior to our interview really angered him, because the unemployment rate had nothing to do with the festival. He recalled the theme of the story being "something to the effect of 'Prior County has the highest unemployment rate in the state, and, uh, here's what they're doing about it.'" The festival had nothing to do with the high unemployment rate—those were two completely separate issues, Nick continued, "but it [the television station] was tying them together." Because local people read those stories and see them on television, Nick said, some residents develop a sense of hopelessness:

> As a community, you're beat down and you're beat down and you're beat down, and it becomes your mindset that there's nothing we can do about it, we might as well accept it. And sometimes a little bit of optimism can go a long way. Perception's everything, and if the community is beat down to the point that they don't think they can pick themselves up by their bootstraps and improve their situation, then they're probably not going to.

Nick saw the provision of that "little bit of optimism" as an important role newspapers like his fill in struggling rural communities. It becomes difficult for a community to be vibrant, he said, when all the news its residents receive is negative. The idea that media have a responsibility to create a strong community environment was especially poignant coming from Nick and his boss, *PPE* publisher Bill, who, of the eleven journalists interviewed for this project, were by far the most likely to publish stories that challenged local officials and the local status quo. Unlike *Greenburg Star* editor Sandra, who thought of community promotion in terms of building up local businesses, Bill and Nick viewed community promotion in terms of generating conversation. "We think people have a right to know," Bill, who founded the *PPE* in the mid-1970s, said. Bill's journalistic philosophy has not been wholly embraced in Priorsville, he explained:

That's got us in trouble a few times through the years. We had a mayor of this town at one time that called down here and said "I'd like to buy that paper. How much? How much do you want for it?" I say, "Well, it's not for sale but why would you want a newspaper?" She says, "so I can close the damn thing down." [laughs] It rubbed people the wrong way, telling the truth. And it's been painful sometimes.[6]

Telling the truth about poverty can sometimes be difficult. A lack of time was rarely the reason for the difficulty at the *PPE*. Nick said he had never felt so rushed to meet a deadline that he could not make time to report out a deeper issue piece. To the contrary, he said, he sometimes had a difficult time finding news during weeks when there was not much "spot news" going on. "If it can fill column inches [space in the newspaper], generally it's going to be a story," he said. News about poverty would often generate criticism from local leaders, Nick and Bill said, but that did not seem to serve as a deterrent—at times, both men seemed to relish in their ability to rile up the town's leadership. The challenge they faced was writing about social conditions in a way that *built up* the community rather than discouraging it. Some stories about joblessness and local need that were published at the start of the recession probably would not be written later on "just because it's been beat to death," Nick said. He continued:

You write something over and over and over and eventually you get tired of it, and people get tired of reading it. But I mean, a lot of it still gets covered. The job numbers come out every month, and that's always a story, usually a front-page story. Every month it mentions that we're still the highest unemployment rate in the state and that we're not making the same progress that a lot of other communities are making. Every month that makes our mayor mad at me. But it is what it is, and he'll get over it.[7]

Nick observed that the community reaction to statistics about poverty was "largely indifference," which could be frustrating. Nick said that his efforts to "facilitate a discussion" about "what needs to be done, what needs to be changed in order to make the community better" were often unsuccessful, a challenge he faced both in his role as editor of the newspaper and as a member of the chamber of commerce board of directors:

> Sometimes it's difficult to get people to be proactive. You can run a story every week, in every edition of the paper, about shortcomings the community has and things it needs to improve on, but if people aren't willing to stand up and do anything about it, after a while you start to feel like you're kind of wasting your breath, or wasting your ink, or whatever. That is a problem, I guess the apathy of the community is a problem. . . . You write stories where you think, "man this is important, this is going to draw a reaction." And you hear nothing. And that can be frustrating.

When it came to writing about poverty specifically, both Bill and Nick said the voices of individuals who experience poverty first-hand were not sought out for stories. Nick, who would be more likely than Bill to take on such a reporting project, said, "We don't go out and talk to a lot of people in the community to talk about that aspect." When asked why, he said "there hasn't really been a need to, to do the stories we've done." Nick said the director of the chamber of commerce was the first source he would contact for a story about poverty. Bill, the *PPE*'s publisher, said the newspaper did not actively seek out stories about poverty in the community at all. "They come to us. Because there is a lot of pride, and some shame in being in that position [of being poor]," he said. Poverty in and of itself, Bill explained, has little news value because it is a part of everyday life: "I don't look at poverty. We live with it. I don't look for it. It's just part of our lives here." Both Bill and Nick said community organizations and individuals in Priorsville were quick to come to the aid of neighbors in need. But Bill expressed little optimism that any institution in Priorsville could materially change living conditions for the poor. The newspaper, the chamber of commerce, and local leaders were always looking for ways out of poverty, largely through the recruitment of industry, he said. "And little by little you do," he added, "but it doesn't last long." Bill said he wanted to see the newspaper crusade for jobs, but "I don't know how you do that." He believed Nick was "in the process of cultivating Prior County. What I mean by that is its image, not just for the people who live here, but for the people who visit here." Bill and Nick's position on the *PPE*'s ability to act as an agent of change was particularly interesting compared to the stance of Ed and Jim at the *Priorsville Record*. Ed and Jim did not see pushing for change and discussion in the community as important parts of their jobs, and they (especially Ed) were wary of disturbing the status quo. Perhaps because of their training and socialization into journalistic norms, Nick and Bill were more likely to see advocacy and the promotion of possibly contentious discussion as part of their jobs at the *PPE*, although Bill's optimism about the potential results of that work seemed to be waning. Bill and Nick saw *themselves* as agents of change, but to achieve that change, they were more inclined to partner with local officials and business leaders and less inclined to empower poor people in the community to become agents of change themselves.

In March 2014, Nick's short-term editorial plans for the *PPE* included some "thought-provoking pieces that will get people to just start talking about how they can make their community better." The community had talked for so long about how jobs weren't available, he said, "but at some point you've got to start talking about things you can do to pick yourself up, stop waiting on the guys from the state or Washington to come in and do it for you, but pick yourself up and put yourself back on a road to a brighter future." Most of those stories, he suspected, would draw the same kind of negative reaction his 2013 piece on jobs received. He mentioned several times plans for a story about food stamp fraud ("that's not going to go over well"), and he was also planning a story about litter, which would take the angle that roadside trash is bad for the area's tourism economy ("That does tie into poverty," he said, "because you don't see that if you go into more affluent communities").

Bill and Nick were, by far, the most socially progressive journalists interviewed for this book, in that they recognized problems in their community and wanted to address them, even if that meant occasionally incurring the ire of local leaders or alienating readers or advertisers. Both men suggested that influencing people's attitudes toward change in Priorsville was key to creating real social progress in the community, and Nick thought about the community's joblessness in that context. Still, they seemed to see poverty mainly in the context of its impacts on people who *were not* poor. Addressing issues such as food stamp fraud or litter are worthwhile from a journalistic perspective. But Nick and Bill seemed to be at a loss when it comes to taking on the underlying problem of quiescence in Priorsville, which, they saw, was tied to the lack of economic opportunity that exists there. It appeared that, in the short term at least, their approach would be to continue to fight the good fight, largely relying on the same sets of voices to address local issues.

Knowledge of the professional backgrounds and educations of the four men who provide Priorsville's local news can help us understand why they make the coverage decisions they make. Bill and Nick had thought about what journalists should try to accomplish for a long time and saw their work as a social service of sorts. Ed and Jim viewed the newspaper more as a place to work and were less likely to relay a sense of social responsibility. However, this comparison of the staffs at the *Record* and the *PPE* should not be understood as an indictment of journalists who do not receive formal journalism training. Of the four newspapers in this study, the *PPE* took the most aggressive role as an advocate for change in its community, and its publisher and editor were both career journalists with college degrees in the field, factors that create their own constraints on how journalists do their work. However, concerned individuals with backgrounds in other fields can use media to attempt to generate conversations about social problems in their communities, as the online Deer Creek Advocate will show.

Deer Creek: "I'm Essentially a Positive Person"

Just before he told the story of his poorly received report on Albert Hodgekins, the homeless man who walked the streets of his town, *Deer Creek Chronicle* owner and senior editor Gregory made this observation about local poverty: "Poverty, poverty is a problem everywhere, I think, in [this state], and there's [pause] it's much more dramatic in other areas than it is right here." He suggested that poverty was less prevalent there because the presence of the local college created an environment where people were expected to take part in higher education. "Now most of them do not stay here. They go elsewhere, where the jobs are. But I think it's mainly the education factor," Gregory said. According to the U.S. Census Bureau, the percentage of Deer Creek residents who had at least a high school diploma (77 percent) or a college degree (15 percent) at the time of our discussion were both below the state average. At the end of the story about Albert, Gregory was asked whether he had written many other stories about poverty. His answer reflects the core reason readers of the *Chronicle* got so little news about the community's poor economic conditions:

No, we do not. We, we have lacks in this community. I think you'll read about the lacks—maybe the lack of affordable good housing, and the lack of certain community services—but you will not read a lot about it. Because the Albert Hodgekins incident happened probably about fifteen years ago, and since then, as I said, I just haven't seen the homeless.

Gregory repeatedly said poverty in Deer Creek was less of a problem than it was in other areas, but income statistics tell a different story. So do many of the people who live in Deer County, including Gregory's secretary Trish, a college graduate who, in her mid-twenties, still lives with her mother because neither can afford to live alone. There was tremendous dissonance between what Gregory saw in his community—be it local poverty rates, homelessness, or educational attainment—and what others in Deer Creek experienced. That difference influenced the way he covered economic matters in his newspaper, and as the next chapter will show, it influenced the ways people in the community reacted to the *Chronicle*.

Gregory once observed that he was "essentially a positive person," and he often noted that he felt it was important for the newspaper to reflect Deer Creek in a positive way. If good things were happening in the community, he said, the newspaper would praise those things. If he perceived some facet of community life to be bad, he would say so. "But in general there's a lot of good people and they're doing a lot of positive projects to move us ahead," he concluded. Recognizing the people behind those "positive projects," particularly "regular people in a small community who are doing good deeds," was one of Gregory's top priorities. He said he initiated the "Shining Stars" feature because he identified a core group of forty or fifty local leaders and civic club members in the community who were in the newspaper all the time. He wanted to create a space for others to be recognized.

The newspaper's emphasis on the positive, especially as it related to economic conditions, was echoed by others involved in its production as well. "We go out of our way here to print the positive of everything we can, you know, except for obits and courthouse [crime] news," said Eric, Gregory's son and the newspaper's general manager. "Other than that, we try desperately to print the good stuff, the happy stuff, the stuff that makes people go 'Yeah, it's nice living in a small town,' and things like that," he said, later adding, "We try to keep it positive because we get enough negative by turning on the nightly news. It's just nice to know that Deer Creek's going to move on and we're doing as well as we possibly can." Quinn, a former reporter at the *Chronicle*, said, "When the community would come together [to help an individual in need], that kind of stuff we covered. But as far as the downside of things, or how dreary it was, we didn't cover stuff like that." Eric observed that coverage of poverty largely consisted of publishing press releases from local service agencies. "As to Dad saying, 'Eric, we need a story about the poverty over on River Street,' he's never given me that kind of a broad story to do something on," Eric said. "As a matter of fact, I'm sitting here thinking, 'how would I start that story?'" When Gregory was asked if it was possible to discuss negative aspects of social life in a positive way, using prescription drug abuse as an example, he responded, "To be honest with you, I don't follow it that much. I mean, we report on meth labs and things like that that the police give us."

Other *Chronicle* employees (who, with the exception of his son Eric, usually referred to Gregory as "Dr. Lastname") said Gregory makes all major decisions about what will be published in the newspaper. He said he has "some general parameters of what we want" in each issue: Political news (usually in the form of columns from the area's U.S. senator or congressman), social news ("we have a lot of very nice ladies who live in small communities" and send in updates from those places, he explained), sports news (produced by a new sports editor who also worked a full-time job in the public sector in another county), news about local government, and news about cultural events such as historical reenactments, concerts, and plays in other parts of the state. The cultural news, Gregory remarked, was of particular interest to people who work at the college and in the oil and gas industry (he often returned to those segments of the community when he spoke of his most important constituencies). Gregory published many press releases from state government agencies, mainly because he often struggled to find local content to fill the pages of his newspaper. "I like to try to stick at, like, sixteen pages, even though it should be like twelve pages [because of advertising sales]. I do like to stick at sixteen pages because it gives more for the reader to read," he explained. "I realize that I'm paying more, but I think that the more you put into something, the more you're going to get out of it. This is what the readers tell me: that they appreciate getting a statewide view." Much of the information published inside the newspaper was pulled from the Internet, he said.

When asked what his newspaper's core mission in Deer Creek was, Gregory answered:

> I think the newspaper, more than anything else, should number one, reflect the community, the various components of the community. And that's why we put a lot of college news in, we put a lot of oil and gas industry news in, if we get anything about prisons or corrections or new concepts on how to prevent recidivism among the inmates, we put it in. And we put in, of course, all of the basic community news, and that's very important. And the other thing is, uh, I don't like to sound moralistic, but it's the job of the small newspaper to be a leader within the community, to bring progress. And we do that mainly, here, through editorials and news stories.

When asked how a newspaper editor or publisher might go about becoming a leader, he answered this way:

I would say go to it. The Local Millionaire[8] here, every time I see him, and I see him about once a month, he always tells me the same thing. I always ask him the same question: "Would you give me a news story? Would you give me an update?" He always says, "Oh man, you've got the power with the newspaper. You just keep writing. You're going in the right direction." Of course, one of the things is that, in a community, in reflecting your community, you have to, whether you like it or not, you have to defend the local big industry, and that's oil and gas here. Before that, it was coal. If I had been in [Appalachian town where he previously worked] and had been against coal, all of my windows would have been broken down there. And occasionally, small problems came up with coal, mainly that, you know, the tearing up of roads by the coal trucks. So I would write an editorial, you know, that truck drivers have got to be more careful and all of that. Well, when I'd write an editorial about that, when the coal trucks would come by the newspaper office, they would just lay on their horns, ERRRRR, ERRRR. And the staff would come back: "They did it again, Dr. Lastname, they did it again." It was their way of getting back at me, you know. But I was essentially for the coal industry. Of course, those were the days before global warming. I'm sort of wavering on that issue now.

I really think that most people would be like our millionaire here, that they think that the newspaper has a lot of power. So you don't have to write an editorial, but you can go out there as a community journalist and write stories, and you can really almost win a Pulitzer Prize just by, let's say, writing stories about poverty. If I had the time to do it, I would go out here and find poverty and do stories about families living in poverty and how they got there, and I might win a Pulitzer Prize. You never can tell. But the community journalist has the ability because of the public perception of the newspaper,[9] that the newspaper is influential and it is powerful. And those journalists can make a difference.

Gregory's description of the local journalist as a community leader is revealing on several levels. It shows the pressures that newspaper professionals face in communities where resource extraction (or any other industry, for that matter) is the major source of jobs and income. It reflects the constituencies he recognized as important: the three main employers in the community. It also betrayed the company he kept, and provided some clues as to how that company influenced his attitude toward the community. Gregory saw the local college and the oil and gas industry (and in particular the Local Millionaire who owned the largest oil and gas company in Deer Creek) as central to the betterment of the community for which he advocated. To suggest that most people in Deer County, which experiences more poverty than 90 percent of the counties in the United States, would be "like our millionaire" in any way is a stretch. The millionaire had access to powerful people locally, but many Deer Creek residents said they did not. The millionaire's concerns and interests were reflected in the local newspaper, but middle-class and low-income community members said it did not reflect their concerns. Gregory talked to the millionaire regularly—they saw each other. Gregory did not see Deer Creek's poor. He suggested that to find extreme poverty, he would need to spend a large amount of time exploring the most remote corners of Deer County. In reality, he could walk out of his office and find it without getting into his car.

Gregory observed that many of his efforts to make a difference involved trying to overcome a general resistance to change that, he argued, was present in all small communities. One of the best ways to do so, he said, was to offer *contextual* information about current news events that was often overlooked (or, in the case of the *Priorsville Record*, actively eschewed) by local newspapers.

He suggested his liberal arts education helped him make context-reliant cases for change in a way that was sometimes effective. He recalled a specific example involving the construction of a small downtown park, which many in Deer Creek had opposed:

> If you can say, "you know, the history of parks is this: They provide places of recreation and entertainment and relaxation for people and families and for individuals for lunch breaks and stuff like that." If you can bring that out, the history of parks, then it helps the good progressive people in, like Deer Creek, to push forward and get this park done. And they did.

Gregory's contextual exploration of local news issues such as the park controversy was largely absent from local coverage in Greenburg and Priorsville during the period studied for this book. Although Gregory rarely applied it to social need because he rarely wrote about social need, it was evident in some of the syndicated material he published. In the cases where that context was present, the writers were able to make effective arguments about broader social impacts of poverty on issues such as health and school achievement.

Later, Gregory returned to the topic of battling a resistance to change, which he referred to in that part of the interview as "the Appalachian Way":

> I think the slowness to accept new ideas is one of the things I'm working on right now. You know, let's accept some new ideas and let's back these new businesses that are starting up. Because, you know, the Appalachian Way is we're going to stay back in our hollow and we're going to do what we've been doing for the last 20, 30, 40 years, and we're not gonna do anything new. And, you know, this is not good for new businesses, especially new small businesses like the new restaurants in town. So many new businesses have gone out

of business because people haven't given them a chance and it's because of this hollow mentality. So, you know, I am critical of that.

Overcoming the "hollow mentality" could mean other things: impressing upon people the benefits of education or entrepreneurship (which, Gregory could argue, he does through news about the local college), or creating a platform where their voices, concerns, and experiences could be addressed. But overcoming the "hollow mentality" in Deer Creek, in this instance, instead involved getting people to come out of the woods to spend money (which he presumed they had).

When I worked as a newspaper reporter and editor, I often interviewed people who were clearly telling me what they thought I wanted to hear, a problem also sometimes encountered by social scientists. I experienced that in a few of the interviews I conducted for this study. But my sense was that Gregory genuinely believed the things he told me, and that he usually did not recognize the social problems around him. The people who influenced him seemed to be a fairly small group of affluent people. He did not see local poverty in the way that the numbers bore it out, or in the way others in the community described it. Gregory talked often about being a community leader and setting an agenda for Deer Creek, duties a newspaper publisher should be willing to accept. However, because of his limited exposure to others in Deer Creek, he ended up with a good-natured but very tunnel-visioned approach to community leadership.

The Deer Creek Advocate: "The Messenger of Citizens"

Several people in Deer Creek said they saw the online Deer Creek Advocate (DCA) as a viable news alternative to the local newspaper. After some initial contact, Lance, the founder of the Advocate, decided not to take part in interviews for this study. However, some story posts and comments on his web site offer clues to his journalistic motives. In a 2011 response to criticism of the site, Lance wrote that DCA "is just the messenger of citizens." In a separate response to another set of criticisms in 2010, Lance told readers that the site intended "to provide a much needed platform for our community" so residents could "express themselves without fear of retribution." While Lance readily provided his own views of local issues, he wrote in the 2010 column that opposing comments were also welcome, as long as they met the site's commenting policies: "On DCA, one can say what one wants. You don't have to pay for it or use your power to use it. Thoughts are printed without editing. Anyone, rich, poor, black, white, red, yellow, domestic, foreign, educated, non-educated, has the same chance." In early 2012, a post entitled "Forces at work to stop the DCA's Advocacy for Transparency and Accountability?"[10] called Lance's web site "a formidable champion for good in the County [*sic*]." The writer of that piece noted that the local newspaper was unwilling to "root out corruption" in Deer Creek and praised the DCA for giving people a platform to voice their concerns. Some community members said they read the DCA more often than the *Chronicle*.

Like Theresa at GreenburgToday.com, Lance offered through the DCA a platform for the establishment of a counternarrative about the local community. Both digital entrepreneurs launched their web sites in part to fill a void they saw in their local media ecosystems: Theresa wanted to create an outlet for positive news about Greenburg, and Lance developed a place where individuals could gather to voice concerns and criticisms that seemed unwelcome in the local newspaper. What set the DCA apart from GreenburgToday.com, and from the four newspapers described in this book, was the public engagement that it facilitated.

Individuals who said they had no other local voice could post their opinions and ideas on the site with little concern about social or political retribution. Because of that freedom and engagement, the DCA's posts and comment sections presented narratives about social issues in Deer Creek that differed dramatically from those expressed in the *Deer Creek Chronicle*.

The engagement the site facilitated also led to the greatest criticism of the DCA. *Chronicle* editor and publisher Gregory, who was often criticized on the DCA, said he believed the site was damaging to the community in that it allowed salacious gossip to spread, but he said he took no umbrage at the personal attacks he experienced there—"I just laugh at them," he said. Quinn, a local secretary and former *Chronicle* reporter, said the DCA site was "good and bad." The site did provide news that readers couldn't find elsewhere, she said. But she believed that comments were sometimes deleted if they did not align with Lance's viewpoints. "The news is pretty good, but if you read the comments, you'll get a one-sided kind of opinion," she concluded. Quinn's suggestion that Lance selectively edited comments was made by others interviewed for this project, and occasionally raised by people who commented on the site. As the next chapter will note, other residents voiced concerns about hostility in the DCA's comment sections as well.

The Factors that Influence Encoding

Attempting to critique the journalistic encoding of *individual stories* about poverty that appear in local media in Greenburg, Priorsville, and Deer Creek is perhaps a futile task because there are so few of them and because news staffs took a hands-off approach to the production of much of the content that did make it into the newspaper. However, journalists' routines, priorities, and attitudes toward their work and toward need in their community provide important insight into the encoding of the *overall news product*, which is just as valuable, if not more so.

Some journalists interviewed for this book said they recognized the ties between poverty and other newsworthy matters, such as local drug abuse in Greenburg or community pride in Priorsville. However, those matters rarely were connected to poverty in stories. There are several reasons for that. In Greenburg, the limitations were partly the result of corporate practices, but philosophies also came into play in important ways. Sandra's attitudes toward community development and her desire to shelter the poor from public ridicule led to the absence of news about realities that many Greenburg residents saw daily. The same could be said for the *Priorsville Record* and GreenburgToday.com, where journalists for the most part provided a platform for others who had the time, resources, and initiative to provide news to them. Dominant local attitudes related to poverty will remain dominant until they are challenged, and neither GreenburgToday.com, the *Record*, nor the *Star* did much to challenge dominant attitudes by actively pursuing alternative voices, or by inviting those voices to come to them. At the news outlet in this study that seemed most poised to explore social alternatives, the *Priorsville Post-Examiner*, journalists were willing to challenge the status quo. However, they also seemed unsure of how to do so in a way that would move people to action. At the *Deer Creek Chronicle*, Gregory simply was largely isolated from the economic realities many of his neighbors faced. One day over lunch at a small diner two blocks from his office, Gregory said, "You are derelict of your duties as a newspaper publisher if you do not consider the work that you do in part, in greater part, as a public service, rather than just strictly as a business." Gregory provided a great deal of service in Deer Creek, but relatively little of it applied to those in his community who looked to the newspaper to help them understand or address poverty. Instead, it mostly catered to an elite crowd, and in the process it ostracized many other local residents.

To wholly understand the approaches of the journalists here, one must balance their professional philosophies against the outside factors at play in the region in which they work. In Greenburg and Priorsville, local journalists compete with regional narratives that set them apart as backward, inept, lazy, or deviant. Residents in Greenburg and Priorsville almost universally said that they would expect a regional newspaper or television story about their community to be negative.[11] Almost every interview participant in Greenburg said they would expect a regional news story featuring the community to be about drug abuse. Most Priorsville residents interviewed said they would expect the story to be about job losses or poverty. The community journalists featured in this book recognized that coverage as incomplete and detrimental to their communities and saw themselves, to varying degrees, as counterbalances to those narratives. They also face a much broader negative narrative when media report on Appalachia. *PPE* editor Nick, who had lived in the region his whole life, explained his feelings about Appalachia's media portrayal this way:

Someone, I think it was in east Kentucky or somewhere, wrote a really good piece, thought-provoking, about how every time the national media comes in [to Appalachia] and covers a story they look at it from the standpoint of the negative. And that's what they're after: They're chasing the things with the poverty, they're going out to the old coal mining towns and getting pictures of the clapboard houses. And they [the author of the story he read] say, "you really don't stop to think about it." And, a friend of mine who is a veterinarian in town said the same thing. And I don't remember the story that she was referring to, but it was a story, I think, in the *Wall Street Journal*. I could be wrong about that, but they did this tour through eastern Kentucky,

West Virginia, down into Tennessee, and she said, "They're totally ignoring, you know, they may be pockets, but there are pockets in Appalachia where people are working hard and trying to change their community for the better." People aren't necessarily just willing to sit around and be on the government draw. But that seems to be the big thing. When the *Washington Post*, or one of the big papers, comes into Appalachia, they're focusing on the high rate of government assistance and things like that, and it seems like they always find the person who's sitting down at the store, down at the hangout, just sitting there waiting for their check to come. That seems to be what they focus on. It's not just the poverty, it's the high welfare rates, the high disability rates, things like that.

The community journalists interviewed for this book were largely in agreement that counteracting specific negative reports about the towns where they worked was part of their job. Theresa said she started GreenburgToday.com in response to regional and national coverage of a local political controversy that she believed was unfairly critical of the community. As noted earlier, Nick believed the *PPE* could provide a positive counterbalance to media messages about Priorsville's suffering economy. There was much less agreement on the impact of negative media images of Appalachia. Nick said he took personal offense to negative mountain stereotypes, but he reasoned stories in the *Wall Street Journal* or the *Washington Post* made little difference locally because few people in Priorsville read those stories. Nancy, the former Henderson Media editor, took a different position, arguing that it was "bizarre" to think that Appalachia was completely culturally different from the rest of the world. "I mean, there are some things here that are different here than other places, but I don't think it's any reflection on intelligence or creativity," she said. "It's important to me to change the way people perceive us here."

Gregory, Bill, Nick, and Sandra all saw themselves as part of a leadership structure that included local government and business leaders, a leadership structure that often excludes people at the lower end of the socioeconomic ladder. Journalists' reluctance to write about poverty, and to interview and feature the poor in their communities, also was rooted in most cases in the rather large assumption that the economically disadvantaged would experience shame or embarrassment if they were "outed" in the newspaper. The *compassionate* thing to do, some journalists interviewed for this book reasoned, is to let them be and focus on other matters. The consequences of that assumption are many: Class-based social isolation and voicelessness remain unchallenged, understandings of poverty as first and foremost an individual responsibility are reinforced, and public discussions about solutions to economic conditions remain largely one-sided with the wealthy and middle class talking *to* or *about*, rather than *with*, their less-wealthy neighbors.

But what if those struggling to make financial headway in Greenburg, Priorsville, and Deer Creek *are not* ashamed of who they are, what they have, or the choices they have made? What if the telling of their stories serves not to isolate them, but rather to integrate them into a community that often *sees* them but rarely *knows* them? Do those who cope with financial hardships firsthand, those who work to help the poor, and others in these communities where need is prevalent understand the dominance of the community response frame and the absence of personal stories as acts of journalistic compassion, or as the ongoing maintenance of a status quo in which some voices matter more than others? Interviews with local residents in the three communities suggests that the decoding of local news coverage of poverty results in an interesting collection of what British sociologist

Anthony Giddens called "unintentional outcomes" that feed back into the problems of apathy and stratification present in Greenburg, Priorsville, Deer Creek, and other rural communities in Appalachia and elsewhere.[12]

CHAPTER 5

Decoding Poverty Coverage and Broader Images of Appalachia

At a nonprofit thrift store that operated out of an old school about a mile from downtown Greenburg, I met two local women, Jenn and Brandy. Jenn was operating the cash register behind the U-shaped counter, where men and women of all ages came to pay a dollar or two for a pair of pants, a toy, tennis shoes, window treatments, a toilet seat, or any other item chosen from the variety of gently used pieces of merchandise donated for the shop to sell. Brandy was nearby, sweeping the tile floors between racks of donated blouses and slacks.

Brandy, in her mid-twenties, had a nine-month-old daughter. Jenn, in her late teens, had a two-year-old son and a six-month-old daughter. None of the three children had fathers who were actively involved in their lives ("They [fathers] all run," Jenn remarked). Both women were born and raised in Greenburg and still lived with their parents because they could not afford places of their own. Both had tried to start new lives in other towns, but their financial realities and the draw of family kept them in Greenburg. Brandy had lived in another town about two hours from Greenburg for a year, before her daughter was born. "It drove me insane, because I was used to seeing all my family every day," she said. "You go eight months without seeing them, or longer, then it's hard. This place has got a pull on you. It brings you back, no matter what."

Stuck in Greenburg without the time, money, or training to commute to jobs in other towns, both women struggled to find work (after two years of unemployment, Brandy had been excited to learn the day before we met that she was going to get a job at a fast food restaurant in Greenburg; Jenn was hoping to get on at a local pizza parlor). Both recalled receiving free school supplies as children from a now-defunct nonprofit agency. On the March day I met them, both women were working at the thrift shop to earn that month's $400 welfare check. And both women were keenly aware of how all of those facts made them look to others, particularly Greenburg's more well-to-do residents. Brandy told me that, at the social service agency where she previously "worked off my welfare," her supervisor had called her, and all the other women who were there for the same reason, "welfare trash." "It's just how it is," she said.

Brandy said she sometimes looked at the *Greenburg Star* when she visited her grandmother, who subscribed to the newspaper. Jenn read it much less frequently—she said the news that most interested her was who'd been arrested, information she could get from the web site of the local court clerk. When they read the newspaper, Jenn and Brandy did not see a reflection of their lives, or of the lives of others they knew who struggled financially. Brandy observed:

> The only thing they put in the newspaper is how they're trying to make everything beautiful around here. They get grants for beautification in Greenburg. I'm sorry, but if you're getting money, a grant, to buy flowers for your town, don't you think you want to fix the potholes so you don't lose half your car instead of putting a bucket of flowers outside so people can see it? That is the thing that I don't understand.

The hanging baskets of petunias that, to *Star* editor Sandra, represented economic advancement were seen by Brandy as a boondoggle, evidence that the concerns of a large segment of the community did not really matter. "These are the issues that drive me nuts, because nobody ever does anything about it, no matter how much you talk about it," she said.

Jenn and Brandy saw compelling stories about the social contradictions in their lives every day. They watched men who did not pay their child support lose their driver's licenses in court, and, as a result, they became unable to drive to work and even less able to financially support their children (this happened to the father of Brandy's child). They knew homeless people who had been hassled by the police for pitching tents under a local bridge without the required city permit (there is no homeless shelter in Greenburg). They knew about situations where three or four families were living in houses built to accommodate one family because there were so few low-income apartments in Greenburg. "If they actually put in the paper, made a story about how life really is here . . . if they put that in the paper and more people talk about it and talk about it, it might spread and it might actually do some good," Brandy said. Some people in the community—namely, those with money—would not be swayed, she argued. But others, particularly low-income residents, might benefit if sustained community discussions about conditions for the poor turned into real action. "But I ain't going to hold my breath on that," she said. Jenn largely agreed. "If it [news about needs in the community] is lame, people are going to walk right past it," she said. When I asked her what "lame" looks like, she replied, "just the same old stuff." Most of what is in the newspaper, she concluded, is "the same old stuff."

Jenn and Brandy essentially read the absence of the news they described as evidence that *poverty is business as usual*, an interpretation they largely accepted at the beginning of our conversation. That interpretation reinforces a dominant "culture of poverty" view of social need that implies poverty is the result of individual choices made by the poor. It does not suggest that communities, or society as a whole, bear any broader responsibilities to address matters such as opportunity and inclusion. It lends credence to the idea, voiced by Bill at the *PPE* and others in this study, that poverty is an unavoidable fact of life in these rural, remote communities. Residents of Greenburg, Priorsville, and Deer Creek recognized the fact that, for the most part, local news organizations were silent when it came to economic matters such as local poverty, unemployment, and homelessness. The lack of reliable news coverage of those matters led some to suggest that there were no real public means in their communities for people to express new ideas or challenge prevailing notions about local poverty, or other social issues, for that matter.

The interpretation of a lack of local news coverage as evidence that poverty is a natural way of life was not isolated to the thrift shop where Jenn and Brandy worked. It was suggested by others, rich and poor, in Greenburg, Priorsville, and Deer Creek. Residents in all three communities understood the absence of news about poverty to mean that poverty was not a problem that was important for the community to address, an interpretation that is especially problematic for Jenn, Brandy, and others who cope with it daily. Other residents read into news coverage an understanding that only certain voices were welcome in the newspaper, and that only certain individuals and groups (mainly churches, nonprofits, or the government) were in the business of discussing solutions. In Priorsville, residents saw positive stories about the local economy as an attempt at community-building through the expression of positive news, although some said they believed those efforts benefited a few powerful people and not the community as a whole.

However, Brandy and Jenn (and a few others) also saw *their own* potential to articulate a different view of their community. As we continued to talk about life in Greenburg and the ways the poor were viewed and treated, their attitudes toward possible change appeared to shift and they seemed to develop a sense of self-efficacy and confidence that their take on matters such as the flower baskets downtown *did matter* to someone. Brandy and Jenn stopped, if only for a moment, seeing their condition as an inevitable by-product of the situation into which they were born. As we spoke, they became more and more confident in their opinions, and more willing to voice them. There are ways that local media (either print or online) can help their economically disadvantaged readers develop a public voice and take part in discussions about possible solutions, and this chapter will argue for why it is in the local media outlet's best interests to do so.

This chapter also explores residents' perceptions of media portrayal of Appalachia. People in Greenburg, Priorsville, and Deer Creek were largely in agreement that those representations were negative, but there was less agreement on whether they were damaging to individuals or communities in the region. Many expressed the opinion that there was little point in trying to combat images of the region that suggested it was in some way deviant or inferior. Their *that's-just-the-way-it-is* mentality, and the perceived lack of agency it suggests, in many ways mirrors the lack of power the poor felt to influence news coverage of poverty at the local level.

Greenburg: Limited Expectations

Many non-journalists in Greenburg expressed limited expectations of their daily newspaper and, for the most part, their new hyperlocal news web site. For most, those limited expectations mirrored their attitudes toward the possibility of social change that would materially improve the lives of Greenburg's poorest residents. Brandy's remarks that negative views of those on welfare were "just the way it is" was representative of a widely held impression that challenging Greenburg's status quo was an insurmountable task. Some local residents suggested the town's wealthy were uninterested in discussing changes to the status quo and enjoyed protections and a voice that would not be available to their less-wealthy neighbors. Frank, a former pastor in his early sixties who lost his job and had been unemployed for three months at the time of his interview, said, "Money's a big thing in Greenburg. If you have it, they will like you and listen to you. If you don't have it, you're not going to be a mover and a shaker." In another interview, Mary, a social service worker in her late fifties, discussed a local political controversy that she believed was downplayed by the *Star*. "If it was somebody that had no social standing in the community and they get in trouble, then it's all over the paper, it's front page, it's right there," she explained. When asked if personal wealth was the main reason for the difference, she answered, "It's not necessarily just money, it's who your family is, and other things. But I think everybody knows those rules and has learned to live with those rules, and around them." Floyd, who runs the county's largest nonprofit social service organization, said many local poor people are suspicious of the motives of the rich, and vice versa. "Communication is the big thing," Floyd said. "We don't communicate well, as groups or newspapers or anything."

The *Greenburg Star* and, to a lesser extent, GreenburgToday.com were seen by many residents as protectors of that status quo. Some saw little room for the voices of Greenburg's working-class and low-income populations, groups that rarely appeared in stories or photos. Mary said the newspaper "does a real good job of just reporting on the surface" but does not challenge the ideas or actions of the local elite. But, like others in Greenburg, she sympathized with the newspaper's staff. Mary believed local residents "have a right to know those things, to know the objective details," but if the newspaper delved more deeply into local problems, she said, "it would just create too much internal turmoil, and they don't get paid enough" to deal with the social consequences. Mary suggested that the newspaper did "as good a job as they possibly can," but she said she believed coverage was limited to protect social standing, an idea that is common in literature on journalistic gatekeeping.[1] "Sometimes they have to take the safe route. They report, but they'll err on the side of safety rather than do, like, investigative stuff or bring stuff to the surface," Mary said. Grace, a cafeteria cook at the local senior citizens center in her mid-forties, said she believed the newspaper workers "do their best" but, like Mary, she suggested they held back information. "A lot of things, people [namely, the newspaper] just keep confidential. The more people know, the more there is to get upset about," Grace said. Dwight, the unemployed pastor, said the newspaper is "just kind of neutral and go-with-the-flow." Floyd said the *Star*'s editor and reporter "don't want to make waves for the county. Sometimes I think waves are good. Let's get it out."

Along those lines, some residents expressed the idea that the newspaper was little more than a mouthpiece for Greenburg's influential decision makers, although that determination did not generate the same level of resentment that a similar sentiment in Deer Creek did (as will be discussed later in this chapter). When asked what kind of poverty coverage she saw in the *Star*, Kathy, a retired secretary, answered, "you don't [see coverage of poverty], unless it's something from a commissioner's report or a report from a local meeting." Clint, a middle-school teacher who grew up in Greenburg, observed that "I don't think they any longer at the *Star* make it a point to go out and get the news. I think they wait for the news to come to them. I think they wait for somebody to call them." Often, he said, the "somebody" who calls provides information with limited utility:

Whenever a report comes out at the state level, they'll have something in the paper, and it'll be very statistically driven, and there's never an answer to the problem, so they're just telling us what we already know. Occasionally they'll say the level of unemployment has gone down and we'll all cheer. But they never really offer any suggestion or they never really have any news about what anyone's doing to keep it down. They're just telling us facts. They're reporting what they've been given.

The reliance on submitted materials was also mentioned by Floyd and Mary, two of the local people Sandra and Susan mentioned as their best sources for news about poverty. Matthew, another frequent source and the manager of Green County's state welfare office, said that, "generally, the *Star* is not publishing anything [about welfare] unless I'm sending them the story." Matthew had strong feelings about the way welfare recipients were viewed in Greenburg: The "vast majority" of Green County residents who got government aid worked and followed the rules, he said, but they still faced a stigma because "people only see the bad apples, the ones that are milking the system and cheating us." However, Green County officials (Matthew's bosses) tended to be politically conservative, he said, and not interested in opening up a public dialogue about welfare locally. In a neighboring county where politics tended to be a little more liberal, Matthew explained, the person in his position (with the support of local leaders there) wrote press releases about how hard it is to pay for basic necessities when your income is at the poverty level, and rebuttals to state or federal reports on poverty. Those press releases usually were published in the neighboring county's newspapers. "I have no problem with what he's doing, because he does keep poverty on the forefront, and on the front of people's minds and eyes," Matthew said. But Matthew did not believe he would get support if he wanted to do the same in Green County. "There's not anybody out there [in Green County government] pushing the welfare angle," he concluded. "I just don't think it comes up that often [among county commissioners]."

Readers' perceptions of the *Star*'s lack of reporting on the community's economic hardships often related back to a lack of faith in the newspaper's ability to generate positive dialogue about those problems. That lack of faith existed not because residents did not trust the journalists who worked at the *Star*—in most cases, Sandra and Susan were viewed positively. Rather, interview participants suggested they had little ability to introduce more voices into social discussion because of broader journalistic barriers. Dwight suggested there was little the newspaper could do to address poverty "and still stay within the confines of the paper." When asked what he meant by that, he explained:

> They can only write what they see, the facts, you know. Philosophy is the domain of philosophers. If you want to theorize, bring theoreticians. If you want to philosophize, bring in the philosophers. But otherwise, report the facts. And there's not a whole lot of facts to report.

Others in the community made connections between their understandings of journalistic conventions and the newspaper's lack of proactive reporting on poverty. Clint, the middle-school teacher, expressed concern that proactive reporting could develop into bias: "I know how it is with papers—you want to report the news, you don't want to make the news." While they would criticize the *Star* for lackluster coverage of social issues and a general unwillingness to challenge the status quo, residents who knew her generally tended not to blame Sandra, the newspaper's editor and general manager, for its shortcomings. This finding is particularly interesting given how synonymous Sandra was with the *Star*— Robert, a local bank executive in his mid-forties, once noted that "Sandra personally *is* the paper, to me." Sandra had visited the nonprofit thrift shop where Jenn and Brandy worked a few days before my visit and had written a community response story about one of its programs. When I asked Brandy if she felt the newspaper cared about the poor in her community, she said:

> It really depends on who the person is. I don't know what her name is, but the lady who came in here and took our

pictures and stuff [it was Sandra], her, I would say, she's closer to us. She's doing stuff to try to help us, the poor. Then there's other people there who don't care.

Other residents who had more experience dealing with the newspaper (and, in some cases, who knew Sandra better), said the coverage shortcomings were the result of a lack of resources at the newspaper, a problem Sandra herself alluded to in her interviews. Kathy said she had sent the newspaper announcements from a community organization with which she works, but never saw them in the paper. She believed that omission was a production problem associated with the newspaper's out-of-town design desk, not an oversight by local staff. "You can't rely on our local paper for local news," Kathy said. She held Henderson Media, not Sandra personally, responsible. "They're constantly changing the [corporate] manager. . . . We have no local clout," she said. "We have no local input in that newspaper." Clint, Grace, and Robert alluded to the fact that the *Star* probably did not have enough people to do the kind of reporting that the editor might want to do. Dan, a local janitor in his late fifties, said the newspaper "is what it is. I'm sure there's more stories [about poverty and local need] out there. Maybe they don't have enough people to do them, I don't know."

Among the Greenburg residents interviewed for this book, the *Star*'s most vocal critic was also one of its most commonly used sources for information about need in the community. Floyd, the manager of the county's largest nonprofit aid agency, said Sandra often visited his agency for stories, which he described as "all feel-good stuff." When Floyd was asked whether those stories made a difference, he shook his head and said they did not. "It's been the same old story for so long," he said. He said the frequent coverage given to donations, food drives, and fund-raisers—the stuff most community response stories are made of—glorified individual efforts and made it difficult to organize larger community-wide help programs for which no one person or group would get credit. He volunteered that the newspaper's reactive coverage did little to challenge the dominant ideas about poverty, or about poor people, in Greenburg: "We know that we're poor, we know that we don't have jobs. Get out there and see—maybe somebody out there might come up with an idea or opinion that would turn things around for us. I'm tired of hearing how poor we are. I know how poor we are." Interestingly, the other voices that spoke most loudly of a desire for more in-depth reporting were also the voices that the *Star*'s staff often turned to for quotes or story ideas. Mary said she believed the newspaper should be more of an advocate for "things that could have a positive impact on the community, but you need to know about them," such as federal laws that limit or expand welfare. The newspaper would not have to take a strong stand on these issues to make a difference, she argued: "They just have to present what they know and let people make their own decisions about it." Matthew suggested stronger analysis of poverty and unemployment news, which would be difficult for him to provide given the political climate in which he worked, would help residents understand the true nature of need and the impacts of local economic conditions. For example, he said if reporters had a better understanding of what welfare statistics meant and what poverty guidelines actually were, he said, they could help challenge existing stereotypes of those who receive government assistance. Matthew suggested that while he did not feel he could initiate more proactive coverage of poverty, he could certainly provide the context reporters would need to execute that coverage themselves. Mary, whose organization was funded by the county government, and Floyd, who depended on church money and private donations to keep his agency's doors open, felt similarly constrained in their ability to push for substantive stories about need in a public way. If the journalists at the *Star* decided to write more aggressively about poverty in their community, sources such as Matthew, Mary, and Floyd would be key allies. The support they expressed for deeper, more proactive reporting suggests they would be willing to provide information needed to make that reporting a reality, if they were asked for it.

More than half of Greenburg residents interviewed said they had read GreenburgToday.com. Floyd said he liked the site because it took the approach that "this is what it is, and [Theresa] doesn't try to smooth it over." Jerry, a Greenburg native in his mid-twenties who worked at a radio station while also studying at a nearby college, said he believed Theresa "has the desire to be" different from the *Star*, but did not have the resources. When it came to poverty and local need, most of the local residents said they saw little real difference between the reporting they read on GreenburgToday.com and the stories they saw in the *Star*.

While Greenburg residents generally felt their news organizations, especially the *Star*, provided lackluster coverage of local need, most were not especially upset about it. To many, the factors that appeared to control what news was included in the paper seemed out of reach or cryptic: Henderson Media's out-of-town executives, journalistic conventions such as the need to avoid bias, or a conservative political climate that limited sources' abilities to say what they might want to say about poverty. Those limitations could not be challenged by folks in Greenburg, some interview subjects explained, so there was little to do but accept them.

Priorsville: Cheerleading for the Community

Like those in Greenburg, residents interviewed in Priorsville said poverty coverage was noticeably absent from their local newspapers. However, many Priorsville residents interpreted that absence in a very different way, and that difference related to the ways they viewed the *Priorsville Post-Examiner* and the people who produced it. This analysis largely focuses on the *PPE* and not the *Priorsville Record* because the *PPE* was the newspaper on which the vast majority of interview participants focused. All of the Priorsville residents who took part in interviews said they read the *PPE* at least occasionally. Those who saw significant differences between the two generally said the *PPE* was the more interesting newspaper, and the one they were most likely to read.

While some participants pointed out that the *PPE* (and its editor Nick specifically) had started to focus more on social problems in the community over the last few years, most said poverty still was rarely discussed in either newspaper. Many Priorsville residents said their local newspapers took great efforts to focus on the *good things* going on in the community, and that they interpreted the absence of regular news and information about poverty as an effort to build community confidence.[2] That effort, which some people referred to as the newspaper's "cheerleader" role, was seen as both good and bad, with the difference largely hinging on perceptions of who might benefit from the agenda for which the newspaper was cheering. Tom, a former local politician in his early sixties who ran a trade school in town, said he liked the Priorsville newspapers because they focused on positive news and did not try to "create scandal." Melody, a Priorsville native in her early twenties who worked as a collection agent at a local payday lender, said the newspaper's coverage of poverty "comes and goes. I guess they're trying to stick to the happier news in the county, instead of that we're suffering." Kevin, a pastor in his early fifties, said the newspapers should "do things that can help build a community and not divide a community." Molly, a local veterinarian in her early forties, said "self-promotion" of the community was an important part of the local newspapers' jobs: "It's very good to be a cheerleader for the things that are going right."

Sharon, the director of the Priorsville chamber of commerce, was perhaps the town's biggest social cheerleader. One of Sharon's main professional aims was to build Prior County's commercial and industrial bases, and she said developing the community's confidence in itself was an important part of that effort. "We say, 'we believe in you [the community and residents]. Yes, we do have problems, here they are.' We identify them. But we have things in place to work on those," she said. "If you're told all the time that you're a failure, you believe that whether you are or not." Sharon said she started establishing a strong working relationship with *PPE* editor Nick, who was on the chamber's board of directors, a few years after he became the newspaper's editor. "There was never a time when we went to Nick and said, 'This is what we want to say,' that he didn't far exceed our expectations," Sharon said. "It doesn't matter what kind of song you write if there's nobody there to sing it." Despite the close relationship between the newspaper and the chamber, both Sharon and Nick insisted that there was no pressure on the newspaper to portray Priorsville in a Pollyanna way. Sharon explained: "Now, Nick is still a news reporter, so when the hard facts come out, he says them. And it hurts, it stings. But we have a chance to come back and say, 'OK, that's true, here's why. But we have a plan to fix that.' And Nick always sings that story for us." Later, Sharon said Nick does a good job of "digging into the roots of Prior County and finding out why this [the community's economic trouble] is the way it is" and trying to promote a public conversation about those findings. She said:

> If you want just a feel-good paper of encouragement, those are good and those are important and there are sections in the paper for that. But the newspaper, the local newspaper, especially for a rural community, it's like a portrait of our county every single week. It's a way to say, "This is who we are—good, bad, ugly, flawed, indifferent. This is who our county is. . . . It tells the community, "This is what you are. Do you like this? If you don't, then change it. If you do, then keep going forward."

Other residents were more skeptical of the motives behind the cheerleading efforts they saw in Priorsville's local newspapers. Scott, the director of a large health care provider in Priorsville, saw the promotional efforts as benefiting a few affluent people in town: "Our local papers are careful, more careful to only show the good things about their sector, or where they have influences. Our local papers . . . they're not without prejudice. Our local papers are not completely without bias." That bias, he said, "comes from man's basic instincts," namely greed and selfishness, and a desire to protect their own privileged position in the status quo. "They don't write *real news*" about how pervasive poverty affects the area's youth, Scott said. "I think we just want to tell people about the ballgame on Friday night." Sally, the nonprofit thrift store manager, said promotional efforts were important, but that they too often overshadowed the realities that Priorsville's needy residents face:

> I want people to understand truth. I don't think there's any shame in the things that have gone wrong here. But we cannot change them until people begin to understand them and see what the issues are. And we do it ourselves— we pretty it all up for the media and try to make it look so good and sound so good, when the truth of the matter is, we're in trouble here. And I know people who will get on me and say, "Do you really have to tell it like that?"[3] Yeah, I really do. Because there's no shame in it.

The *PPE*, Sally suggested, was beginning to talk about those issues "gently and kindly," a welcome change, she said, to local news that had often been unrealistically positive:

> We've all been really afraid to admit, you know, some of the things that are going on here. We know them, but we don't always want to talk about them or read about them.

But I think if sometimes people knew the truth, if people would just hear other people's hearts, you know, I think we could get a lot more done.

Some residents suggested the newspapers were fulfilling a responsibility to protect the poor from social alienation by keeping their names and stories out of the newspaper, an idea that came up in other communities as well. The identities of poor children were of particular concern. Amanda, a social service worker in her early seventies who worked daily with individuals and families in need, found this protection particularly important. She was mindful of making the poor "feel different" and saving their dignity. "You can't talk about certain families," referring to poor families with children, Amanda said:

You don't want to embarrass them. You don't. They're innocent kids. Yeah, if Daddy's in jail and Daddy's done this, yeah, that's news, it's no problem. But to go in and talk about how poor they are and what a rough life they're living and so forth, it's demeaning to a lot of the kids.

The best way to avoid demeaning exposure, Amanda reasoned, was to keep low-income residents out of situations that might draw attention to their economic plights. Doing so, however, was not always easy. She recalled one instance where she believed a large charity's advertising had violated the privacy and dignity of a local family:

That's just like [large national charity], when they came in here they brought us a truckload of boxes, 400 boxes of food and 400 boxes of hygiene [products]. And I asked the local agencies to give me fifty names. And then I made sure they didn't double up. OK, those who were the neediest in this three-county area here came and got these boxes.

These people aren't written about. They don't want their name and picture posted anywhere because they're poor. [Large national charity] came back and wanted families for advertisements, poor families—go in and take a picture of their children. I did it, I helped them. I got permission, I took them in and I got these children. But did that make me happy? No. You don't like to stick a camera in someone's face and them knowing that, 'hey, you're poor and we want to take your picture.' I feel rotten when I do it.

The large national charity gave the family some money and food, "helped them out," Amanda said, and the subjects of the photos did not seem troubled by the attention. "These people [the poor family] were glad to do it, didn't care at all. So if they don't care, then I'll do it for them," Amanda said. However, it still made her uncomfortable.

Steven, a Priorsville native who ran a small local organization that promoted awareness of substance abuse, agreed that coverage of the poor could have damaging effects. "You don't want to take a, even though it's a struggling people, a proud people and try to beat them down more, OK? So there's not a lot [of news] about poverty," he said. Unlike Amanda, who suggested the poor in Priorsville would be better off if they were not identified in stories about poverty, Steven suggested that, with great care, it would be possible to cover low-income residents in a respectful way:

It would, *if* they did it in a way that was not derogatory toward anybody, any culture in this area, any economic background in this area, and they did it in a way that would lead someone not to better themselves, but to find a different way. Our people, like I said, are proud, and they can make it. But they don't need to feel like they're stupid or inadequate the way world media portrays them.

Media narratives that focus on getting someone to change a behavior in order to improve their lives place blame on individuals, Steven reasoned. "Finding a different way" involved the development and expression of a broader community approach to opportunity and education, and showing individuals how they could benefit from those approaches.

Although residents generally spoke positively about the newspapers in Priorsville, several recognized that coverage of social issues generally, and poverty and unemployment specifically, tended to be *reactive* rather than *proactive* in a way that limited the impact news about those issues might have. Molly, a local veterinarian, acknowledged that difference and said that the nonprofits that generate much of the news about poverty in Priorsville generally fall into the same rut. "I feel like that [poverty] is one of the stories that gets done around Christmastime" when charities become more active, she observed. Some "preventative medicine" in the form of news about the *causes of* Priorsville's need rather than the *reactions to* that need, she argued, would be a more effective way to shape people's attitudes and challenge generational poverty. Micah, the owner of a local textile factory, said coverage of unemployment and poverty rarely provided any detail on why things were the way they were: "Usually what happens on the poverty side, the loss of jobs, they [the newspapers] pretty much duplicate what comes from the state." Scott, the manager of the local health care company, said more proactive coverage would help locals focus on issues: "People need to discuss it and be aware that it's going on. I don't think the bad should be hidden, but I don't know, news is just news. We need some direction." Scott's suggestion that "news is just news" is a telling critique of the reaction to the response-driven coverage that generates much of the poverty news in Priorsville's newspapers, and in the other news outlets examined in this study. Reactive coverage put the power to speak in the hands of those who make the news, such as local government officials, charity groups, and business leaders, who already dominated local discussions about poverty and who, in Scott's view, did so with an agenda. Direction in the form of proactive news coverage and an open attitude toward alternative views and voices could provide an alternative to that dominant discussion. For example, if newspapers actively sought out the voices of the unemployed and incorporated their views into stories about chronic unemployment, then those views could add important context to stories and challenge the often-expressed view in Priorsville that unemployment was high because low-income people were unwilling to work.

Deer Creek: Whose Voice Is Heard?

In Priorsville and Greenburg, residents voiced a fairly wide range of opinions regarding the local newspapers and their coverage of social issues. Some people loved their newspapers, others disliked them, most fell somewhere in between, and their opinions were based on a variety of factors, such as ability to get information published, attitudes toward community promotion, or their personal opinions of newspaper workers. In Deer Creek, local reaction to the *Deer Creek Chronicle* and interpretation of the newspaper's coverage and motives was much more negative and much more uniform. Residents' distaste was largely rooted in the common impression that the *Deer Creek Chronicle* was only interested in a certain set of voices. Some residents claimed the newspaper exclusively covered the aspects of community life that interested Gregory, the *Chronicle*'s owner and editor. Others suggested local coverage reflected the interests and desires of the town's wealthiest residents. Both sets of concerns culminated with the understanding among many residents that there was little space in the newspaper for *their* concerns or opinions. The newspaper's approach to community journalism, some residents said, left them with a one-sided picture of social life in Deer

Creek. The online Deer Creek Advocate (DCA) was seen as a valuable alternative because it provided a forum for local residents to voice their concerns freely, although that freedom resulted in a degree of negativity that bothered some interview subjects. The DCA will be discussed in more detail later in this chapter.

The idea that Gregory's personal and social interests drove the bulk of the *Chronicle*'s content was expressed by some current (and estranged) newspaper readers in Deer Creek. Frank, a participant in a publicly funded work training program in his mid-sixties, observed that Gregory "has his own version of what's important, which is probably very typical of any owner/editor." Later, he noted that Gregory "likes to cover all the 'Mr. such-and-such is in for this and that,' you know," as opposed to the "real news" he reads on the DCA. Juanita, a local librarian in her early sixties, made a similar observation: "He [Gregory] owns it [the newspaper], and he can do what he wants to do."

Other residents said Deer Creek's wealthier residents, but not Gregory specifically, seemed to dictate coverage. Stacy, a clerk at a discount shop in Deer Creek in her mid-thirties, said that when she picked up the *Chronicle*, which did not happen very often, she saw stories mainly about the wealthy, including the Local Millionaire, whom she mentioned by name. "He's a multimillionaire, so it's all about him. Which, he's probably the one that started the newspaper," Stacy said.[4] She did not see her own life, which included financial struggles as the single mother of two teenagers, in the *Chronicle*. She grew up in a neighboring county and said she related better to her hometown newspaper, which she still received by mail. It included stories about the place where she used to work and events in which she was interested. A newspaper editor, Stacy said, "should not pick what *they* want to do. They should be aware of a lot more that's going on in a community . . . versus what they personally want to have in that paper, or what they're interested in." Jennifer, a social service worker in her early thirties, said the newspaper "focuses a lot on, in my opinion, some of the higher-class functionings and what they're doing. It doesn't really hit anything I'm interested in." Rebecca, another social service worker in her late sixties, let her subscription to the *Chronicle* lapse several years earlier. The newspaper, she said, "is only about a few businesses, a few people and their families. It doesn't benefit the community as a whole."

The feeling of isolation from the newspaper expressed by its critics was accompanied by the opinion that they had no power to influence its content. Juanita and Frank both said they believed there was little they could do to change the content of the newspaper. "It matters, but what choice do we have? He [Gregory] owns it," Juanita observed. Suzie, who owned a small restaurant in Deer Creek, had a similar complaint. She had problems with errors in newspaper ads for her restaurant and found little editorial value in the newspaper, but she expressed no sense that she had any stake in what was being written. "You know, we're customers [of the newspaper] and they're our customers, so some things are just better left unsaid," Suzie, who was in her mid-thirties, said. "It's a small town. You've got to be careful." When asked about poverty coverage, Suzie said the newspaper rarely addressed the issue. "I think it's one of those things that nobody really wants to talk about. They don't want to be honest, in my opinion, about the situation or how it can get better." When asked why she thought that was the case, she said, "I don't know. It's just, because I think it's a conversation that would just continue, because no one's going to come up with any answers."

The online Deer Creek Advocate came up in many interviews in Deer Creek. When conversation turned to the DCA, participants usually mentioned the comments that readers (at times prolifically) posted at the ends of stories. No one interviewed for this book said they had commented on the DCA, but some said they would be comfortable doing so if they felt passionate about an issue. Residents' opinions of DCA as a local news source seemed driven largely by how they viewed the anonymous readers' comments posted at the ends of stories. Some people, such as Suzie, said they were bothered by the tone of comments, which to her came across as unnecessarily cruel or gossipy. Suzie said she read articles on DCA but never looked at comments because "they're mean, some of the comments. They're meanspirited. It's not right." Crystal, who, in her early sixties, was a participant in a job training program for older residents, said she was turned off by the "rumormongering" that occurred on DCA, and that she considered it "biased news." Other residents who read DCA spoke positively about the site because of its policy of allowing people to comment on news stories. "I think the free trade of information is good, regardless of what people say," said Blake, a college librarian in his early thirties. "It [DCA] gets a lot of flak because they allow people to comment anonymously on stories. But they also publish a lot of news" that the newspaper would not publish. For example, stories and comments on the DCA often were critical of spending practices at the college in Deer Creek, which largely received favorable coverage in the newspaper.

Community participation is perhaps the main factor that set the Deer Creek Advocate apart from its print competitor, the *Deer Creek Chronicle*. Many local residents viewed the *Chronicle* as being out of touch with a large segment of Deer Creek, and they expressed pessimism at any suggestion that the newspaper might foster some type of dialogue that would engage the whole community and not just the affluent. The *Chronicle* was seen by some as a vehicle for a certain class of Deer Creek. The DCA was seen as a more open space for discussion and education, even among some who were bothered by the hostile writings that sometimes appeared in its comment sections. No one in Deer Creek expressed optimism about the idea that the *Chronicle* could help improve living conditions for the town's poorest residents; a few said they thought the DCA might be able to. Blake, the college librarian, observed that newspapers that challenged the status quo risked alienating government officials who supply information or corporate interests that supply advertising. The DCA, Blake said, "is not reliant on outside forces" and therefore is in a better position to challenge local institutions and create meaningful discussion. "I think they [DCA] do [create those discussions], I really do," Blake said. "I'd like to hope and I'd like to think there's a way to improve these things." However, he was not especially optimistic that *any* local media, print or online, could prompt real change: "I just don't see this area ever doing anything for itself, sadly." Blake's pessimism about Deer Creek's future was a direct commentary on powerlessness that was expressed more subtly by other Deer Creek residents, by many in Greenburg, and by some in Priorsville.

Interpreting the National Image of Appalachia

As noted in the previous chapter, many of the fifty-one individuals interviewed for this book said they felt their communities were unfairly stereotyped by regional media outlets. Residents in Greenburg and Priorsville[5] said the metropolitan media outlets that occasionally reported on their communities focused only on the bad things (drug use in Greenburg, unemployment in Priorsville, and poverty in both communities) without describing any of the good things happening in those places. They also live in a region that is often stereotyped by national news and entertainment media as backward, uneducated, poor, and dangerous. In that sense, entire communities may suffer from the same stereotypes, powerlessness, and ostracizing forces to which the poor are exposed at the local level.

Residents of all three communities were asked about those regional and national media representations, and how the representations compared to their lived experiences. Interview participants in Greenburg, Priorsville, and Deer Creek discussed images of Appalachia and at times rural life generally in major news outlets such as the *New York Times* and nightly national news broadcasts, television programs such as MTV's *Buckwild* and The Discovery Channel's *Moonshiners*, and motion pictures such as the 2005 film adaption of the television show *The Dukes of Hazzard* and the 2009 documentary *The Wild and Wonderful Whites of West Virginia*. Residents' opinions of Appalachia's portrayals in those media were fairly uniform: Almost all of them said outside media portrayed Appalachians in mockingly negative and inaccurate ways. However, there was less agreement when participants were asked whether those media images bothered them personally, or if they thought the portrayals were damaging to their communities or the region. Residents often tried to deflect negative imagery by suggesting that it had no direct impact on their day-to-day lives, or by claiming that stereotypes that reflected even the smallest kernel of truth were justified. Absent a platform to challenge images that they found demeaning, those justifications were perhaps the best responses they could muster.

What Does Appalachia Mean to You?

As they discussed local news coverage of social problems and broader regional and national stories about their homeplaces, residents of Greenburg, Priorsville, and Deer Creek who participated in this study were asked about regional identity, usually in the form of this intentionally broad question: "What does the word 'Appalachia' mean to you?" Some considered the idea of Appalachia to be central to their personal or community identities. Others said it meant little to them. A few suggested their communities were "on the fringe" of Appalachia, or that while their towns were part of what the country considered Appalachia, they did not think of themselves personally as Appalachians. Responses to the question, however, can largely be grouped into three dominant frames: Understandings of Appalachia as a *geospatial location*, as a *culture*, and as a *challenging experience*. The language residents use to position themselves within the region is by no means trivial; it can be key to the development of effective counternarratives, as discussed later in this book.

About a quarter of interview participants discussed Appalachia in terms of its geospatial location, defining the area as a space on a map or associating it with the Appalachian Mountains. Several people used this understanding of Appalachia to suggest that their communities were not truly part of Appalachia—they were "more or less on the fringe" of Appalachia (*Priorsville Post-Examiner* editor Nick), or "on the border of it" (Kevin, Priorsville resident in his early fifties). Clint, a Greenburg middle-school teacher, said, "I don't think of myself as an Appalachian at all. I know Green County is part of Appalachia," but he associated "Appalachia" with communities that were more isolated and deeper in the mountains. He recalled the frustration he had felt several years earlier when he received a survey from a group of academic researchers doing a study on "Appalachian kids":

> I don't even know what that [an Appalachian kid] is. Appalachia is a region of the United States. They wanted to know if my kids were Appalachian. I don't know. When a group of kids is sitting in an eighth grade class, I don't know where they were born. . . . I can't look at a kid and say, "that person's an Appalachian."

The understanding of Appalachia as a culture was the most often-referenced expression of regional identity, coming up in two-thirds of interviews about the region. Residents identified several personal values with that culture, including a strong work ethic, perseverance, independence, kinship, and an appreciation for close family ties. Micah, a Priorsville resident in his early sixties, summed the traits up as "mountain grit." Crystal, a Deer Creek resident in her early sixties, said, "Appalachia to me is more that self-sufficient, proud, traditional values, and crafts. I'm really an admirer of someone who can go out into the woods and cut down a tree and make a basket out of it." Suzie, a Deer Creek resident in her mid-thirties, said, "To me, it [Appalachia] means home. It means trees and just the history, the roots of the struggles of the people that have always been here." Family history was an important part of that, Suzie said, "I'm a firm believer in you don't ever forget where you came from. Because once you do, you're lost." Eric, the general manager of the *Deer Creek Chronicle*, explained that when he thought of the region, he thought of people more than a location. "I think of people that are hardworking, but they know that work isn't everything," he said. "They've always got something to do. They're religious, at least enough in their own minds, they're religious." Mary, a Greenburg resident in her late fifties, said Appalachia is "that pride in yourself and being able to make do no matter what—that Hank Williams Jr. 'Country Boy Can Survive' thing. No matter what happens, we can take care of ourselves here."

Most interview participants spoke fondly of those traits, but not all of the cultural aspects attributed to Appalachia were positive. For example, Dwight, a Greenburg resident in his early sixties, defined Appalachia as a place that was rigid, unwilling to change, and "mostly stuck in the present" with no willingness to think about the future. Rick, a Deer Creek resident in his mid-seventies, said that when you think of Appalachia, "you think of people that are isolated, very rigid in their beliefs, rednecks and this and that, whatever."

Some residents said they related less to the idea of Appalachia and more to the cultural labels of "hillbilly" or "redneck." When they spoke of what it meant to be a "hillbilly," they alluded to many of the same traits others used to describe the aspects of Appalachian culture that they valued. Linda, a Greenburg resident in her mid-thirties, said she proudly associated herself with those labels, which she linked to living on a farm, enjoying outdoor recreation, and being able to live a self-sustaining life. Linda said she did not see "hillbilly" or "redneck" as derogatory terms: "I've lived here my whole life. That's how we were raised," she said. Steven, a Priorsville resident in his mid-forties, offered a similar answer:

> Appalachia means a lot to me. I take pride in being called a hillbilly. A hillbilly is somebody that has been forced to make their own way. When in the worst of circumstances, they will figure out a way to feed their family. They have all kinds of family around them. They will figure out a way to survive in the worst of circumstances.

These cultural identifiers seemed to be the aspects of Appalachian identity around which people most easily coalesced. In describing what they valued about their lives and experiences in the region—family ties, simple lifestyles, connections with the outdoors, and other aspects of country life—residents described aspects of the region to which others could relate, regardless of their geospatial understandings of where Appalachia starts and stops.

A smaller group of interview participants focused on the *challenges* associated with living in Appalachia as an expression of regional identity. These expressions were often voiced alongside discussions of the more positive aspects of the region's culture. They were also more common among people who had always lived in the region. Nancy, the former Greenburg media company executive, said, "I think I've always been a person that kind of fights for the underdog. I think I kind of wear the Appalachian thing as a badge of pride." The aspects of the region she most related to, Nancy said, were its work ethic, the endurance of the people who live there, and the region's "untapped potential." Others spoke about the challenges associated with living and working in Appalachia in less romantic terms. Frank, a Deer Creek resident in his mid-sixties, referred to the region as an "internal colony" because of its history of economic and environmental exploitation. When Scott, a Priorsville resident in his late sixties, was asked what Appalachia meant to him, he responded that "for some reason, the people right up the Appalachian Mountains have always been in poverty." Trish, a Deer Creek secretary in her mid-twenties, said that Appalachia "is where I've always been. I hate to say it seems to be the perpetuated stereotype that we're poor, you know. But we are. . . . We're kind of stuck." Nancy was the only person I interviewed who viewed the region's underdog status as an aspect of life worth clinging to. Others spoke of the hardships as something that bound residents together in a rather unfortunate way.

Almost everyone interviewed about Appalachia for this book said that the dominant images that the rest of the country receives about the region did not do it justice. When residents discussed those images, they were sometimes describing news products such as national newspaper articles or segments that appeared on network news programs. More often, they described entertainment media: television programs, movies, and documentaries. No matter the media, most residents said they expected Appalachia and its residents to be misrepresented. "I really hate all of the reality shows that are portraying us in the manner that they are," Greenburg resident Mary said, specifically mentioning the television show *Here Comes Honey Boo Boo,* which first aired in 2012 on TLC. Shows like that "disgust me. People are selling themselves out," Mary said. She continued:

> To me, it's kind of like selling your soul. Instead of making fun of our culture, we should be proud of our culture. There's nothing wrong with it. Call us a hillbilly, whatever you want to call us—there's a lot of good things that have happened in Appalachia and a lot of good things that have come out of this area. But to allow this to happen to ourselves is disgusting to me.

Many residents said the lopsided view of Appalachia presented to the general public did not appreciate the diversity, education, and resources that do exist in the area. Crystal, a Deer Creek resident in her early sixties, noted that some Appalachian communities are home to centers of learning and diversity, but in the media, "it's all lumped together as poverty-stricken." Trish, a Deer Creek resident in her mid-twenties, observed:

> I have watched some of the shows like *Mountain Monsters*[6] and [laughs] some of those other ones [shows] where it's just a bunch of barefoot backwards-talking, plaid-clad, unkempt gentlemen roaming through the woods looking for things that aren't there. That's what people see and think of when they think of us.

Those images, local residents said, shape the ways people who live in Appalachia are viewed. Priorsville resident Steven noted that "if somebody says Appalachia, they're going to think of a toothless hillbilly that doesn't know how to read. That's what's going to pop into 90 percent of people in the country's minds. That's not true, you know." Study participants such as Eli, a factory worker in his mid-twenties from Priorsville, and Clint, the middle-school teacher from Greenburg, told stories about leaving the region and being made fun of because of their accents. Other interview participants shared more stories about instances when outsiders' perceptions of Appalachia led to uncomfortable situations:

> You look at the movie *Deliverance*, which is still on *everybody's* mind. You look at different things coming through the media, in comedy, people always make fun of hillbillies, you know, or whatever. I was in Washington, DC, and was at a bar, a piano bar, just sitting there, and this guy said [using exaggerated accent] "Wow, from [state name]? Did

you come out to get you some supplies?" So, that's kind of what other people out there think about us.

—*Steven, nonprofit manager from Priorsville*

I went on a date with a gentleman from Texas and one of the first things out of his mouth [when he found out where she was from] was, "Are you inbred and have you ever done anything [sexually] with a relative?" I walked out—it was that bad. You experience a lot of that.

—*Jennifer, social service worker from Deer Creek*

I went to [prestigious private university on the East Coast] when I was 17, and I had my neighbor, my suitemate, convinced that we had indoor plumbing put in that week. She was from Connecticut and she would believe anything. She would literally believe anything I told her. If I told her we didn't have a car and we drank moonshine with every meal, she literally believed it, because she had no experience with that. . . . In my mind, she, the very sophisticated private school girl from [town], Connecticut, was behaving a whole lot more like a rube than I was.

—*Molly, veterinarian from Priorsville*

Micah, a textile factory owner in Priorsville, sometimes worked with corporate executives from major clothing companies. He offered this description of the reaction of businesspeople who came in to Priorsville to meet and discuss contracts with his company:

We might have 10 or 15 of these people coming in here every week. They're coming out of San Francisco, they're sometimes coming out of Europe, where the mills are, in France and Italy and different places, very cosmopolitan cities and areas. And here they are coming to a rural community in [state]. You can tell they're a little bit intimidated, a little bit frightful that they're going to get caught up in something they're not ready for [laughs].

Quinn, a Deer Creek secretary in her early forties, said she worried about how dominant media images would affect her children and other young people in the region. "Right now, I think we are portrayed as being poor and stupid and addicted to either pills or meth," she said. Quinn added that she worried that her teenage son might come to see those portrayals as "a normal thing to do because he's a kid in [her Appalachian state]." Quinn also suggested the media images made it difficult for communities to attract new residents or industries, a concern shared by others in Deer Creek, Greenburg, and Priorsville. "If you're not from the area, you don't know [how bad the problem is]. You only know what you read in the paper or see on TV," she said. Problems such as drug abuse are legitimate, she continued, "but there's just a lot more good things going on. But that [the drug abuse and other bad images] is what you hear about the most these days, I think.

Images of people and places in popular culture can constitute an idea of what is and is not normal in America, helping dominant groups carve out an understanding of who is "us" and who is "Other."[7] Appalachians have historically been painted as a national "Other" by media in the United States, and residents interviewed for this book were keenly aware of the continuation of that practice today. When Appalachian residents are overwhelmingly shown as backward, simple, and lawless, it can leave outsiders (and, as Quinn suggested, people in the region as well) with the impression that poor people in Appalachia are poor for *cultural reasons*. Historically, that understanding has led to a view of a normalized and often demeaning "culture of poverty" perception of need in the region. Some participants alluded to the fact that images of Appalachia generally, and their communities specifically, as poor, backward places gave off the impression that mountain residents were not capable of creating better lives for themselves. The internalization of that idea leads to the sense of powerlessness that has been pervasive in much of the region for generations.[8] Most interview participants agreed that Appalachia was portrayed negatively by outside media. However, there was less consensus on the question of whether this was something that individuals or communities in the region should be concerned about. Some residents, such as Quinn, voiced worries about how media images and outsiders' impressions could shape the attitudes of Appalachians and limit opportunities coming in from other places. Jerry, a Greenburg resident pursuing a bachelor's degree in education, said media images of Appalachia "infuriate" him because they limit communities' abilities to attract tourists, as well as the opportunities residents have when they try to leave their communities for professional reasons: "For people that live here, if they try to go away to make something of themselves, they have to fight an uphill battle because they see you're from [region of his state] or [neighboring state]." Greenburg resident Mary said the images were "demeaning" and that, by participating in the production of those images, Appalachian residents were teaching the outside world that it was acceptable to mock the region: "If we allow people to view us as second-class or third-class citizens and we're treated that way, then we've played a big part in allowing that to happen."

However, other residents said they were not concerned about negative stereotypes affecting their lives or their communities' livelihoods. Moments after recalling an instance in which a man from Washington, DC, made fun of him for being from rural Appalachia, Priorsville resident Steven said there was no point in being concerned about the dissemination of negative stereotypes. "They don't affect our lives," he said, adding that he viewed those who would look down on people from Appalachia as "empty, hollow shells of people that do not have any moral standards or anything like that." Steven's view was that the stereotypes and the negative encounters they sometimes cause would not affect *his* view of *himself*, a common interpretation of people who said they were not concerned about how outside media portrayed

Appalachia. *Greenburg Star* editor Sandra said, "I've never thought of it [negative stereotypes] as damaging. I just think when you see that type of stuff on TV, if I were watching that, I wouldn't relate that to Greenburg." Robert, a bank executive in Greenburg, made a similar point: "I don't think it matters to me. It's not going to change anything, I don't think . . . I don't think it affects people long term." Trish, the secretary at the *Deer Creek Chronicle*, said, "I don't think you should let what other people think about you upset you any. I don't think anybody here does, I don't think they let it bother them very much." Molly, a Priorsville veterinarian, doubted efforts to combat the stereotypes would change the ways other people thought:

> There's still a fairly healthy level of "I don't care what they [people outside the region] think of me," because you do have so many people that never leave this area or couldn't care less of what so-and-so in a different state thought of them, that I think they [Priorsville residents] embrace that being put-upon and don't let it matter to them very much.

Molly's comment that some residents "embrace that being put-upon" is consistent with the idea of Appalachian identity as a (shared) challenging experience, a version of Appalachian identity she expressed. It was also a subtle reflection of an idea expressed more directly by people such as Robert and Sandra: Outsiders' opinions of the region are inconsequential. That approach ignores the practical fact that, for some, it actually does matter, in very tangible ways, how others view Appalachians. In a sense, then, what residents may see as an act of personal agency (deciding not to object to negative representation) actually takes the form of quiescence. From a theoretical standpoint, the view places a great emphasis on the development of bonding social capital, which focuses on relationships within groups, over bridging social capital, which strengthens relationships *across* groups. The exclusive emphasis on bonding social capital, over time, can create communities that are unhealthily insular.[9]

A few people, particularly in Deer Creek (the most geographically isolated of the three communities described here), claimed that even the most vulgar stereotypes were grounded in at least a little reality. After saying she did not let negative images bother her, Trish added, "It does perpetuate the stereotype, but it [the stereotype] is not entirely wrong. It's the stereotype for a reason—there's got to be some truth in it somewhere." Blake, a librarian at the college in Deer Creek, expressed guilt about the fact that he watched and enjoyed television shows about Appalachia, adding:

> I don't like the fact that people who have never been here probably envision that the populace is like that, but on the other hand, as I said, stereotypes come from somewhere. I've lived around this area long enough to know that some of that stuff is spot on, and some of it is entertaining.

Eric, the general manager of the *Deer Creek Chronicle*, made a similar observation, and also tied it to the economic priorities of entertainment television:

> I'll watch these programs, like *Swamp People*, and I'll be like, "I know people like that." They're the extreme minority, super-minority, but yeah, I know people like that. I know people like the *Duck Dynasty* people. I know people like the Whites of whatever it was [the documentary *The Wild and Wonderful Whites of West Virginia*], which I only saw about half of and said, "no thank you." I think the Appalachian is really skewed in those kind of views. But you know, the TV companies don't care, as long as a measurable percentage of people are watching them, they don't care whether it's accurate or not.

A sense of powerlessness clearly manifests itself in statements such as these. Even if the stereotypes are bothersome, some residents suggested, they must be accepted at some level as real, either because they are similar to people who really do live there, or because outside media interests will propagate them no matter what anyone says. Residents who saw no point in challenging negative representations of Appalachia live in a habitus built on the view that the poor are somehow destined to suffer because of their own deficiencies,[10] an approach reminiscent of the way poor residents felt about the prospect of challenging dominant local narratives in their own communities. If they are empowered with the opportunity and the platform, residents can develop counternarratives to that dominant idea and express their own understandings of what Appalachia is and who its residents are, embracing the diversity and opportunity in the region through a grassroots communication effort.

Whose Voice Is Heard?

Almost all of the non-journalists interviewed for this book recognized a difference between the poverty they knew existed around them and the poverty they saw in their community newspapers and on local news web sites. Residents expressed preconceived notions about the motives for that difference, and those ideas influenced their decoding of the local newspaper/news web site as a voice for the community. As residents expressed the ideas that news coverage about poverty was unreliable because of personal or class barriers or, in the case of Greenburg, the limitations of the news outlet itself, they also expressed a sense that there were no effective vehicles for people who wanted to express opinions, change attitudes, or offer new approaches to addressing local poverty, or any other social issue. Rural Appalachia has a long history with that type of community powerlessness. Hyperlocal news web sites provide possible options for individuals who do wish to engage in public discussions about poverty and need. People in Greenburg and Deer Creek seemed to express more faith that GreenburgToday and the Deer Creek Advocate could (and would) challenge dominant ideas about need in their communities. Theresa, the founder of GreenburgToday, expressed a desire to facilitate a more positive discussion about life in Greenburg, and some local residents said they were optimistic about her ability to do so, but as of this writing, it is too early to tell just how robust that discussion might be. The Deer Creek Advocate *has* established itself in its community and gets a great deal of attention (both positive and negative) from local residents. The site's founder wrote that he wanted it to be a place open for discussion, and several Deer Creek residents said they perceive it as such, although some seemed to feel overwhelmed by the hostility that took place in the comments section.

Some residents spoke to an idea that poverty was viewed as a fact of life in their communities, and they seemed to decode the lack of media coverage of the issue as evidence of that fact. Mary, a Greenburg social service worker, said this about poverty: "I don't think it's something people in the area want to focus on. I mean, if it's smacking you in the face every day, you're living in [it], so *you don't need the paper to tell you about it.*" The view of poverty as routine and therefore not really worthy of coverage was shared by people in other communities as well. "I think most of the [nonprofit and government aid] programs are standing. The people who need them largely know about them or hear about them from their friend because they've been going to them forever," Trish, the secretary at the *Deer Creek Chronicle*, explained. Trish and her older brother grew up in a single-parent household in Deer County where food stamps (and the stigma associated with redeeming them at the grocery store) were a regular part of life. Trish excelled in high school and graduated from the college in Deer Creek with a bachelor's degree. However, because of a physical disability, she was unable to drive, so she had to find a job in Deer Creek. She said she liked working at the newspaper, but she did not make much money there; she still lived with her mother because neither woman could afford to live by herself. She said:

> I think we've all been in the same state for so long, we just know. It doesn't need to be put out there. We know it [the deadline for aid applications] is going to happen, we know what day it is, we know we have to have it done by this time. I don't even think it needs to be publicized anymore [laughs]. We all just know. We know where to go and what to do.

The idea that poverty is less worthy of public discussion because it has been around for so long feeds a naturalistic perspective of the phenomenon that makes challenging dominant views of the poor difficult to do. In order to overcome a "culture of poverty" approach, media and communities must first agree that the issue is something that warrants discussion. Rebecca, a social service worker in Deer Creek, made this observation: "If you've never wanted for food, never wanted for a house, you will look at people and say they are lazy. They [wealthy people in the community] don't see homelessness or poverty. They think it's a choice." News coverage is one way those wealthy people can be shown other aspects of need. But before that can happen, poverty must be accepted not as a natural state, but as a public issue that warrants discussion.

The idea that the poor were kept out of the newspaper for their own good was expressed, either directly or indirectly, in each of the three communities studied here. It was most strongly voiced in Priorsville, a town where the economy had been under close regional media scrutiny for five years at the time this research was conducted. The protection supposition seems to be built on one or more of the following assumptions:

- that poor people themselves would be unable to eloquently or accurately express themselves and, if given the chance, would likely say or do things that would lead to ridicule;

- that local reporters would twist the words or images of the poor to fit their own agenda or that a lack of care on the part of local journalists would result in inadvertent embarrassment; or

- that the community as a whole would misunderstand the poor or automatically see them as lazy or unworthy of respect, regardless of what they said or how they were portrayed.

No one I interviewed for this story suggested that the poor would be unable to express themselves. The most "stereotypically poor" individuals interviewed for this study—Greenburg residents Brandy and Jenn and Deer Creek residents Trish and Stacy—were thoughtful and eloquent, and had little difficulty describing to me the realities of their daily lives. The second assumption was very relevant when community members addressed coverage of their communities in regional media or stories about Appalachia at the national level. Many interview participants expressed little faith in outside media to tell their stories fairly and accurately, and some believed reporters, filmmakers, and television producers came to Appalachia primarily to exploit rather than learn or educate. However, in Greenburg and Priorsville, residents seemed generally confident in their local reporters' and editors' desires and ability to deal accurately and fairly with story subjects.

That leaves the third option: concerns about the community's preconceived notions about their local poor. That fear seemed to underlie much of the hesitation local residents (and, for that matter, local journalists) had about putting the faces and voices of their neediest resident on the front page. But as Rebecca in Deer Creek noted earlier, the absence of those voices results in the maintenance of a status quo that restricts the ability of the poor to develop social capital in their communities. Keeping low-income residents "under wraps" because of fears that they'll be subjected to scorn in communities that often already scorn them does nothing to improve their social condition. A few residents, including Molly, the veterinarian in Priorsville, spoke to that idea during interviews. Stories about pulling yourself up by your proverbial bootstraps are great, Molly said. Stories about welfare fraud are useful. But stories about people who really need services and are using them correctly are important too. "Those stories need to be told," Molly said, but they would have to be told using "a certain voice" that spoke to the struggle and opportunities in a community without casting blame. Matthew, the manager of the state welfare office in Greenburg, expressed optimism that such stories, if told with compassion, could make a difference in the way low-income people are viewed:

> I think stories like that that are positive where this person is working, trying to get by, doing the best they can, makes a difference with reasonable people who are reading those stories. I don't think it makes any difference to the person that is just absolutely against any kind of government handout, welfare, regardless of what it might be. But you'd hope that most of the people are the reasonable type where if they had some information about this poor person that's struggling to work 30 hours a week and get their kids to daycare but still needs $200 in food stamps to get by, I think most people are fine with that, and understand that that is the way it is, especially in this area. But I have seen that, exactly what you're saying, backfire.

The story Matthew referred to that backfired was a segment that ran on a national network news broadcast a few years before his interview about poverty in the communities around Greenburg. The segment was criticized by some in the region for feeding into stereotypes in its portrayal of rural poverty. The intentions of the journalists who produced that program were good, Matthew argued, but "it just didn't come across very positive on TV, and I think that just reinforced some of that stereotype that these people don't want to work, they just want everything given to them."

Some people in Greenburg and Priorsville saw a clear difference between stories about *poverty as an issue*, which were rare in the newspapers reviewed for this book, and stories about *community responses* to need that dominated local charity coverage. When asked about local poverty stories, Amanda, a Priorsville social service worker in her early seventies, said, "You know, you just don't see them. I don't see them. You see [stories about] special programs." Even the people who ran those programs, such as Amanda in Priorsville and Floyd in Greenburg, saw the limits of coverage that focused exclusively on things community members were doing to help those agencies. One likely reason for their popularity is that it is easy for community response stories to be viewed as *positive stories* that will be well-received by most readers, and easy to criticize issue stories as *negative stories* that journalists might be hesitant to write.

Some residents had little concern about whether news about the community was positive or negative, as long as it was true. Others acknowledged that the binding of community members through the expression of common, positive experiences and beliefs was one of the important responsibilities of a local news outlet. When Blake, the college librarian in Deer Creek, was asked what he thought a local newspaper should accomplish in the community, he answered this way:

> I'd love to think that it's there to spark debate, but it's not. That could probably be the most important aspect that it can do, but none of them do it. The second most [important

function] is basically support the community, and that's what they do. The realistic part of it is they give people a sense of self-worth, the good aspects of it, reports on children's activities, you know. People love seeing themselves in the paper, whether it be a baseball accomplishment, an academic accomplishment, you know, winning the spelling bee. As corny as it might sound, I think the fact of the matter is that these local newspapers basically just help prop people's egos more than anything. And that is important in a way, because a depressed populace isn't exactly what we need either.

Perhaps a newspaper can share the stories of the poor who are struggling in a community in a way that is empowering rather than shaming. And perhaps social issues can be discussed in ways that express the true gravity of problems while still being constructive. The remainder of this book will focus on best practices for journalists and community members who want to try to accomplish those goals.

If newspapers and web sites actually do these things, will it make a difference? I cannot honestly say. But the time I spent with Jenn and Brandy at the counter of the Greenburg thrift shop left me hopeful about the prospect of change and where it can come from. When Jenn, Brandy, and I first started talking, they were not especially optimistic about the possibility of changing things in Greenburg, nor did they seem especially interested in my project. The more we talked, the more willing they said they might be to try to be a part of local change. They stopped expressing themselves as people who were content to scrape by, or as folks who were satisfied with the "that's just the way it is" response to poverty. At one point near the end of our discussion, Brandy said, "I do think if we could get more people around here to quit being afraid and speak up, then we could make changes around here, instead of everybody just hiding behind their shadow bitching and complaining about it, actually get out and try to do something." When I asked Jenn and Brandy if they would ever feel comfortable writing about their experiences and opinions in the newspaper, Brandy quickly said she would:

> I mean, I think if we could get, like the girls that work here [referring to the other women who "worked off their welfare" at the thrift store], if we could get all of us to write it out and actually sign it, stating that we all believe that this is the way it should be, then yeah, I'd feel very comfortable doing that.

I followed that question by asking them if they thought such an act might make a difference in Greenburg. Jenn responded, "It might, as long as we keep talking about it." Brandy quickly added:

> Yeah, don't just put one thing in the newspaper and just leave it, you know, and let it [gestures as if she's throwing something out the window]. Because people are going to forget about it. Every couple of weeks, once a month, something, put something in the newspaper about it. If we keep talking about it, eventually, something might happen.

In that moment, Brandy and Jenn hardly sounded like women who did not have voices, or who needed to be sheltered from a community that might ridicule them. The truth is, they already faced stigma and social and economic isolation. They were capable of standing up for themselves, and for others they knew who were experiencing the same hardships. They did not need a reporter from the *Star*, or from a metropolitan television station, or me, to tell their stories. Given the platform and opportunity, they were, and are, perfectly capable of telling those stories themselves.

CHAPTER 6

How Local Media's Silence Influences Views of Poverty

In 1983, Bill, the owner and publisher (and, at that time, editor) of the *Priorsville Post-Examiner*, wrote a stirring personal column about Ernest Miller, a local laborer in his sixties known locally as "Pap." Pap Miller, who had died the week before, was the type of man many found easy to ignore. He worked for the city, digging holes and doing other odd jobs for the public works department. He also drank coffee at the same morning hangout spot Bill and his friends frequented and, over the years, Pap had become a member of that group, albeit one who never engaged in much conversation. In the remembrance, Bill wrote about his early impressions of Pap: "At first, I was taken aback by his appearance," his "dirty clothes," and his "scraggly, bearded face." He wrote about the impetus for his column—after Pap died, a friend suggested Bill write a tribute to him, an idea Bill initially resisted, he wrote, because he did not really know much about Pap. In his column, Bill wrote:

> As if reading my thoughts, my friend said: "You know, it's a shame that someone can live sixty-some-odd years and then die and nothing is ever written down about him. He deserves more than that. Pap deserves more than that."
>
> That made me feel sort of guilty. That made me feel as though, because I had gone off to school and learned the fundamentals of journalism and came back home to edit a little weekly newspaper, that I had a responsibility to

chronicle such events like the passing of Pap Miller. And while I was feeling guilty, I decided that, yes, maybe I do have that kind of responsibility. Maybe Pap Miller does deserve more than an obituary notice to mark his passing from this life. And maybe there are a lot of other people who are born and struggle through life and leave it without anybody ever taking much more notice of them, much less recording it for the sake of history.

In the column, Bill described his personal interactions with Pap, which mostly consisted of Pap listening as other men at the coffee spot chatted. He wrote about watching Pap at work, as he dug holes for street projects. He wrote about the time the coffee crowd got Pap a surprise birthday cake ("I wasn't the only one who noticed the tear come to his eye and I don't suppose I was the only one who almost cried along with him."). The point Bill made in his column, which won a state press association award the year after it was published, was that men and women like Pap were often seen but rarely known in Priorsville. At the conclusion of the column, Bill wrote:

> Because of his appearance, because he was from the other side of the tracks, because he was born and died a poor man, there were a lot of people who ignored Pap Miller. There were a lot of people, I guess, who knew of him, but thought little about him. And, I suppose, there were a lot like me who were sorry the day he died because they hadn't got to know him better.
>
> Pap deserved more than that. Pap deserved better than he ever got.

Bill's column has been reprinted in the *PPE* several times since 1983. It represented a rare published glimpse into the life of a man so poor his family could not afford a grave marker when he died, and it presented a deeper message that, to Bill, still resonated thirty years after Pap's death.

Profiles of people from Pap's social class were largely absent from the four newspapers described in this book. So were more analytic views of the extent to which poverty and related issues impacted the community as a whole, as well as the voices of those who dealt with the repercussions of those issues firsthand. In their absence, audiences were left with the long-standing, dominant view of Appalachian poverty as a cultural deficiency. The "culture of poverty" attitude Cynthia Duncan discussed can be an accurate way to describe the conditions associated with poverty. However, it often leads to victim blaming and social stratification that further separates the poor from opportunities to engage their communities economically or socially. The poor stay poor, Duncan wrote, "because the social institutions, civic norms, and politics that make up the social context in their communities deny them opportunities to learn and get good jobs."[1] Community newspapers are important social institutions in small towns in rural Appalachia and across the world because they play critical roles in the constructions of the "social context" Duncan described.

When he published *Power and Powerlessness* in 1980, John Gaventa was not entirely sure what effects "non-coverage or degrading coverage" of disenfranchised individuals would have. He speculated that rural Appalachians who saw primarily negative collective self-images in media would "develop a sense of inadequacy," and that the lack of coverage would also keep "members of [subordinate groups] isolated from one another, unaware that others similarly situated share common concerns or are pursuing challenges upon common issues."[2] This book reinforces those assumptions and provides even greater detail on the impacts of media silence on the issue of poverty. In the communities described in this book, the *absence* of poor voices in news stories is interpreted in ways that reinforce the culture of poverty perspective. That absence is encoded into local news coverage in part because of the routines and beliefs of journalists and sources and, in some cases, because of the business constraints under which they work. Journalists said they believed their approaches to poverty were beneficial for their communities in that they gave people the information they needed but did not embarrass low-income residents or depress the community as a whole. Many residents, however, decoded local media approaches to poverty quite differently, seeing it as a suggestion that poverty is a normalized way of life, and that the public conversation of poverty included only certain kinds of voices. The powerlessness and exclusion amplified by journalistic conventions are unintended consequences that still systematically and unconsciously feed back into further acts—in the case of this study, further news coverage and the continuation of journalistic practices that lead to silence and exclusion.[3]

History, economics, and inequalities combine to shape the ways residents of Appalachia view poverty, progress, and community. High poverty combined with a lack of economic diversity lead communities to become culturally attached to exploitative enterprises such as extractive industries.[4] Class relations dictated by inequality in rural environments may stand in the way of broader community efforts to address social issues.[5] Middle classes aligned with the rich and powerful may, as a larger social group, come to see the lower class as lazy, immoral, and dangerous.[6] Legacies of poverty, division, rampant negative stereotyping, and a sense of powerlessness have clear consequences at the individual level as well: apathy and excessive fatalism, low levels of self-efficacy regarding education and career aspirations, experienced discrimination, and a growing skepticism—particularly among Appalachian youth—of individual ability to engage society in a meaningful way.[7] Poverty and problems associated with poverty, such as a lack of access to resources and public spheres, also help shape the discursive styles of individuals, a matter that is of special importance to this study of local media. In their work on democratic deliberation in Indian villages, Rao and Sanyal saw that shaping process unfold as "pleading tones" used by members of the lower caste and allegiance to community harmony.[8] Geographically, rural India is certainly a world away from rural Appalachia. However, there are similarities between the villagers in Rao and Sanyal's study and the residents of small, economically depressed communities such as the ones described in this book. Both groups find themselves on the economic outside looking in, defined by cultural understandings of what it means to be "poor" that work to their disadvantage. However, the public forums where Indian villagers from all walks of life can gather to discuss local issues "provide ordinary citizens a place to think about and voice their concerns about broader policy issues and abstract principles that closely touch their lives."[9] In those environments, villagers are able to express their needs and wants by discussing what it means to be poor. The Indian system is far from perfect—power from above stands in the way of the meetings taking truly deliberative forms. Nonetheless, the forums do serve as an arena where poor individuals may seek dignity through participation. Local news outlets acting inclusively, proactively, and intentionally can provide similar platforms for their communities.

Newspapers and local news web sites are and will continue to be important vehicles for the construction and maintenance of attitudes and opportunities in rural communities such as Greenburg, Priorsville, and Deer Creek. This work describes some of the structural aspects of social life and journalistic practice that limit the poor's ability and/or willingness to engage in local discussions about poverty through those media and the ways their absence contributes to feelings of powerlessness and stratification. It is important to note that these actions are not *solely* responsible for alienation and voicelessness in communities. In the cases of poverty coverage in Priorsville, Greenburg, and Deer Creek, a group of actors—certainly reporters, editors, and publishers, but also local officials, chamber of commerce directors, and social service agents—made decisions that, individually, seemed rational, but collectively resulted in a consequence that was irrational for all of them. When they discussed poverty coverage, journalists described a range of internal and external forces that both enabled and constrained their work from day to day. Giddens argued that most individual action is driven by the knowledge actors have of day-to-day life, and that knowledge, and the action it precipitates, gives form to the structural properties of social spheres. As human beings, journalists and editors are capable of recognizing the routines and attitudes that give life to those structural properties and, if they choose to, they may disrupt those routines and create different structural properties that may in turn lead to different outcomes (Giddens referred to this ability as the "dialectic of control"). If actors can be made to look at their routines differently, change is possible. The ideal solution to the problem of finding a better approach to local poverty reporting would be for journalists with an established platform, community advocates with knowledge, and residents with lived experiences to collaborate on a new public view of local economic need that could lead to more robust community discussions. If those groups can work together in new, effective ways, they may facilitate more inclusive public discussions about issues that address problems without condemning individuals or communities.

Internal Communication: Becoming More Inclusive

Local newspapers live and die by their ability to connect their communities and provide perspective and support for their readers, a role that, from a community perspective, fills a need for *internal communication*. Some journalists and publishers said they also saw themselves as spokespeople for the community, filling a need for *external communication* to show outsiders that their hometown was, in most cases, a good place to live and do business. Nancy, the former corporate newspaper manager from Greenburg, brought up the idea of a local newspaper as both an internal communicator and an external communicator during one conversation:

> I think that primarily, the *Star* is the good old community newspaper that everyone knows and loves that tells you what Suzie Q is doing down the street, and it's quaint and people like that style of news in rural areas, while we're still gathering state, local, and international news to educate our readers. But [we] also try to get information about our readers out to the wider audience.

Later, Nancy said:

> I think all newspapers are starting to become more external. That doesn't mean that their internal is diminishing, especially if they're getting additional resources. In my mind, that just means we get to keep everything we have and expand. I think with technology the way it is today, you almost have to try to *not* get things out to a broader audience.[10]

If publishers and editors open newspapers to people who currently do not get in, they at least acknowledge the presence of economic diversity in the community and begin to tell different stories about the people they cover. If, rather than exploit those people as "poor folks," local journalists show that they have the same hopes and dreams as everyone else (as was the case with the profile of Dan), then newspapers attempt to help integrate them into the community. Engaging low-income residents and advocates in a new form of *internal communication* not only helps the community understand the issue of need from a different point of view, but it also empowers residents who often find themselves at a social disadvantage because of their social class. Journalists and local residents expressed concern that the poor would be humiliated were they to appear in the newspaper. That view reinforces an understanding that there is something inherently wrong with an individual who deals with poverty. Sally made this observation during one of our conversations: "As a community, as a whole, we're looking at this [being poor] as, there's something wrong with this. We believe that those things, it's like we look at that as a negative instead of looking at it as just what it is. There's no shame in this."

As local journalists consider ways to create a more proactive, inclusive approach to reporting on social issues, community members can attempt to create news coverage (and public dialogue) by taking advantage of established news routines. Some journalists interviewed for this book noted that poverty often is not covered because it does not come up in the meetings or other routine events they write about. That reactive coverage, as noted previously, is not conducive to a strong media-facilitated discussion of poverty. However, members of the public may be able to take advantage of it by creating events at which poverty is discussed in new ways. Such events generate opportunities for discussions that fit more tightly into daily and weekly journalists' own conception of what news *is*. Journalists who cover those events may feel more inclined to report on what is said without growing concerned that they are inappropriately "editorializing," a fear that arose when Nancy described the *Star*'s reluctance to develop social issues stories that were not based on a spot news element. Activists in some parts of the region already engage with community groups and media outlets to develop positive coverage of marginalized groups. For example, a community task force in Morristown, Tennessee, worked to generate more robust coverage of the town's growing Latino community by finding success stories and actively sharing them with the community. William Isom, an activist and member of the task force, said the stories, which were about "this Latino student [who] got a scholarship to Yale, or this Latina student [who] got straight A's and had perfect attendance in school, or this business owner [who] feeds homeless people on Sundays and doesn't ask for anything in return," were published in the newspaper.[11] Most of the people on that task force were middle-class locals who had already established social capital in their community—"a lot of these small-town newspapers will listen to middle-class folks," Isom said.[12]

The availability of the Internet has made it possible for active citizen journalists to take root in Deer Creek and Greenburg. Those new online enterprises show that both journalists (in the case of GreenburgToday.com) and non-journalists (in the case of the Deer Creek Advocate) can attract audiences, and produce at least a little revenue, by providing alternatives to dominant local narratives about community life. Both web sites were valued in their respective communities, although neither was uniformly praised. Some Greenburg residents suggested GreenburgToday. com was too similar in tone and content to the *Greenburg Star*.[13] In the six months' worth of content analyzed for this book, GreenburgToday.com rarely reached out to sources that were not also regularly featured in the *Star*. GreenburgToday.com did not allow readers to comment on stories, which also limited participation. The Deer Creek Advocate (DCA) did allow comments, and readers often contributed a great deal of content to the web site. Some DCA readers criticized the site (particularly its commenters) for providing too much negative commentary. Screening critical comments or taking other steps associated with stronger top-down moderation (such as requiring users to include their real names alongside their posts) would not be advisable because it would drive many alternative opinions out of the public discussion.[14] It would be more productive to encourage a sense of virtual community on the site by taking active efforts to show commenters their contributions are valued and encouraging interactivity and the exchange of information.[15] Research has shown that residents who feel forums are hostile are still more likely to continue to participate in those forums if they feel a sense of virtual community.[16]

Their weaknesses aside, both web sites provided valuable services to community members who longed for alternatives to local media narratives that many found unfulfilling. Both were drawing readers away from the established print products in their communities; two interview participants in Greenburg said they thought GreenburgToday.com could eventually put the *Greenburg Star* out of business. I come from a newspaper background, and I believe newspapers can and should be vocal advocates for their community. Because of their established business models and the social capital they already possess, many community newspapers are still in a strong position to advocate in the ways described in this study. Unfortunately, many newspapers do not do that. This study is largely newspaper-centric because most participants still found traditional newspapers to be more influential local voices than online news sources.[17] That can shift, and it very well may in Deer Creek and/or Greenburg. If more residents get an opportunity to voice their concerns as a result, then those communities would be well served by the change.

For those opportunities to be realized, broadband Internet access must become more widely available in rural communities. In each of the three communities studied here, high-speed Internet was available in incorporated areas, but connectivity (even through mobile devices) was extremely limited even a mile or two outside of town. Some study participants in Deer County said that access limitations outside of town were a major barrier to the DCA's reach and influence. Research has found that, on the whole, rural Americans are far less likely than urban or suburban residents to adopt high-speed Internet. Seventy percent of the rural residents who responded to a 2013 survey conducted by the Pew Internet & American Life Project reported having either a smartphone or home broadband. Eighty percent of urban residents and 83 percent of suburban residents who responded to the same survey reported having access to either broadband or a smartphone. Household income was also a strong predictor of adoption: 95 percent of the respondents with annual household incomes over $75,000 reported having either home broadband or a smartphone. Seventy-nine percent of those with annual household incomes between $30,000 and $49,000 reported having either home broadband or a smartphone, and for individuals in households that made less than $30,000, adoption dropped to 67 percent.[18] Access to high-speed Internet in Appalachia is limited, particularly in the coal fields of central Appalachia. Nationwide, 98 percent of rural Americans had access to some high-speed Internet technology in 2013, but 91 percent of rural West Virginians and 93 percent of rural Kentuckians had access. Access to mobile Internet is even more limited in those areas. In 2013, 96 percent of rural Americans had access to mobile broadband, but only 87 percent of rural Kentucky residents and 79 percent of rural West Virginia residents had access.[19] A 2011 study of broadband adoption in Appalachian Ohio suggested that access to broadband was a bigger barrier to adoption than the price of the service. Twenty-three percent of rural residents in Appalachian Ohio told the nonprofit advocacy group Connect Ohio that they did not adopt high-speed Internet because it was not available where they lived; Ohioans as a whole reported lack of access as a barrier only 8 percent of the time. The price of broadband was reported as a barrier by 20 percent of rural Appalachian Ohioans and 25 percent of Ohioans overall.[20] A 2014 study of broadband access in Ohio noted that broadband networks had developed much more slowly in Appalachian Ohio than in the rest of the state.[21]

When he published *Bowling Alone* in 2000, Robert Putnam challenged journalists, media owners, and Internet gurus to develop ways to create more opportunities for communion among a growingly isolated and apathetic public: "Let us foster new forms of electronic entertainment and communication," Putnam wrote, "that reinforce community engagement rather than forestalling it."[22] Putnam envisioned digital media such as the Deer Creek Advocate and GreenburgToday.com, which hold a great deal of potential to encourage engagement and help communities develop social capital. It is far too early to abandon the notion that traditional community newspapers can promote those conversations as well. Doing so will require the women and men who work at those newspapers to see themselves as concerned friends interested in developing stronger, more inclusive communities. At times, it will require them to rethink traditional journalistic roles and practices. Importantly, as Priorsville textile factory owner Micah observed, they will need to view themselves not as mouthpieces for actors in a community, but as actors themselves:

> We can go 'til Judgment Day reporting all the deficits and all the things that's wrong in life. But now there's a great difference in telling a story and then going out and trying to do something to impact that, and change it. And I believe that takes people of character and vision and resolve—people that are not just talking the talk, they are willing to walk the walk. They are saying, "The problem is there, what can we do? It's ugly, and everybody knows it's ugly. Is there something we can do to make it better?"

External Communication: Telling a Different Story

Sally, the owner of the nonprofit thrift shop in Priorsville, said she often felt regional media—the metro newspaper and television stations an hour and a half down the interstate—provided a negative view of the town she called home. When asked what she wanted the journalists who made that drive to know about

Priorsville, she answered, "I think there's a lot of stereotypes about a community like ours. And I know that a lot of people think that there are people who just don't care, and have got this lazy attitude, and just a bunch of hicks up in the hills. And they need to see the difference." The "difference," she went on to explain, were the dedicated teachers, the active educational and social programs, and the local residents who volunteered to keep those programs running. If reporters would dig deeper into local society, she said, they would find a community much more complicated than the stereotypes often employed to describe Priorsville and rural Appalachia.

Individuals vie for economic and social capital on what French sociologist Pierre Bourdieu called a *cultural field*, a field on which rural Appalachian residents have for generations struggled to compete. Identities such as "poor," "Appalachian," "poor Appalachian," and "hillbilly" are all, Stuart Hall would have told us, "constructed within, not outside, discourse"[23] and developed to reinforce difference and exclusion. The exclusionary aspect of identity construction helps individuals realize that they "are what everybody else on the globe is not," Hall wrote, a knowledge that helps individuals place themselves as well as the Others they encounter.[24] The construction of a national Appalachian identity has been dominated by outside interests with cultural or economic interests in Othering the region. However, identity may be constructed from the inside, and often-Othered groups—including the Amish and Mennonites in North America, Aboriginal groups in Australia, and Iranians in London—have used print and electronic media to craft their own versions of "us."[25] The media described in those studies are largely intended to be *internal communications* in that they produce community narratives made by and for members of those groups. However, such efforts can also be effective tools for *external communication* when members of a group see the dominant narratives about them in outside media as destructive forces.

Newspaper publishers and editors, local leaders, and others who appear in this book emphasized the importance of a positive local media narrative to counter regional media stereotypes such as the one Sally described in Priorsville. In some ways, the structural aspects that limit low-income individuals' ability to engage their communities in Greenburg, Priorsville, or Deer Creek are microcosms of Appalachia's struggle to combat negative stereotypes that dominate popular media images of the region. The vast majority of those interviewed for this project acknowledged the negative imagery associated with the region, as well as with monikers such as "hillbilly." They differed on how representative the idea of "Appalachia" was to their area, and to a degree on how damaging the stereotypes were to their communities. Almost everyone interviewed, regardless of whether they found Appalachian stereotypes to be problematic or not, expressed a general sense of powerlessness as it related to those stereotypes. Those who were troubled by the images seemed at a loss for ways to address them. Some others dismissed the stereotypes as *the way it is*, a reaction strikingly similar to the way some interview participants expressed powerlessness about the portrayal of the poor in their local newspapers.

In 1993, Appalachia scholar Jean Haskell Speer wrote a column for the *Journal of the Appalachian Studies Association* suggesting strategies that might be used to slow the use of negative hillbilly representations in the media. Most of her strategies involved pressuring television networks, advertisers, producers, and media regulators such as the Federal Communications Commission. Filing FCC complaints about programming, for example, "may be useful for convincing legislators to put pressure on media producers" to end negative portrayals, as could using the threat of eminent FCC complaints to sway local network affiliates, she suggested.[26] Speer suggested the Appalachian Studies Association, as an advocate for the region, should take a lead "in highly visible media, such as the *Washington Post, New York Times*, national magazines, and television" by writing op-ed pieces and offering televised commentary, and then "funnel these same concerns and positions to local media in our own [geographic] areas."[27] Speer's top-down approach to challenging negative Appalachian stereotypes did not take hold, but perhaps a bottom-up campaign could, if nothing else, establish a strong counternarrative to the Appalachian hillbilly stereotype found by so many in the region to be offensive. If local newspapers and other community media did began to contribute to a more nuanced understanding of the lived experience of the rural poor in Appalachia, as I suggest they should, it would create new opportunities to contribute to a more robust national understanding of the region and its people. The process of challenging that narrative is, in some ways, quite similar to challenging dominant ideas about poverty at the local level.

In order to attempt to develop a strong counternarrative about Appalachia's rural communities, and particularly the rural poor, it must be made clear that the dominant narratives are often harmful to social life in the region. It is problematic when individuals assume all poor people in Greenburg, Priorsville, or Deer Creek are culturally or socially deficient and solely responsible for their own poverty. It is equally problematic when people outside the region come to see poor people in the region as culturally backward. The Othering of a region and its people has tangible social consequences that transcend an individual's experience. When a regional identity such as Appalachian is believed to be real, then its consequences—including structures that enable inequality—also become real.[28] Getting the attention of the local newspaper editor may be relatively easy in small towns such as the three described here. On the other hand, changing the minds of national media executives, filmmakers, and television producers who employ regional stereotypes is a task that seems insurmountable for the vast majority of Appalachian residents. However, technology makes it increasingly easier for the region's people to tell their own story in their own words, to create a different picture of the region, its problems, and its successes. Horace Newcomb's biting analysis of commercial television's treatment of "hillbillies" in the 1970s made the point that the

> negative aspects of the broad images do reinforce negative attitudes and contribute to the model of "cultural imperial-ism." But the positive images serve in part to counter that model. It is a slow process of cultural and social change. The faster process is one in which we contribute our own images to the mixtures.[29]

Even that process of contributing our own images is fraught with cultural peril, Newcomb noted: Documentaries, journalism, long-form nonfiction, and even books such as this one still need to "sell" in one sense or another and, as such, run the risk of doing so using stereotypes by focusing on "the unusual or the almost forgotten."[30] A nonprofit Appalachian media cooperative like the one described in Appendix B would seem to be a forum less sus-ceptible to those types of pressures. Local advertisers would already have "paid" for much of the content as it appeared in newspapers, and it would be disseminated not with the goal of accumulating more economic capital, but rather of building bridging social capital for the region and countering prevalent negative stereotypes. The development of a platform where people from the region could learn about the challenges and successes of communities similar to their own could lead to increased interac-tion and cooperation among residents of those communities and the exchange of information that could help residents address local problems in new ways. Local newspapers and online news organizations in Greenburg, Priorsville, Deer Creek, and hundreds more communities in Appalachia already create volumes of content promoting the positive things going on in those communities. As those local narratives become more robust and more inclusive, the opportunity arises to create broad counternarratives to the dominant picture of Appalachia.

Being "the Last Refuge of Unfiltered America"

In a column entitled "Why I Love My Hometown Newspaper" published in his hometown newspaper, the *San Pedro Valley* (Arizona) *News-Sun*, poet Baxter Black wrote that he thought of local newspapers "as the last refuge of unfiltered America. A running documentary of the warts and triumph of real people unfettered by the spin, the bias and the opaque polish of today's homogenized journalism."[31] The local news outlets in Greenburg, Priorsville, and Deer Creek often seemed to struggle to live up to Black's ideal. I did not write this book to criticize the newspapers I studied, or to put down the hardworking, intelligent, dedicated individuals who produce them on a daily or weekly basis. They find themselves in a difficult position. The editors and reporters in those three towns want to foster unity and community pride. However, poverty—a highly divisive issue—sits in their communities like an elephant in the room. Some journalists seemed to view its coverage as an either/or proposition: Do they ignore poverty or downplay it, and in the process further distance the poor from the rich and middle class? Or do they discuss it aggressively, and risk creating internal conflict, alienating themselves from another segment of their readership? It is my hope that this study will encourage journalists to recast that dichotomy or eliminate it altogether and consider how they can reorient discussions about social issues. The men and women who work in local media in Greenburg, Priorsville, and Deer Creek expressed the desire to help the people around them live more fulfilled lives. Many other reporters, editors, publishers, and online news providers approach their work with the same desire as concerned friends. It is my hope that this study will help journalists reevaluate the ways they have acted on those desires.

Media scholar and former journalist Don Heider suggested that, for meaningful changes in the way class is covered in media to occur, reporters, editors, and owners would have to be on board.[32] The good news for others who wish to see change is that in rural communities, these major players are often within reach. If individuals in a community such as Priorsville or Deer Creek want to influence the newspaper's editorial voice, they do not need to seek out a CEO in a faraway city, a board of directors, or shareholders. Rather, they need to convince one or two people who work for community newspapers and actually live in those communities.[33] As the Deer Creek case shows, new media can emerge to create alternative discussions when existing community news outlets seem unwilling or unable to address community needs. Niche publications and community news outlets that operate outside the normative practices of mainstream media can serve as platforms for community members to challenge dominant narratives, a process that can have the effect of community cohesion.[34] Media have an extraordinary capacity, communication scholar James W. Carey noted, to expand individual abilities and opportunities to share knowledge and experience.[35] As they go about that work, journalists involved in that process should consider who they themselves are including and leaving out of that process.

The recommendations set out in this book would help facilitate the building of bridging social capital and bonding social capital in rural Appalachian communities such as Greenburg, Priorsville, and Deer Creek. As Putnam noted in *Bowling Alone*, bonding social capital undergirds the strong communal ties that enable reciprocity and solidarity that hold groups together. Bridging social capital, on the other hand, makes possible relationships among different groups for the exchange of information or resources.[36] Healthy communities have a need for high levels of both bridging social capital *and* bonding social capital. Communities with high levels of both kinds of social capital tend to be inclusive, with strong internal connections as well as ties to the outside. Communities that experience weak bonding *and* bridging social capital tend to be defined by apathy. Communities with high levels of bonding social capital but low levels of bridging social capital are sometimes plagued by factions and intolerance. Communities with high levels of bridging social capital and low levels of bonding social capital are often less self-sufficient than communities with higher levels of bonding social capital, and their residents may feel less connected to one another.[37]

Community news organizations like the ones described here are more typically associated with bonding social capital than with bridging social capital, but they can encourage both bridging and bonding social capital by being intentionally inclusive and reflexive. More inclusive outreach and sourcing practices and comprehensive news coverage help encourage bridging social capital by giving more local residents the opportunity to feel they are a part of the community. Bridging social capital is evident when individuals who find themselves on the fringe of social life are able better integrate into a community. Some of the individuals interviewed for this study viewed themselves as community out-siders. A few, namely Dan in Greenburg and Sally in Priorsville, became more integrated into the community and experienced an increase in personal social capital after they were featured in their local newspapers. As those individuals feel more a part of a com-munity, they develop stronger bonding social capital.

News organizations, both print and online, are important institutions in small communities, but they are only one part of a larger social structure that dictates how individuals in a bounded place see and understand one another. Health care groups, edu-cation networks, law enforcement systems, and other bodies that help constitute what we might broadly refer to as "social life" in a community have important roles to play in public discourse about social issues. This study explores the edges of some of those relationships, but it does not fully explain the interactions among them that may contribute to stratification and stigmatization regardless of what the local media do or do not do. I chose to study the news because news is what I know, and because I strongly believe newspapers and electronic media can foster important public dialogue. It is doubtful, however, that a newspaper could cause wholesale change in a community on its own. *Priorsville Post-Examiner* editor Nick, who pushes his sources' and readers' boundaries more than any other journalist in this study, put it well when he said:

> At the end of the day, it comes back to [the fact that] the community has got to get involved. If the community's not willing to get involved, the newspaper can't [pause], the newspaper's only, in that role of being able to make a difference, the newspaper can only do what the community's willing to do. So after you've been the voice, you've been the mouthpiece and you've facilitated the discussion, at that point, if people aren't willing to get involved, and maybe that's because you as a newspaper haven't done your job well enough to convince people to get involved, but if they're not willing to get involved, it's hard to make a difference.

This study represents snapshots of three communities at a single moment in time. It focuses on perceptions, which are important but also very fluid. Long-term community issues such as the unemployment trend in Priorsville can influence those perceptions, as can more immediate and concrete matters such as the closure of a local hospital or a natural disaster. Longitudinal studies of communities like Greenburg, Priorsville, or Deer Creek could offer a more robust explanation of how attitudes toward poverty and the poor evolve over time, and what types of public discussions (either in media or independent of them) contribute to those perceptions.

Theoretical understandings of the ways people incorporate media into their understandings of daily life are especially pertinent when one considers the history of Appalachia. Media have been important historically in the construction of Appalachia as a land full of outsiders who are poor, uneducated, and in need of civilizing. National and local media are instrumental in shaping the public's beliefs, and they clearly continue to play a role in the development and maintenance of the Appalachian narrative. Community news outlets have the ability to foster more inclusive discussions of social matters that are (or should be) of grave local concern, and the people who live in the communities they serve deserve those discussions. Much existing coverage does little to help communities see solutions to their problems, and it does little to integrate the poor into local discussions. People like Jenn and Brandy in Greenburg and Stacy in Deer Creek, largely invisible except to those who would look down upon them, deserve more than that. People like Trish in Deer Creek, who struggle to get by through no fault of their own, yet sometimes get lumped into the heap of "those people" who need assistance, deserve more than that. People like Stacy and Micah in Priorsville and Floyd in Greenburg, who have ideas about changing things but find themselves yelling into the wind when they try to voice them, deserve more than that. People like the late Pap Miller who, because of their social standing, never get a public voice until after they are dead, deserve more than that.

The people of rural Appalachia, who in many cases live in communities that have been exploited for the economic benefit of the rest of a country and Othered for their social benefit, deserve more than that.

APPENDIX A

Research Methodology

Most of this book is based on fieldwork conducted in the winter of 2013 and the spring of 2014. My primary goals were to examine rural community journalists' professional approaches to poverty, to describe how the resulting coverage resonated with their readers, and to consider how news contributed (or could contribute) to local community attitudes toward poverty and to broader views of Appalachia as a region. To provide for a robust analysis, I chose to write about three communities in the central and north-central Appalachian regions. The three communities are similar in that they are all part of Appalachia as it is defined by the federal government, and in 2013 and 2014, each experienced high levels of economic distress as defined by the Appalachian Regional Commission. All three communities are rural; none of the three is inside a U.S. Census Bureau–defined Metropolitan Statistical Area. As I was selecting cases for analysis, I placed a great deal of value on analyzing communities with somewhat diverse media environments, with the expectation that different media ecosystems might produce somewhat different results. For example, frequency of local newspaper publication (daily versus weekly), media ownership (local versus corporate), and competition within local media markets (i.e., a single publication, multiple publications, publications and hyperlocal online media, etc.) were taken into consideration when selecting sites.

Taking those factors into account, I identified communities in different states as possible sites for this research and began contacting newspaper workers in those communities. Newspaper managers were the natural points of entry into individual cases for several reasons. Most notably, the participation of newspaper personnel was a vital component of each case study; if editors, publishers, and journalists had not been willing to participate in interviews, then the communities in which they worked would not have been the best subjects for this project. The three communities described here were my first three choices for the project.

Collection and Analysis of Interview Data

This study examines data collected through interviews with fifty-one residents of Greenburg, Priorsville, and Deer Creek. Interviews conducted for this study were largely unstructured in nature. I went into each interview with some specific topics in mind, but conversations with research participants were largely allowed to run their own courses. Interviews ranged in length from fifteen minutes to three and a half hours. I attempted to interview every media worker who influenced editorial content (reporters and editors), as well as publishers, general managers, and other supervisors who made editorial decisions. Interviews conducted with media workers focused on their attitudes toward poverty in the communities they covered, the ways they approached poverty and associated issues in news coverage, and the roles they saw their media outlets playing in their communities. Participants chose the interview sites; almost all of the journalists interviewed chose to speak at their offices.

The study also included interviews with between thirteen and fourteen people who lived in each of the communities that are the focus of this study. The sample interviewed consists of local stakeholders with a specific interests in poverty (such as nonprofit managers, pastors, government officials, and social workers), residents recruited through a snowball sampling method (stakeholders were asked to recommend other people who could provide useful viewpoints and information), residents recruited through my own personal networks, and other residents I approached during my site visits. I attempted to interview a broad cross-section of residents for this book, and the non-media participants described in the preceding pages were diverse in terms of biographies and lifestyles. Some were lifelong residents of their communities, and others were newcomers or, in a few cases, people trying to leave for personal or economic reasons. Some held jobs many of their neighbors might covet: factory managers, bank executives, and teaching positions at local public schools. Others worked for low wages or did not work at all. Some held positions in local government, and others said they viewed themselves as social outcasts. Interviews conducted with community members focused on the representations of poverty they observed in local media, their experiences with local media, and the roles they believed local media played (or should play) in the creation of community dialogue about social issues. As was the case with journalists, non-media interview participants chose the locations for our interviews—I talked with them in their homes, their offices, in local schools and libraries, at diners, and in community organization offices. I conducted interviews in each community until I reached what Strauss and Corbin called the point of "theoretical saturation"[1]—that is, the point at which interviews ceased to reveal new information of significance to the study.

Anonymity was extended to all interviewees (journalists and community members) to encourage honesty and candor, and research participants were assigned pseudonyms for the purposes of telling their stories. Audio recordings were made of most of the one-on-one interviews and those recordings were coded for common themes. Five participants asked that our conversations not be recorded. In those cases, I took notes by hand and coded those notes after the interview. Sixteen of the interviews were conducted over the telephone; the rest were conducted in person. All participants had opportunities to learn more about the study and to ask questions. Signed informed consent was obtained from all participants interviewed in person in Greenburg, Priorsville, and Deer Creek. Residents who took part in phone interviews provided verbal informed consent.

Collection and Analysis of Media Content

This book describes many different types of local news stories, from front-page items to small announcements buried deep inside the publication. The description of these texts provides important perspective—it is enlightening in and of itself, and it helped inform many of the interviews included in the book. I analyzed content published over a six-month period in the three weekly newspapers, and over a four-month period in the one daily newspaper, the *Greenburg Star*, reviewing the publications for news and information relating to local poverty and need. The *Greenburg Star* sample included the eighty-five newspapers published between November 1, 2013, and February 28, 2014. The *Priorsville Post-Examiner* sample included the twenty-six newspapers published between October 3, 2013, and March 27, 2014. The *Priorsville Record* sample covered the same dates but included only twenty-five newspapers, because the *Record* does not publish a newspaper during the week of Christmas. The *Deer Creek Chronicle* sample covered the twenty-five issues published between November 7, 2013, and April 24, 2014. Online news content was examined on a daily or semi-daily basis. Media content were subjected to three separate readings. The first reading included all editorial and advertising content produced during the sample period, regardless of its relevance to the study. During the initial reading, content that pertained to poverty, even tenuously, was identified. That content was subjected to a second reading, in which common themes were identified and frames began to emerge. I used the third and final reading to refine those frames and to consider how they fit within the study's broader theoretical perspective. Although the textual analysis was qualitative in nature, some frequencies were recorded and reported (for example, the percentage of front-page stories that specifically address poverty). That data, while not the immediate focus of the study, are important in that they speak to the dominance and/or absence of certain ideas and messages. I recorded basic quantitative data about stories that appeared on the front pages of the newspapers for a content analysis, coding for story placement, story topic, the inclusion of photos, whether the story made mention of poverty, and what sources were quoted in the story. To test the reliability of the coding instrument used for the quantitative content analysis, a second person coded the front pages of fifteen issues (ninety stories) randomly chosen from the sample. Reliability estimates using Scott's pi were .75 for both story classification and references to poverty, which are high enough to draw tentative conclusions.[2]

In addition, other popular local media content were subjected to a secondary analysis. "Popular" is a subjective idea, particularly as it relates to the huge, ever-evolving world of social media. To select digital media for the secondary analysis in this study, I asked all participants in this study which web sites and social media presences they visited for local news and information. If a site or social media account was mentioned by three or more community members, it was subjected to a secondary analysis. That approach yielded two hyperlocal news web sites, GreenburgToday. com and the Deer Creek Advocate, which were studied alongside local newspapers. The GreenburgToday.com sample included 197 stories—everything published between November 2013 and the end of February 2014 (the same time frame used for the *Greenburg Star*). The sheer quantity of posts published on the Deer Creek Advocate and the slow load time of the site made calendar-based sampling impractical. Instead, I created a purposive sample by searching for posts that included the following keywords: poverty, poor, welfare, unemployed, unemployment, and homeless. The search focused on stories posted between November 1, 2013, and April 30, 2014 (the same period used in my analysis of the *Deer Creek Chronicle*). I filtered out news items that included those words but were not relevant to the study (for example, horoscopes, movie reviews, and reports on fishing conditions). That approach yielded ninety-nine posts for analysis.

I excluded radio and television coverage from the analysis for several reasons. Television coverage of the three communities I studied was largely produced by journalists in the nearest metropolitan areas. Only one of the three communities I studied had local public-access television, and residents told me local television programming that aired on that channel had no real news value. Commercial radio stations operated in two of the three communities I studied, but the news-gathering capabilities of those stations was extremely limited, and few local residents told me radio was an important part of their local news diet.

Historical data from each community, collected through local libraries and historical societies, also shaped this book in important ways. The historical information described here is largely descriptive in nature, but it provided important contextual information about communities and their media ecosystems and informed my understanding of interview subjects' views of poverty.

My Position within This Work

Social scientists (particularly those who do qualitative research) since the 1970s have wrestled with the spoken or tacit understanding that a researcher's personal experience might shape his or her scholarly work. Understanding and acknowledging the fact that personal identity and professional pursuits in academia are inextricably intertwined attacks head on the "positivist fiction of an objective observer."[3] Social science, like social life, is inherently messy. The selection of research topics, research methods, research questions, and publication venues all involve subjective choices based on the goals of the researcher, which are inseparable from her or his individual identity. When researchers contemplate those matters in a public fashion, it allows the research audience (and in fact the researcher herself or himself) to incorporate biography into the interpretation of study findings.

I grew up in a rural community and have spent much of my life living in areas that one might colloquially refer to as "out in the country." Most of that time was spent in the U.S. South, where I grew up and lived as an adult around people who were, for the most part, like me: lower-middle to middle-class working folks, farmers, small business owners, and rural-to-urban commuters, many of whom had never lived anywhere else in their lives. For me, the exploration of the research questions outlined in this study was also a personal exploration of the ways I have been pushed to understand my own regional identity, and the ways I as a professional journalist, who often wrote about rural people and issues, pushed others to understand theirs. As a local newspaper reporter and editor during the first half of my career, I usually tended to write and report from the community journalist's perspective described in this book. As a metropolitan newspaper reporter during the second half of my career, I was more often an outsider looking in, although my outsider status was lessened when I would report on the communities I had previously covered as a community journalist. In both cases, I made decisions about how to portray people that had tangible social consequences—I will never forget the woman who called me, outraged about the fact that I had referenced the thickness of her glasses in a story as a coy way of emphasizing her age. I sometimes wonder about the people who did not call because they did not believe reaching out to me would have made a difference.

The people and places discussed in this study are familiar to me biographically in some ways. I went into this study with a few personal contacts in two of the three communities, and all three are full of people to whom I feel I relate to a degree. However, as similar as I may perceive myself to be to many of the individuals who appear in this book, I remain an outsider to their communities. The end result of my work there is a written portrayal of the ways their lives, problems, and opportunities are portrayed by other writers, and the ways they understand those portrayals. In the process of crafting that portrayal, I ran the risk of subjecting the participants in this study to what sociologist Pierre Bourdieu called the "symbolic violence" associated with fieldwork:

> It is the investigator who starts the game and sets up its rules, and is usually the one who, unilaterally and without any preliminary negotiations, assigns the interview its objectives and uses. (These, on occasion, may be poorly specified—at least for the respondent.) This asymmetry is reinforced by a social symmetry every time the investigator occupies a higher place in the social hierarchy of different types of capital, cultural capital in particular.[4]

Symbolic violence exercised by the researcher objectifies the research participant for the sake of the research project. It also creates an environment, Bourdieu argued, in which participants recognize the social chasm between themselves and the researcher and, because of the understood difference, may be inclined to "play along" with the research process—that is, to become the *subjects* the researcher wants them to be rather than the *individuals* they understand themselves to be.[5]

To address those issues, I returned to Bourdieu's 1999 analysis of social suffering, in which he advised researchers to make the participants' problems their own problems. As Bourdieu noted, every act of social science involves at least a small degree of intrusion. The key to reducing the symbolic violence associated with that intrusion is to recognize the distance between researcher and research participant and to mitigate it as much as possible by making the participant's problems your own through active listening and concerted efforts to put yourself in the place of the interviewee: "social proximity and familiarity provide two of the conditions of 'nonviolent' communication."[6] Such understanding does not begin and end with the interview process. It must be actively exercised throughout the entire research process, especially during the writing of results and conclusions. Throughout this research project—from conception to data collection to the penning of findings, impressions, and conclusions—I have worked to dispel any notion that this book is a detached, clinical case study. I rather choose to view it as a collaborative effort involving myself and the fifty-one women and men who chose to help me complete it.

APPENDIX B

Action Steps for Journalists

1. Seek Out Diverse Sources

By reaching out to people in their communities who might not normally get their names and opinions in the newspaper, journalists can establish more inclusive and welcoming discursive environments. "Reaching out" can mean different things. For starters, it can mean simply conversing with people who experience social issues such as poverty firsthand. During interviews for this book, local residents were asked what advice they would give a local journalist who wanted to help address problems in their communities. Trish, the newspaper secretary in Deer Creek, first said she'd tell that person to talk to the people who run the two largest nonprofit organizations in town. Then, she said, "maybe, you know, just talk to some of the people around town. Ask them what they want, what would they like to know or have. Just go straight to the source and see what it is they'd like to see. People are pretty forthcoming here."

I did find people in Deer Creek, Greenburg, and Priorsville to be very forthcoming about what they would like to see their newspapers accomplish. But few of those people seemed to feel they were in a position to relay those desires to the people who ran the newspaper, either because they thought their ideas were unimportant or because they felt there was too much social distance between themselves and the newspaper and its employees. This was particularly problematic in Deer Creek, where many residents felt Gregory could not relate to their concerns. When we talked, Gregory expressed a strong desire to lead his community and promote change through the newspaper.

I believe he was genuine in his desire to do that, and to help people in his community. But when he tried to lead in a vocal way, he did so almost exclusively through his own voice. His readers noticed this, and it made them reluctant to attempt to engage the newspaper.

The voices of residents who are willing to talk about firsthand experience with issues such as government aid, unemployment, or homelessness will provide deeper meaning and context to stories about those topics. One effective way to build a network of possible sources is to work with social service agencies, nonprofit groups, and individual activists in communities who can and will help journalists establish those relationships. First, journalists must seek out those groups and individuals. Then, journalists should effectively explain the goals of their stories or columns to the people who operate those agencies and get the agency heads to support their efforts. At that point, agency workers can work as recruiters of sorts, reaching out to individuals who use their programs and connecting those people with journalists.

Transparency is the key to avoiding exploitation and building healthy relationships with sources. Journalists should show their sources how they fit into stories about social issues. People who agree to talk about their personal experiences for stories about poverty and other matters should have an understanding of why they were asked to do so in order to make a sound decision about whether to participate in an interview. Journalists should explain in great detail to sources what they hope to accomplish in writing about them (i.e., "I want to write a column that helps people understand the challenges of raising a family on minimum wage") rather than offering an abstract descriptions of a story (i.e., "I'm writing about the minimum wage"). Research has shown that some news stories framed *thematically* (that is, stories based on trends, policies, or abstract ideas) tend to lead audiences to assign responsibility for poverty to societal factors, while stories framed *episodically* (that is, stories based on a specific event or individual) may lead audiences to hold the poor responsible for their own poverty.[1] Introducing

thematic concepts into stories alongside more personal perspectives may help readers consider alternative views of poverty while
at the same time exposing them to individuals in their community
who may challenge their preconceived notions of what it means, for
example, to live in government housing.

Local journalists can also look for opportunities to empower
their community sources, making sure they have a say in how they
are portrayed. Journalists often recoil when sources ask them to
review stories prior to publication. However, if a reporter is concerned about how an interview subject will "come off" in a story,
then sharing all or part of the story with the source can ensure
that the source is comfortable with her or his portrayal. It also can
build the source's confidence in the newspaper's ability to fairly
represent his or her issues. Another option that will sometimes be
more effective is to encourage sources to tell their stories in their
own words. Give individuals the opportunity to express their own
realities without journalistic interpretation. Those expressions can
come in the form of editorial page columns, or as passages written
down or transcribed by a journalist for inclusion in a news story.
When journalists do that, they "end up with different stories with
different emphases that, rather than leaving people feeling like they
can't accomplish anything, leave people feeling empowered to step
in and do something about their own world," said Peggy Holman,
co-founder and executive director of the media nonprofit Journalism
that Matters.[2]

2. Do not exclusively rely on spot coverage for poverty news

Poverty and local need most often made their way into the media
in Greenburg, Priorsville, and Deer Creek as "spot news"—news
reported of events as they happen. Spot news is, by definition,
reactive rather than proactive: An external event (i.e., a check

donation, the release of new unemployment figures, or a city council vote) occurs, and a journalist creates an account that relays news of that event to the public. Those stories and photos have news value in that they provide information that readers may need. Donation photos, nonprofit social service workers interviewed for this book said, often lead to increased awareness of local agencies and spikes in financial donations. However, when spot news is the dominant (or exclusive) image of poverty a community receives, there are negative consequences. Daily struggles can come to be seen as the norm, only certain voices end up speaking about poverty in public forums, and remedies to associated social issues such as drug abuse or housing shortages sometimes focus on symptoms rather than core problems. "These issues, they're not going away. They're not changing," Sally, the nonprofit thrift store manager in Priorsville, said. "By not addressing them, not dealing with it, we're not changing anything."

Local newspapers can instead look for ways to write about need in a proactive way. Editor Nick at the *Priorsville Post-Examiner*, a newspaper struggling to find "fresh angles" to pervasive unemployment and poverty, expressed the importance of proactive reporting this way:

> You can go out and seek out information from outside. So many times within the community it becomes just isolated and closed off, people talking in the coffee shop and developing their opinions about what's going on. And that's any issue, it's the same with the economy, things like that. But as a newspaper, you can go outside and get those outside opinions, see what other communities are doing, and separate fact from fiction, that sort of thing. . . . As a newspaper, you can go out and chase those stories and look at what other communities are doing, and bring that back and tell people about that and say let's try this.

When asked if the *PPE* did a good job of that, Nick answered frankly: "We can do better." When asked, how, he answered:

> Thought-provoking, maybe getting people a little riled up. That's something we've not done a lot of in the past. It's easier just to, just write a jobless story. Numbers, people are used to seeing. And so we've covered it. When you've got to step outside of your comfort zone and do a story on, for example, food stamp fraud that might not only get some of your neighbors mad at you but might also get one of your advertisers mad at you too if he's helping to facilitate that food stamp fraud, you know, especially in a small town, that makes it a little more uncomfortable sometimes. But there comes a point where you've got to do it if you're going to do your job right.

New ideas and proactive stories can come through the efforts of local journalists such as Nick, or they can come from other places. The *Deer Creek Chronicle* rarely published stories or columns about need during the time period analyzed for this study, but it did give readers two stories produced by a state news organization about new research on poverty. Newspapers can also find new ideas by opening up their pages to the rest of the community, reaching out to regular sources who have ideas but have never been asked (Jennifer in Deer Creek or Floyd in Greenburg), residents who have strong opinions but rarely appear in the newspaper (Micah or Sally in Priorsville or Blake in Deer Creek), or local residents who deal with the realities of poverty every day (Jenn and Brandy in Greenburg or Trish in Deer Creek).

3. Think About the Meanings of "Positive" and "Negative" News

None of the recommendations in this section should be taken to mean that local newspapers should stop publishing news about the good things happening in their communities. Positive stories about what former community journalist Jock Lauterer called the "triumphs of life" have news value and help bind people together in a way that builds community.[3] Defining "positive news" can be fairly easy. Defining "negative news" can be more difficult. Is a story "negative" when we do not like the issue at hand, or when we think the subject of the story reflects poorly on us as a community? I do not believe that was the case in Greenburg, Priorsville, or Deer Creek, because I did not get the sense that people who *did* want to see issues such as poverty brought to the forefront would view a story about unemployment as inherently negative. It might be more constructive to reconceptualize "negative coverage" of social issues as news coverage that does one or both of the following things:

- Suggests a problem where none really exists. Much stereotypical reporting and journalism that is basely inaccurate falls into this category.

- Discusses the problematic nature of an issue, person, or group without explaining the realistic scope of the problem or solutions, or without attempting to help other people develop them.

By pointing out problems and offering narratives that propose realistic, grounded solutions, news organizations can produce content that moves their communities toward solutions. Media groups such as the Solutions Journalism Network (SJN) encourage reporters and editors to seek out solutions for the problems that plague their communities through training and the provision of online reporting tools. SJN advises journalists to identify issues of concern (such as persistent poverty), consider what information is missing from the public conversation about that issue, and look for places that have handled that issue well.[4]

When residents in Greenburg, Priorsville, and Deer Creek discussed negative news coverage created by outside media, they for the most part acknowledged that a social issue (such as drug abuse or unemployment) *did* exist, and that it was problematic. What bothered them was the fact that the problem was *all* they saw in media reports. Local newspapers may respond to such coverage in one of three ways:

1. Ignore it. News outlets often do this. It is easy, and it does not cause conflict within the community because it does not require the newspaper to take a position on a potentially polarizing issue such as poverty.

2. Refute it, an option that does take time and effort. Theresa founded GreenburgToday.com because she wanted to refute negative coverage of a political controversy Greenburg.

3. Recast it. Scholars such as Lillian S. Robinson and Linda Steiner have chronicled social groups' ability to express concerns in their own language and on their own terms through niche media and thus capitalize on alternative framing opportunities. Steiner studied oppositional decoding in Ms. magazine's "No Comment" section, a space where the magazine printed reader-submitted media items that debased women. She argued that the submission of texts to "No Comment"—even without commentary—represented resistance through expression. Groups have the ability, she concluded, to "actively play with the texts of the larger culture, responding to and reworking both positive and negative images of the group in the dominant media. The group here deconstructs in order to reconstruct its own story."[5]

If a local newspaper is going to try to foster an oppositional reading (option 2 or 3) to a negative code that suggests its residents are poor because of a personal or cultural deficiency (a culture of poverty argument), then it must produce evidence of alternative options. Perhaps the alternative argument is that the community has a collective responsibility to try to change things—the way its members see themselves (as a community, not as individuals), as well as the ways that others see them.

4. Consider your opportunity to set agendas

Some community journalists, such as George McLean, have embraced their roles as change agents. In the 1940s, McLean was the publisher of the *Daily Journal* in Tupelo, Mississippi, an isolated town then mired in job loss and poverty. McLean was brazen both in person and through his newspaper, and his approach to journalism rubbed some members of Tupelo's elite the wrong way—his newspaper's support for workers involved in local labor disputes, for example, made him a villain in the eyes of some local business owners. Despite those at times adversarial community relationships, McLean built support among community businesses for a progressive program aimed at convincing Tupelo's more well-heeled citizenry to invest their money in improving the lives of the county's poorest residents and creating an atmosphere where local people from all backgrounds could address local problems. McLean was able to appeal to those who did not trust him by convincing them that, as he told one local hardware store owner, "As long as your customers are poor, you're going to be poor."[6] By bringing Tupelo's poorest residents up, he reasoned, the entire community would prosper.

McLean had advocated for change in the *Daily Journal* before, to little avail. To make his vision for community development a reality, he built trust between himself and his town's leaders, and between those leaders and Tupelo's broader population, a process that would take years.[7] By the late 1990s, Lee County, of which Tupelo is a part, had become the second wealthiest county in Mississippi, home to eighteen Fortune 500 companies and forty-five international corporations.[8] George McLean started small, focusing on bettering the lives of Lee County's poorest farmers by raising money from local businesses to fund a dairy project. In 1946, the *Daily Journal* created a series of "rural community development councils" that worked together to nurture new leaders by mobilizing farmers and getting them involved in community development.[9] Two years later, he led the formation of a local Community Development Foundation that became "the linchpin of community life in Tupelo and its surroundings, the organization through which things got done." In their case study of Tupelo's growth in the middle of the twentieth century, Vaughn Grisham and Rob Gurwitt observed that

> in any other community, a group of citizens taking that role upon themselves would have been called "the power elite" and would undoubtedly have been self-selecting, wealthy, and given to acting behind closed doors. In Tupelo, anyone with the inclination and the dues—which varied according to one's income—could join in.[10]

McLean helped give shape to the structure that enabled Tupelo's growth, but a large collection of residents ultimately made it possible. McLean died in 1983, but he left a lasting legacy. As a journalist, he sought out solutions and fought for equality in his community. Grisham and Gurwitt noted that his newspaper, now called the *Northeast Mississippi Daily Journal*, continued to keep community development in the public discussion into the 2000s.[11]

The turnaround Tupelo underwent in the twentieth century has become a model for progressive rural development efforts. McLean started turning his community around by trying to change people's preconceived notion about their poor neighbors. "The opportunity to bring a message is important, if you can use it well," said Peter Hille, president of the Mountain Association for Community Economic Development in Berea, Kentucky. Local media can play a critical role in both "informing the public and also shaping a set of perspectives for people and messaging that creates a frame in which people can see what they could do differently and how doing things differently would make things work differently for people in their community," Hille said.[12] News organizations can do that by providing their readers with basic information about how their local economies work in their news sections, and by taking critical looks at local problems from a variety of different perspectives on their opinion pages.

Such an approach may be seen to stand at odds with the journalistic notion of objectivity—the idea that the reporter must be detached and unbiased.[13] "A lot of news folks in our country have grown up with a set of beliefs about objectivity, that if they step in and get involved, then that crosses a line into advocacy. Therefore, they've tended to hang back," said Peggy Holman of Journalism that Matters.[14] Holman encourages journalists to question their own roles in a community—particularly whether they want to work, as McLean did, to make their towns thrive. "If that's what they're about, what does that mean for every practice of journalism from where the stories come from, who gets interviewed, the nature of the questions themselves, the forms of the storytelling, how distribution happens, how the stories are used and circulated and the conversations that happen around them?" Holman said. "The range of possibilities is really pretty stunning."[15]

The journalists interviewed for this study were often very mindful of working with "journalistic integrity," as former Greenburg editor Nancy put it, to avoid being seen as outwardly advocating. Some in their community, however, were supportive of the idea that a local media outlet could be an outspoken community leader. Local journalists can seek out ways to do that incrementally, without trying to overhaul their communities overnight. They may do it by becoming change agents themselves, as George McLean did. Or they may use their news outlets to create an environment that is conducive to the creation of new change agents. By giving more sets of community members access to public platforms, publishers and editors may help new leaders emerge.

5. Seek out partnerships and band together

Large-scale reporting projects are often daunting propositions for small news organizations with only one or two reporters. Organizations such as the Whitesburg, Kentucky-based Center for Rural Strategies can and do help produce data that local media organizations can localize by interviewing sources in their communities. The center has produced and distributed data on, among other things, the economic impact of Social Security in rural areas, increases in college graduation rates, and the economic impact of food stamps. Often, community journalists struggle "to get a hundred feet above it all and write that story," said Dee Davis, president of the Center for Rural Strategies. "We can aggregate this data in ways that we can then put into stories and get it out."[16] The food stamp data, produced in 2014, was used by 450 news outlets in forty-five states, with a combined reach of about a million people.[17] Other media have partnered with nonpartisan organizations to create meaningful opportunities for their audiences to express themselves and interact with one another. For example, West Virginia Public Broadcasting's "What's Next, West Virginia," executed with the West Virginia Center for Civic Life and the West Virginia Community Development Hub, encourages residents across the state to take part in conversations about the West Virginia's economic future.

Individually, local newspapers cannot challenge the dominant narrative about poverty in Appalachia. We cannot idealize these businesses and the people who work in them beyond their practical contexts. However, a coalition of news organizations in Appalachia, local activists, universities in the region, and nonprofit organizations could aggregate content that was already being produced by local news organizations into a larger body of content that would reflect a different story about Appalachia, told by the men and women who live there. The content could take many forms: stories written by participating local news organizations such as GreenburgToday.com or the *Priorsville Post-Examiner*, films and other media produced by nonprofit groups, citizen journalism (perhaps produced by local residents who have received media training from universities, communications students at those universities, and/or nonprofit groups), or opinion columns on the region produced by residents or academics. By providing a space for commentary on the ways outside media outlets cover the region, the Appalachian media coalition could help residents of the region find a voice in a nation that often speaks *of* them but rarely speaks *to* them. The aggregated materials, which could be housed on a web site managed by one or more universities, would not attempt to paint a uniform picture of Appalachia, because there is no uniform picture of Appalachia. Instead, the media initiative would reflect the geographic, economic, and cultural diversity of the region that is often portrayed by outsiders as homogenous. Based on discussions with residents for this study, I would suggest that such stories focus on *cultural aspects* of Appalachian identity rather than geographic aspects or commonality through struggle, because people seemed most willing to coalesce around those cultural aspects of Appalachian identity. News organizations can involve themselves by contributing content as they are able, but other material would be produced by members of the public or the academy. As a result, the site could be largely unencumbered by concerns of the expression of opinion or advocacy that sometimes make local newspaper staffs hesitant to write about broader issues in the region.

Notes

1. POVERTY AND COMMUNITY MEDIA IN RURAL APPALACHIA

1. Lauterer, *Community Journalism*, 20.

2. Walls and Billings, "The Sociology of Southern Appalachia," 136.

3. Duncan, *Worlds Apart*.

4. Ibid., 103.

5. Ibid., 189.

6. Gaventa, *Power and Powerlessness*.

7. Benson, "News Media as a 'Journalistic Field'"; Bourdieu and Wacquant, *An Invitation to Reflexive Sociology*.

8. Eller, *Uneven Ground*.

9. Shuford, "What Happens When You Don't Own the Land?"

10. Gaventa, *Power and Powerlessness*, 218.

11. Ibid., 226.

12. Duncan, *Worlds Apart*, 34.

13. Dean, "The Journalist as a 'Committed Observer.'"

14. Sen, *Development as Freedom*, 277.

15. Ewick and Silbey, "Narrating Social Structure," 1328.

16. Hall, "Introduction: Who Needs 'Identity'?" 4–5.

17. Hall, "Encoding/Decoding," 128–38.

18. Ibid., 129.

19. Ibid., 130.

20. Bourdieu, *The Field of Cultural Production*; Bourdieu, *Language and Symbolic Power*.

21. Bourdieu, *Distinction*, 6–7. See also Bourdieu, *The Field of Cultural Production*.

22. Hall, "Introduction: Who Needs 'Identity'?" 13–14.

23. Hall, "Encoding/Decoding," 138; Steiner, "Oppositional Decoding as an Act of Resistance," 3.

24. Giddens, *The Constitution of Society*.

25. Ibid., 281–84.

26. Shilling, "Reconceptualising Structure and Agency in the Sociology of Education," 75.

27. Ibid.

28. Hall, "Signification, Representation, Ideology," 95.

29. Wheatley and Kellner-Rogers, "The Paradox and Promise of Community," 17.

30. Walker, Lewis, McBrien, and Wessinger, "It Has to Come from the People," 27.

31. Richards-Schuster and O'Doherty, "Appalachian Youth Re-envisioning Home, Re-making Identities," 86–87.

32. Lippman, *Public Opinion*, 54–55.

33. Eller, *Uneven Ground*; Straw, "Appalachian History"; Peterson, *Magazines in the Twentieth Century*.

34. Eller, *Uneven Ground*, 1–2.

35. Carey, "University Invitations and Inexhaustible Resources."

36. Frank, "When Bad Things Happen in Good Places."

37. Bowler, "'That Ribbon of Social Neglect,'" 239; emphasis in original.

38. Maggard, "Cultural Hegemony," 72.

39. Wray, *Not Quite White*; Harry, "'Trailer Park Trash."

40. Williamson, "The White Ghetto."

41. Lippmann, *Public Opinion*, 96.

42. See, among many others, Seiter, "Stereotypes and the Media: A Re-evaluation"; Merskin, "The S-Word"; Rendleman, "I Know Y'all Think I'm Pretty Square, But Tuh, I Believe What I Believe'"; Reed, "Lesbian Television Personalities"; McCloud, "From Exotics to Brainwashers"; Westerfelhaus and Lacroix, "Seeing 'Straight' Through Queer Eye"; Kama, "The Quest for Inclusion."

43. Dyer, *The Matter of Images*, 1.

44. Dyer, "Stereotyping," 277.

45. Lasorsa and Dai, "When News Reporters Deceive."

46. Gans, *Deciding What's News*.

47. Shelby, "The 'R' Word," 160.

48. Scott, "The Sociology of Coal Hollow," 13.

49. Precourt, "The Image of Appalachian Poverty," 103.

50. Maggard, "Cultural Hegemony," 72.

51. Lewis, "Beyond Isolation and Homogeneity," 22.

52. Ledford, "A Landscape and a People Set Apart," 49.

53. Tickamyer, "Space Matters!" 810.

54. Gaventa, *Power and Powerlessness*, 14.

55. Sen, *Development as Freedom*; Bachrach and Baratz, *Power and Poverty*.

56. Duncan, "Understanding Persistent Poverty"; Duncan and Lamborghini, "Poverty and Social Context in Remote Rural Communities."

57. Precourt, "The Image of Appalachian Poverty," 106.

58. Eller, *Uneven Ground*, x.

59. Gaventa, *Power and Powerlessness*, 15.

60. Kendall, *Framing Class*; Kitch, "Mourning 'Men Joined in Peril and Purpose'"; Hancock, *The Politics of Disgust*; Gilens, *Why Americans Hate Welfare*.

61. Mantsios, "Media Magic." Mantsios offered the following critique of the "down on their luck" frame, which, he argued, is largely applied to the white poor: "These 'Yule time' stories are as much about the affluent as they are about the poor: they tell us that the affluent in our society are a kind, understanding, giving people—which we are not" (102).

62. Kendall, *Framing Class*, 99.

63. Champaign, "The View from the Media," 54. Analysis by social scientists is vulnerable to the same shortcomings, as is government policy, as Sen noted in *Development as Freedom*: "A system of support that requires a person to be identified as poor (and is seen as a special benefaction for those who cannot fully fend for themselves) would tend to have some effects on one's self-respect as well as on respect by others" (136).

64. Hancock, *The Politics of Disgust*, 87.

65. Gilens, *Why Americans Hate Welfare*, 132.

66. Reader, "Community Journalism"; Donohue, Olien, and Tichenor, "Structure and Constraints on Community Newspaper Gatekeepers."

67. Janowitz, *The Community Press in an Urban Setting*.

68. Shaker, "Community Newspapers Play Significant Role in Election"; Lauterer, *Community Journalism*.

69. Williamson, "Australian Special-Interest Magazines"; Cover, "Community Print Media"; Viswanath and Arora, "Ethnic Media in the United States"; Carey, "Expression of Culture in the Amish Press."

70. Berger and Luckmann, *The Social Construction of Reality*, 149–50.

71. Terry, "Community Journalism Provides Model for Future," 71–83.

72. Lowrey, Brozana, and Mackay, "Toward a Measure of Community Journalism."

73. Reader, "Distinctions that Matter"; Janowitz, *The Community Press in an Urban Setting*.

74. Wotanis, "Community Journalism as Ritual," 299.

75. Curran, "What Democracy Requires of the Media," 128. See also Colistra, "The Rumble and the Dark."

76. Vidich and Bensma, *Small Towns in Mass Society*, 84.

77. Hatcher, "Were Those the Days?"; Hull, "Beacon of Light."

78. Carey, *Communication as Culture*, 15.

79. Ibid., 33. It is important to note that Carey did not suggest that this societal maintenance was the sole role of newspapers; he also spoke to their position as providers of information.

80. Buffington, "Our Job Isn't to Build Communities," 11–13.

81. Auyero and Swistun, *Flammable*.

82. Sen, *Development as Freedom*, 39–40.

83. Bourdieu, "Understanding," 614.

84. Ibid., 621.

85. Guenther, "The Politics of Names"; Scott, "Beyond Tokenism"; Marwell, "Privatizing the Welfare State"; Eckstein, "Community as Gift-Giving."

86. Later in this book, I will criticize the community journalists studied here for excluding the poor from news coverage out of an at times misguided sense that, in doing so, they are protecting them from social ridicule. It is fair to ask whether I, by assigning study participants pseudonyms and obscuring their geographic locations, am doing the same in this work. That is an especially problematic question for a community of journalists (of which I consider myself a part) that wrestles daily with the question of how and when it is appropriate to offer sources anonymity. It is true that the journalistic use (perhaps misuse is the better word) of anonymous sources has at times produced inaccuracies and outright fabrications that have eroded public trust in media institutions. At the same time, many important stories may never have been told were participants in those stories not allowed to describe their knowledge and experiences anonymously. Were the men and women interviewed for this study given the choice of appearing in this book under their real names or not appearing at all, some would have chosen the latter for fear of professional and/or social repercussions. One of this book's key goals is to articulate the perspectives of those individuals. The creation of an environment where they felt comfortable participating in this project necessitated the extension of anonymity.

2. GREENBURG, PRIORSVILLE, AND DEER CREEK: COMMUNITY CASE STUDIES

1. Shortly after fieldwork began, Nancy left her job as managing editor at Henderson Media for a job in public relations at a nearby university. Henderson Media assigned a newspaper editor from another part of the country to replace her. The new managing editor did not respond to my requests for interviews.

2. Most of the *Record*'s five employees, including Jim and Ed, worked part-time.

3. The *Record* launched its first news web site in June 2014. Its first attempt at an e-edition was delivered by e-mail.

4. I had an opportunity to witness firsthand Gregory's ability to turn everyday objects into news collection tools. I accompanied him to a local business mixer not long after we met. He took several photographs at the event with plans to publish them in the next week's paper. On that night, he took notes on the back of a bank deposit slip.

3. DOMINANT FRAMES IN LOCAL POVERTY COVERAGE

1. Entman, "Framing: Toward a Clarification of a Fractured Paradigm," 142.

2. Scheufele and Tewksbury, "Framing, Agenda Setting, and Priming"; Entman, "Framing: Toward a Clarification of a Fractured Paradigm."

3. The remaining four stories were about other local issues and referenced local poverty only in passing. For example, a January 2014 story about a city council meeting noted the council's interest in applying for a grant for local revitalization. The grant, the story noted, "is targeted to distressed communities where residents fall into the low to moderate income bracket." The reference to the grant was the story's only mention of Greenburg's economic condition, but because it was mentioned, it was counted as a reference to poverty.

4. The same was true of the *Star*'s Facebook page, which was updated less frequently.

5. Check presentations and other philanthropic achievements were published, but they appeared on inside pages of the newspaper.

6. Unemployment was less pronounced in Deer Creek, and the newspaper there published only one unemployment story over the six-month study period. That story, which included state numbers and no quoted sources, was similar to the ones that appeared in the other newspapers.

7. Nick's general view of himself as an advocate for the community and his role with the local chamber of commerce heavily influence his writing. The next chapter will explore those influences in more detail.

8. Appadurai, "The Capacity to Aspire," 67.

9. Duncan, *Worlds Apart*, 189; Swidler, "Culture in Action."

10. Appadurai, "The Capacity to Aspire," 67; Duncan, *Worlds Apart*.

11. Appadurai, "The Capacity to Aspire," 83.

12. As noted in the preceding chapter, Gregory often included information about his personal life in his newspaper. Interestingly, there were almost as many photos of Gregory in the newspaper (seven) as there were stories that referenced poverty over the six-month study period (November 2013–April 2014).

13. Gregory often used the phrase "we editors" to state the newspaper's opinion on issues, even in his own personal columns. Others at the paper who wrote and/ or edited copy told me Gregory made the decisions about such matters himself.

14. Another columnist featured in that issue of the newspaper had written a column about a couponing class she had attended.

15. Ettema and Peer, "Good News from a Bad Neighborhood," 849–50.

16. The reporter who wrote Dan's profile died in the mid-2000s.

17. Sen, *Development as Freedom*, 20.

18. Mantsios, "Media Magic," 102.

CHAPTER 4: PRESSURES, PHILOSOPHIES, AND THE ENCODING OF MEDIA MESSAGES

1. Donohue, Olien, and Tichenor, "Structure and Constraints on Community Newspaper Gatekeepers."

2. Abernathy, "The Rise of a New Media Baron," 61.

3. Iyengar, "Framing Responsibility for Political Issues," 21–22.

4. It should be noted that the poor are not the only groups with limited media access. Media routines that rely heavily on government sources for information limit the voices of other groups within a community as well. For analysis, see Hopmann and Shehata, "The Contingencies of Ordinary Citizen Appearances in Political Television News."

5. Susan said overtime was discouraged at the *Star*. She said she was routinely sent home early on slow days to account for extra hours she has already worked, or in anticipation of long hours later in the week. The day before I interviewed her, for example, she had worked only four hours in an effort to balance out her timecard.

6. When Bill said "it's been painful," he meant socially, economically, and at times physically. He said he was once physically attacked in his office over a story he wrote about a group of Prior County cockfighters. He said he had been threatened many times over his nearly forty-year journalism career. During one conversation, he recalled a local man who once came into his office with a gun in his hand. The man had sued his own son over a civil issue (Bill could not remember the specifics of the case), and Bill had written a story about it. Bill recalled the encounter this way: "The old man comes up here and he says, 'Did you know that he [the man's son] hadn't even seen that before you made a major story out of that? He hadn't even seen the papers yet!' And I said, 'No, I didn't know, but it doesn't make any difference because what I wrote was the truth.' He said, 'The truth don't enter into this. You're breaking up a family.' What are you going to say? So I just kept talking to him and finally he gave up and left. But I thought I was going to get shot."

7. When I interviewed Priorsville's mayor, he said he felt the *PPE* did take an unnecessarily negative position on the local economy. He was the only person I interviewed who raised that concern about either newspaper in Priorsville.

8. Several people in town, including Gregory, referred to the owner of Deer Creek's largest oil and gas company as "the Local Millionaire" in casual conversation. I reached out to the Local Millionaire, but was unable to get in touch with him. At one point, Gregory suggested that he might be able to arrange a meeting between me and the millionaire, but he was not able to follow through on that suggestion.

9. Gregory was asked if he believed that perception was accurate. His answer: "To some degree. As you know, we can sometimes write until we're blue in the face about an issue and it seems like no progress is ever made. On certain issues, yes, you can really make a difference."

10. This post did not include an author's name, and there is no indication that Lance himself wrote it. A line at the end of the story read: "author and source on file." The practice of withholding bylines was not uncommon at DCA—Lance wrote in another post that he knew the identity of all writers and commenters, but allowed some to write anonymously so that they could speak freely without fear of retribution.

11. Likely because of its size and relative geographic isolation, most people in Deer Creek told me their community rarely receives attention from regional media outlets.

12. Giddens, *The Constitution of Society*, 8.

5. DECODING POVERTY COVERAGE AND BROADER IMAGES OF APPALACHIA

1. Donohue, Olien, and Tichenor, "Structure and Constraints on Community Newspaper Gatekeepers," 810–11.

2. Carson, Priorsville's mayor, was the only interview participant who said poverty was a regular focus of local media, and he thought the newspapers there reported on unemployment specifically in an unfairly negative way: "It seems like they try to make it very negative. When there's a positive side, they try to offset the positive side with negativity." For example, he said the *PPE* had at one time suggested that the local unemployment rate was falling because jobless people were dropping out of the workforce once their unemployment benefits ran out (the story he referenced did not appear in the sample of stories examined for this study). He argued that suggestion was incorrect, and that the real reason the rates were dropping was that the county's population was aging. Of the people interviewed in Priorsville, Carson was the strongest critic of the local newspapers, although he did say that he had a good relationship with both. He also acknowledged that the *PPE*'s Business Spotlight feature was helping to portray the town in a more positive light.

3. Sharon, the chamber of commerce director, was one of those people. Because of her work with local organizations, Sally had a public platform, and she was not shy about using it to express opinions like the ones she shared with me. Sally and Sharon both told me they'd had amicable discussions about whether Sally's vocal position was helping or hurting efforts to improve morale in the community. Both women said they worked well together, but it was clear that neither fully bought into the other's point of view.

4. Stacy and Chad, who ran the store where Stacy worked, were the only people interviewed in Deer Creek who did not know who Gregory was.

5. Residents in Deer Creek said they were rarely covered by the larger metropolitan newspapers or television stations in their area.

6. *Mountain Monsters* first aired on the network Destination America in 2013. According to the network's web site, the program follows "a band of hardcore hunters and trappers native to West Virginia and known as The Appalachian Investigators of Mysterious Sightings" as they search for mythical beasts such as the Devil Dog, Wampus Beast, and Mothman "in the hope of helping local mountain communities rest more easily when night falls and nature comes out to play."

7. Bourdieu, *Distinction*; Hall, "Introduction: Who Needs 'Identity'?"

8. Gaventa, *Power and Powerlessness*, 221.

9. Flora and Flora, "Social Capital," 219–20; Putnam, *Bowling Alone*.

10. Bourdieu, *The Field of Cultural Production*, 133.

6. HOW LOCAL MEDIA'S SILENCE INFLUENCES VIEWS OF POVERTY

1. Duncan, *Worlds Apart*, 116.

2. Gaventa, *Power and Powerlessness*, 220–21.

3. Giddens, *The Constitution of Society*, 11.

4. Bell and York, "Community Economic Identity"; Cunningham, "Sustained Outrage"; Wilson, "Riding the Resource Roller Coaster."

5. Duncan, *Worlds Apart*; Schulman and Anderson, "The Dark Side of Social Capital."

6. Duncan, *Worlds Apart*.

7. Gaventa, *Power and Powerlessness*; Ali and Saunders, "The Career Aspirations of Rural Appalachian High School Students"; Bennett deMarrais, "Urban Appalachian Children"; Hansen and Cooke-Jackson, "Hillbilly Stereotypes and Humor."

8. Rao and Sanyal, "Dignity Through Discourse," 160.

9. Ibid., 163.

10. One key line in that quote is "especially if they're getting additional resources." Few newspapers are getting additional resources; most (including all four of the newspapers examined in this study) are instead trying to do their jobs with *fewer* resources as advertising revenues and circulations decline. The recommendations made in Appendix B take those financial challenges into account and attempt to provide a framework for positive change that could be instituted without a great deal of expense.

11. William Isom, interview with author, January 6, 2017.

12. Ibid.

13. Professional socialization is a possible explanation for the similarity. Theresa, the editor of GreenburgToday.com, had a bachelor's degree in communications and was a former reporter at a newspaper owned by Henderson Media, which also owned the *Greenburg Star*.

14. Chua, "Why Do Virtual Communities Regulate Speech?"

15. Parks, "Social Network Sites as Virtual Communities"; Blanchard, "Developing a Sense of Virtual Community Measure."

16. Meyer and Carey, "In Moderation."

17. Local radio stations in Greenburg and Priorsville did not have strong news presences. Deer Creek did not have a local radio station.

18. Zickuhr and Smith, "Home Broadband 2013."

19. National Telecommunications and Information Administration, "Broadband Statistics Report."

20. Connect Ohio, "Technology Barriers and Adoption in Rural Appalachian Ohio."

21. Feran, "More in Ohio Can Get High-Speed Internet."

22. Putnam, *Bowling Alone*, 410.

23. Hall, "Introduction: Who Needs 'Identity'?" 4.

24. Hall, "The Local and the Global," 174.

25. Carey, "Expression of Culture in the Amish Press"; Rose, "For the Record"; Sreberny, "Media and Diasporic Consciousness."

26. Speer, "From Stereotype to Regional Hype," 15.

27. Ibid., 17

28. See Tickamyer, "Space Matters!"

29. Newcomb, "Appalachia on Television," 328.

30. Ibid.

31. Lauterer, *Community Journalism*, 25.

32. Heider, "Epilogue," 338–43.

33. Gaining access to most of the publishers, editors, and reporters interviewed for this study seemed to be fairly easy in most cases, if you could visit their offices during working hours. Nick, the editor of the *PPE*, Sandra, the editor of the *Star*, and Gregory, the editor of the *Deer Creek Chronicle*, worked in offices right off their newspapers' lobbies. During my later visits, I would enter the *Chronicle* building (a house converted into an office) and go straight to Gregory's office without even checking in at the front desk. Occasionally, Gregory would answer the phone when I called the *Chronicle*'s main line.

34. Steiner, "Finding Community in Nineteenth Century Suffrage Periodicals"; Novek, "'Heaven, Hell, and Here.'"

35. Carey, *Communication as Culture*.

36. Putnam, *Bowling Alone*, 22–23.

37. Flora and Flora, "Social Capital"; Putnam, *Bowling Alone*.

APPENDIX A: RESEARCH METHODOLOGY

1. Strauss and Corbin, *Basics of Qualitative Research*, 65.

2. Riffe, Lacy, and Fico, *Analyzing Media Messages*, 131.

3. Lindlof and Taylor, *Qualitative Communication Research Methods*, 285.

4. Bourdieu, "Understanding," 609.

5. The process of objectification of interview subjects is not the exclusive terrain of the social scientist; journalists may be guilty as well. In "The View from the Media," Patrick Champagne made the following observation about residents of the Vaulx-en-Velin suburbs in Paris, who were regular subjects of news stories about violent outbreaks in the early 1990s: "These districts are presented as insalubrious and sinister, their residents as delinquents. . . . This journalistic vision of the suburbs is strongly rejected by a small section of the population of these districts, generally the most politicized or the most militant, and arouses their indignation. . . . Still, most of the inhabitants, notably because they are culturally deprived, take to heart the vision of themselves produced by these interested and somewhat voyeuristic spectators that journalists necessarily are ('it's a ghetto here,' 'we don't count for anything,' etc.)" (55).

6. Bourdieu, "Understanding," 610.

APPENDIX B: ACTION STEPS FOR JOURNALISTS

1. Iyengar, "Framing Responsibility for Political Issues, 21–24.

2. Peggy Holman, interview by author, January 10, 2017.

3. Lauterer, *Community Journalism*, 26.

4. Bansal and Martin, "The Solutions Journalism Toolkit," 12. The Solutions Journalism Network offers a great deal of useful reporting advice on its web site, http://solutionsjournalism.org/.

5. Steiner, "Finding Community in Nineteenth Century Suffrage Periodicals," 1; Robinson, "Women, Media, and the Dialectics of Resistance."

6. Grisham and Gurwitt, *Hand in Hand*, 14. The case study of Tupelo laid out in *Hand in Hand* is instructive for those in the fields of both community development and journalism.

7. Ibid., 15–16.

8. Ibid., 18.

9. Ibid., 25.

10. Ibid., 27.

11. Ibid., 62.

12. Peter Hille, interview by author, January 4, 2017. Hille said he often discusses Tupelo, and McLean, when he talks to communities about local economic development approaches.

13. Kovach and Rosenstiel, *The Elements of Journalism*.

14. Holman, interview.

15. Ibid.

16. Dee Davis, interview by author, January 5, 2017.

17. Ibid.; Marema, "Editor's Note."

Bibliography

Abernathy, Penelope Muse. "The Rise of a New Media Baron and the Emerging Threat of News Deserts." Center for Innovation and Sustainability in Local Media, University of North Carolina. http://newspaperownership.com/wp-content/uploads/2016/09/07. UNC_RiseOfNewMediaBaron_SinglePage_01Sep2016-REDUCED.pdf.

Ali, Saba Rasheed, and Jodi L. Saunders. "The Career Aspirations of Rural Appalachian High School Students." *Journal of Career Assessment* 17, no. 2 (May 2009): 172–88.

Appadurai, Arjun. "The Capacity to Aspire: Culture and the Terms of Recognition." In *Culture and Public Action*, edited by Vijayendra Rao and Michael Walton, 59–84. Stanford, CA: Stanford University Press, 2004.

Appalachian Regional Commission. "Source & Methodology: Distressed Designation and County Economic Status Classification System, FY 2007–FY 2014." Appalachian Regional Commission. www.arc.gov/research/SourceandMethodologyCountyEconomicStatusFY2007FY2014.asp.

Auyero, Javier, and Débora Alejandra Swistun. *Flammable: Environmental Suffering in an Argentine Shantytown*. New York: Oxford University Press, 1999.

Bachrach, Peter, and Morton S. Baratz. *Power and Poverty: Theory and Practice*. New York: Oxford University Press, 1970.

Bansal, Sarika, and Courtney Martin. "The Solutions Journalism Toolkit." Solutions Journalism Network. http://solutionsjournalism.org/wp-content/uploads/2015/01/FINAL-Journalism-Toolkit-singles.pdf.

Bell, Shannon Elizabeth, and Richard York. "Community Economic Identity: The Coal Industry and Ideology Construction in West Virginia." *Rural Sociology* 75, no. 1 (March 2010): 111–43.

Bennett deMarrais, Kathleen. "Urban Appalachian Children: An 'Invisible Minority' in City Schools." In *Invisible Children in the Society and Its Schools*, edited by Sue Brooks, 89–110. Mahwah, NJ: Lawrence Erlbaum, 1998.

Benson, Rodney. "News Media as a 'Journalistic Field': What Bourdieu Adds to New Institutionalism, and Vice Versa." *Political Communication* 23, no. 2 (2006): 187–202.

Berger, Peter L., and Thomas Luckmann. *The Social Construction of Reality: A Treatise in the Sociology of Knowledge*. New York: Anchor Books, 1966.

Blanchard, Anita L. "Developing a Sense of Virtual Community Measure."
CyberPsychology & Behavior 10, no. 6 (2007): 827–30.

Bourdieu, Pierre. *Distinction: A Social Critique of the Judgment of Taste.*
Cambridge, MA: Harvard University Press, 1984.

———. *The Field of Cultural Production.* New York: Columbia University
Press, 1993.

———. *Language and Symbolic Power.* Cambridge, MA: Harvard University
Press, 1991.

———. "Understanding." In *The Weight of the World: Social Suffering in
Contemporary Society* by Pierre Bourdieu et al., 607–26. Cambridge:
Polity Press, 1999.

Bourdieu, Pierre, and Loïc J. D. Wacquant. *An Invitation to Reflexive
Sociology.* Chicago: University of Chicago Press, 1992.

Bowler, Betty Miller. "'That Ribbon of Social Neglect': Appalachia and the
Media in 1964." *Appalachian Journal* 12, no. 3 (Spring 1985): 239–47.

Buffington, Mike. "'Our Job Isn't to Build Communities.'" *ISWNE: The
International Society of Weekly Newspaper Editors* 40, no. 5 (August
2015): 11–13.

Carey, James W. *Communication as Culture.* 2nd ed. New York: Routledge,
2009.

Carey, Michael Clay. "Expression of Culture in the Amish Press: Media and
Community Maintenance in a Religious Diaspora." *Journalism &
Communication Monographs* 18, no. 3 (August 2016): 112–57.

———. "Universal Invitations and Inexhaustible Resources: Portrayals of
Rural Life in Popular Magazines of the Late 1800s." Paper presented at
the annual meeting of the Association for Education in Journalism and
Mass Communication, Washington, DC, August 10, 2015.

Champagne, Patrick. "The View from the Media." In *The Weight of the
World: Social Suffering in Contemporary Society* by Pierre Bourdieu et al.,
46–59. Cambridge: Polity Press, 1999.

Chua, Cecil Eng Huang. "Why Do Virtual Communities Regulate Speech?"
Communication Monographs 76, no. 2 (2009): 234–61.

Colistra, Rita. "The Rumble and the Dark: Regional Newspaper Framing of
the Buffalo Creek Mine Disaster of 1972." *Journal of Appalachian Studies*
16, no. 1/2 (2010): 79–100.

Connect Ohio. "Technology Barriers and Adoption in Rural Appalachian
Ohio." http://connectohio.org/sites/default/files/connected-nation/Ohio/
images/oh_adoption_barriers_final_12022011.pdf.

Cover, Rob. "Community Print Media: Perceiving Minority Community in
Multicultural South Australia." *Continuum: Journal of Media & Cultural
Studies* 27, no. 1 (February 2013): 110–23.

Cunningham, Brent. "Sustained Outrage." *Columbia Journalism Review* 50,
no. 4 (November/December 2011): 90–94.

Curran, James. "What Democracy Requires of the Media." In *The Press,*
edited by Geneva Overholser and Kathleen Hall Jamieson, 120–40. New
York: Oxford University Press, 2005.

Dean, Walter. "The Journalist as a 'Committed Observer.'" American Press Institute. www.americanpressinstitute.org/journalism-essentials/what-is-journalism/journalist-committed-observer.

Donohue, George A., Clarice N. Olien, and Phillip J. Tichenor. "Structure and Constraints on Community Newspaper Gatekeepers." *Journalism Quarterly* 66, no. 4 (Winter 1989): 807–12.

Duncan, Cynthia. "Understanding Persistent Poverty: Social Class Context in Rural Communities." *Rural Sociology* 61, no. 1 (March 1996): 103–24.

———. *Worlds Apart: Why Poverty Persists in Rural America*. New Haven: Yale University Press, 1999.

Duncan, Cynthia, and Nita Lamborghini. "Poverty and Social Context in Remote Rural Communities." *Rural Sociology* 59, no. 3 (September 1994): 437–61.

Dyer, Richard. *The Matter of Images*. New York: Routledge, 1993.

———. "Stereotyping." In *Media and Cultural Studies: Key Works*, 2nd ed., edited by Meenakshi Gigi Durham and Douglas M. Kellner, 275–82. Malden, MA: John Wiley & Sons, 2012.

Eckstein, Susan. "Community as Gift-Giving: Collective Roots of Volunteerism." *American Sociological Review* 66, no. 6 (December 2001): 829–51.

Eller, Ronald D. *Uneven Ground: Appalachia Since 1945*. Lexington: University of Kentucky Press, 2008.

Entman, Robert M. "Framing: Toward a Clarification of a Fractured Paradigm." *Journal of Communication* 43, no. 4 (December 1993): 51–58.

Ettema, James S., and Limor Peer. "Good News from a Bad Neighborhood: Toward an Alternative to the Discourse of Urban Pathology." *Journalism & Mass Communication Quarterly* 73, no. 4 (Winter 1996): 835–56.

Ewick, Patricia, and Susan Silbey. "Narrating Social Structure: Stories of Resistance to Legal Authority." *American Journal of Sociology* 108, no. 6 (May 2003): 1328–72.

Feran, Tim. "More in Ohio Can Get High-Speed Internet." *Columbus Dispatch*, June 7, 2014. http://www.dispatch.com/content/stories/business/ 2014/06/07/more-in-ohio-can-get-high-speed-internet.html.

Flora, Cornelia Butler, and Jan L. Flora. "Social Capital." In *Challenges for Rural America in the Twenty-First Century*, edited by David L. Brown and Louis E. Swanson, 214–27. University Park: The Pennsylvania State University Press, 2003.

Frank, Russell. "When Bad Things Happen in Good Places: Pastoralism in Big-City Newspaper Coverage of Small-Town Violence." *Rural Sociology* 68, no. 2 (Spring 2003): 207–30.

Gans, Herbert. *Deciding What's News: A Study of CBS Evening News, NBC Nightly News, Newsweek, and Time*. New York: Pantheon Books, 1979.

Gaventa, John. *Power and Powerlessness: Quiescence and Rebellion in an Appalachian Valley*. Urbana: University of Illinois Press, 1980.

Giddens, Anthony. *The Constitution of Society*. Berkeley: University of California Press, 1984.

Gilens, Martin. *Why Americans Hate Welfare: Race, Media and the Politics of Antipoverty Policy*. Chicago: University of Chicago Press, 1999.

Grisham, Vaughn, and Rob Gurwitt. "Hand in Hand: Community and Economic Development in Tupelo." The Aspen Institute. https://assets. aspeninstitute.org/content/uploads/files/content/docs/pubs/Tupelo_0. pdf.

Guenther, Katja M. "The Politics of Names: Rethinking the Methodological and Ethical Significance of Naming People, Organizations, and Places." *Qualitative Research* 9, no. 4 (September 2009): 411–21.

Hall, Stuart. "Encoding/Decoding." In *Culture, Media, Language: Working Papers in Cultural Studies, 1972–79*, edited by Stuart Hall, Dorothy Hobson, Andrew Love, and Paul Willis, 128–38. London: Hutchinson, 1980.

———. "Introduction: Who Needs 'Identity'?" In *Questions of Cultural Identity*, edited by Stuart Hall and Paul du Gay, 1–17. London: Sage, 1996.

———. "The Local and the Global: Globalization and Ethnicity." In *Dangerous Liaisons: Gender, Nation, and Postcolonial Perspectives*, edited by Anne McClintock, Aamir Mufti, and Ella Shohat, 173–87. Minneapolis: University of Minnesota Press, 1997.

———. "Signification, Representation, Ideology: Althusser and the Post-structuralist Debates." *Critical Studies in Mass Communication* 2, no. 2 (June 1985): 91–114.

Hancock, Ange-Marie. *The Politics of Disgust: The Public Identity of the Welfare Queen*. New York: New York University Press, 2004.

Hansen, Elizabeth K., and Angela F. Cooke-Jackson. "Hillbilly Stereotypes and Humor: Entertaining Ourselves at the Expense of the Other." In *Ethics and Entertainment: Essays on Media Culture and Media Morality*, edited by Sandra Borden and Howard Good, 263–80. Jefferson, NC: McFarland and Company.

Harry, Joseph C. "'Trailer Park Trash': News, Ideology, and Depictions of the American Underclass." In *Class and News*, edited by Don Heider, 213–39. Lanham, MD: Rowman & Littlefield, 2004.

Hatcher, John A. "Were Those the Days? Revisiting the Pulitzer-Winning Efforts of Community Newspapers in the 1970s." *American Journalism* 24, no. 1 (Winter 2007): 89–109.

Heider, Don. "Epilogue." In *Class and News*, edited by Don Heider, 338–43. Lanham, MD: Rowman & Littlefield, 2004.

Hopmann, David Nicolas, and Adam Shehata. "The Contingencies of Ordinary Citizen Appearances in Political Television News." *Journalism Practice* 5, no. 6 (2011): 657–71.

Hull, Dana. "Beacon of Light: An Ambitious, Award-Winning Weekly Gets a New Owner." *American Journalism Review* 28, no. 1 (February/March 2006): 12–13.

Iyengar, Shanto. "Framing Responsibility for Political Issues: The Case of Poverty." *Political Behavior* 12, no. 1 (March 1990): 19–40.

Janowitz, Morris. *The Community Press in an Urban Setting: The Social Elements of Urbanism.* 2nd ed. Chicago: University of Chicago Press, 1967.

Kama, Amit. "The Quest for Inclusion: Jewish-Israeli Gay Men's Perceptions of Gays in the Media." *Feminist Media Studies* 2, no. 2 (2002): 195–212.

Kendall, Diana Elizabeth. *Framing Class: Media Representations of Wealth and Poverty in America.* Lanham, MD: Rowman & Littlefield, 2011.

Kitch, Carolyn. "Mourning 'Men Joined in Peril and Purpose': Working-Class Heroism in News Repair of the Sago Miners' Story." *Critical Studies in Media Communication* 24, no. 2 (June 2007): 115–31.

Kovach, Bill, and Tom Rosenstiel. *The Elements of Journalism: What Newspeople Should Know and the Public Should Expect.* 2nd ed. New York: Three Rivers Press, 2007.

Lasorsa, Dominic, and Jia Dai. "When News Reporters Deceive: The Production of Stereotypes." *Journalism & Mass Communication Quarterly* 84, no. 2 (Summer 2007): 281–98.

Lauterer, Jock. *Community Journalism: Relentlessly Local.* 3rd ed. Chapel Hill: University of North Carolina Press, 2006.

Ledford, Katherine. "A Landscape and a People Set Apart: Narratives of Exploration and Travel in Early Appalachia." In *Confronting Appalachian Stereotypes: Back Talk from an American Region,* edited by Dwight B. Billings, Gurney Norman, and Katherine Ledford, 47–66. Lexington: University of Kentucky Press, 1999.

Lewis, Ronald L. "Beyond Isolation and Homogeneity: Diversity and the History of Appalachia." In *Confronting Appalachian Stereotypes: Back Talk from an American Region,* edited by Dwight B. Billings, Gurney Norman, and Katherine Ledford, 21–43. Lexington: University of Kentucky Press, 1999.

Lindlof, Thomas R., and Brian C. Taylor, *Qualitative Communication Research Methods.* 3rd ed. Thousand Oaks, CA: Sage, 2011.

Lippmann, Walter. *Public Opinion.* New York: Harcourt, Brace, and Company, 1922.

Lowrey, Wilson, Amanda Brozana, and Jenn B. Mackay. "Toward a Measure of Community Journalism." *Mass Communication and Society* 11, no. 3 (Summer 2008): 275–99.

Maggard, Sally Ward. "Cultural Hegemony: The News Media and Appalachia." *Appalachian Journal* 11, no. 1/2 (Autumn/Winter 1983–84): 67–83.

Mantsios, Gregory. "Media Magic: Making Class Invisible." In *Privilege: A Reader,* edited by Michael S. Kimmell and Abby L. Ferber, 99–109. Boulder, CO: Westview, 2003.

Marema, Tim. "Editor's Note: One Newspaper at a Time." *Daily Yonder,* November 25, 2014. http://www.dailyyonder.com/rural-news-one-newspaper-time/2014/11/25/7627/.

Marwell, Nicole P. "Privatizing the Welfare State: Nonprofit Community-Based Organizations as Political Actors. *American Sociological Review* 69, no. 2 (April 2004): 265–91.

McCloud, Sean. "From Exotics to Brainwashers: Portraying New Religions in Mass Media." *Religion Compass* 1, no. 1 (January 2007): 214–28.

Merskin, Debra. "The S-Word: Discourse, Stereotypes, and the American Indian Woman." *The Howard Journal of Communication* 21, no. 4 (October 2010): 345–66.

Meyer, Hans K., and Michael Clay Carey. "In Moderation: Examining How Journalists' Attitudes Toward Comments Affect Participation and the Creation of Community." *Journalism Practice* 8, no. 2 (2014): 213–28.

National Telecommunications and Information Administration. "Broadband Statistics Report." http://www.broadbandmap.gov/download/Broadband%20Availability%20in%20Rural%20vs%20Urban%20Areas.pdf.

Newcomb, Horace. "Appalachia on Television: Region as Symbol in American Popular Culture." In *Appalachian Images in Folk and Popular Culture,* edited by W. K. McNeil, 315–29. Knoxville: The University of Tennessee Press, 1995.

Novek, Eleanor M. "'Heaven, Hell, and Here': Understanding the Impact of Incarceration Through a Prison Newspaper." *Critical Studies in Media Communication* 22, no. 4 (October 2005): 281–301.

Parks, Malcolm. "Social Network Sites as Virtual Communities." In *A Networked Self: Identity, Community and Culture on Social Network Sites,* edited by Zizi Papacharissi, 105–23. New York: Routledge, 2011.

Peterson, Theodore. *Magazines in the Twentieth Century.* 2nd ed. Urbana: University of Illinois Press, 1964.

Precourt, Walter. "The Image of Appalachian Poverty." In *Appalachia and America: Autonomy and Regional Dependence,* edited by Allen Batteau, 86–110. Lexington: University of Kentucky Press, 1983.

Putnam, Robert D. *Bowling Alone: The Collapse and Revival of American Community.* New York: Touchstone, 2000.

Rao, Vijayendra, and Paromita Sanyal. "Dignity Through Discourse: Poverty and the Culture of Deliberation in Indian Village Democracies." *The Annals of the American Academy of Political and Social Sciences* 629, no. 1 (May 2010): 146–72.

Reader, Bill. "Community Journalism: A Concept of Connectedness." In *Foundations of Community Journalism,* edited by Bill Reader and John A. Hatcher, 3–20. London: Sage, 2012.

———. "Distinctions That Matter: Ethical Differences at Large and Small Newspapers." *Journalism & Mass Communication Quarterly* 83, no. 4 (December 2006): 851–64.

Reed, Jennifer. "Lesbian Television Personalities—A Queer New Subject." *The Journal of American Culture* 32, no. 4 (December 2009): 307–17.

Rendleman, Todd. "'I Know Y'all Think I'm Pretty Square, but Tuh, I Believe What I Believe': Images of Evangelicals in American Film." *Journal of Media and Religion* 7, no. 4 (October 2008): 271–91.

Richards-Schuster, Katie, and Rebecca O'Doherty. "Appalachian Youth Re-envisioning Home, Re-making Identities." In *Transforming Places: Lessons from Appalachia*, edited by Stephen L. Fisher and Barbara Ellen Smith, 78–91. Urbana: University of Illinois Press, 2012.

Riffe, Daniel, Stephen Lacy, and Frederick G. Fico. *Analyzing Media Messages: Using Quantitative Content Analysis in Research*. Mahwah, NJ: Lawrence Erlbaum, 1998.

Robinson, Lillian S. "Women, Media, and the Dialectics of Resistance." In *Class, Race and Sex: The Dynamics of Control*, edited by Amy Swerdlow, Hanna Lessinger, and Johanna Lessinger, 308–24. Boston: G. K. Hall, 1983.

Rose, Michael, ed. *For the Record: 160 Years of Aboriginal Print Journalism*. St. Leonards, NSW: Allen & Unwin, 1996.

Scheufele, Dietram, and David Tewksbury. "Framing, Agenda Setting, and Priming: The Evolution of Three Media Effects Models." *Journal of Communication* 57, no. 1 (March 2007): 9–20.

Schulman, Michael D., and Cynthia Anderson. "The Dark Side of Social Capital: A Case Study of Restructuring and Social Capital." *Rural Sociology* 64, no. 3 (September 1999): 351–72.

Scott, Ellen K. "Beyond Tokenism: The Making of Racially Diverse Feminist Organizations." *Social Problems* 52, no. 2 (May 2005): 232–54.

Scott, Rebecca R. "The Sociology of Coal Hollow: Safety, Othering, and Representations of Inequality." *Journal of Appalachian Studies* 15, no. 1/2 (Spring/Fall 2009): 7–25.

Seiter, Ellen. "Stereotypes and the Media: A Re-evaluation." *Journal of Communication* 36, no. 2 (June 1986): 14–26.

Sen, Amartya. *Development as Freedom*. New York: Anchor Books, 1999.

Shaker, Lee. "Community Newspapers Play Significant Role in Election." *Newspaper Research Journal* 32, no. 1 (Winter 2011): 6–18.

Shelby, Anne. "The 'R' Word: What's So Funny (and Not So Funny) About Redneck Jokes." In *Confronting Appalachian Stereotypes: Back Talk from an American Region*, edited by Dwight B. Billings, Gurney Norman, and Katherine Ledford, 153–60. Lexington: University Press of Kentucky, 1999.

Shilling, Chris. "Reconceptualising Structure and Agency in the Sociology of Education: Structuration Theory and Schooling." *British Journal of Sociology of Education* 13, no. 1 (March 1992): 69–84.

Shuford, Chuck. "What Happens When You Don't Own the Land." *Daily Yonder*, www.dailyyonder.com/what-happens-when-you-dont-own-the-land/2009/07/03/2205.

Speer, Jean Haskell. "From Stereotype to Regional Hype: Strategies for Changing Media Portrayals of Appalachia." *Journal of the Appalachian Studies Association* 5 (1993): 12–19.

Sreberny, Annabelle. "Media and Diasporic Consciousness: An Exploration among Iranians in London." In *Ethnic Minorities and the Media*, edited by Simon Cottle, 179–96. Philadelphia: Open University Press, 2000.

Steiner, Linda. "Finding Community in Nineteenth Century Suffrage Periodicals." *Journalism History* 1, no. 1 (Summer 1983): 1–15.

———. "Oppositional Decoding as an Act of Resistance." *Critical Studies in Mass Communication* 5, no. 1 (March 1988): 1–15.

Strauss, Anselm, and Juliet Corbin. *Basics of Qualitative Research: Grounded Theory Procedures and Techniques*. London: Sage, 1990.

Straw, Richard. "Appalachian History." In *A Handbook to Appalachia: An Introduction to the Region*, edited by Grace Toney Edwards, JoAnn Aust Asbury, and Ricky L. Cox, 1–26. Knoxville: University of Tennessee Press, 2006.

Swidler, Ann. "Culture in Action: Symbols and Strategies." *American Sociological Review* 51, no. 2 (April 1986): 273–86.

Terry, Thomas C. "Community Journalism Provides Model for Future." *Newspaper Research Journal* 32, no. 1 (Winter 2011): 71–83.

Tickamyer, Ann R. "Space Matters! Spatial Inequality in Future Sociology." *Contemporary Sociology* 29, no. 6 (November 2000): 805–13.

Vidich, Arthur J., and Joseph Bensma. *Small Towns in Mass Society: Class, Power and Religion in a Rural Community*. Princeton: Princeton University Press, 1968.

Viswanath, Kasisomayjula, and Pamela Arora. "Ethnic Media in the United States: An Essay on Their Role in Integration, Assimilation, and Social Control." *Mass Communication and Society* 3, no. 1 (Winter 2000): 39–56.

Walker, Maxine, Helen M. Lewis, Clare McBrien, and Carroll L. Wessinger. "'It Has to Come from the People': Responding to Plant Closings in Ivanhoe, Virginia." In *Communities in Economic Crisis: Appalachia and the South*, edited by John Gaventa, Barbara Ellen Smith, and Alex Willingham, 19–28. Philadelphia: Temple University Press, 1990.

Walls, David S., and Dwight B. Billings. "The Sociology of Southern Appalachia." *Appalachian Journal* 5 (Autumn 1977): 131–44.

Westerfelhaus, Robert, and Celeste Lacroix. "Seeing 'Straight' Through Queer Eye: Exposing the Strategic Rhetoric of Heteronormativity in a Mediated Ritual of Gay Rebellion." *Critical Studies in Media Communication* 23, no. 5 (December 2006): 426–44.

Wheatley, Margaret J., and Myron Kellner-Rogers. "The Paradox and Promise of Community." In *The Community of the Future*, edited by Frances Hesselbein, Myron Goldsmith, Richard Beckhard, and Richard F. Schubert, 9–18. New York: The Peter F. Drucker Foundation for Nonprofit Management, 1998.

Williamson, Kevin D. "The White Ghetto." *National Review Online*, January 14, 2014. www.nationalreview.com/article/367903/white-ghetto-kevin-d -williamson.

Williamson, Rosemary. "Australian Special-Interest Magazines: A Case Study in Community Formation and Survival." *Media International Australia, Incorporating Culture & Policy* 150 (February 2014): 122–29.

Wilson, Lisa J. "Riding the Resource Roller Coaster: Understanding Socioeconomic Differences between Mining Communities." *Rural Sociology* 69, no. 2 (June 2004): 261–81.

Wotanis, Lindsay Lee. "Community Journalism as Ritual: A Case Study of Community and Weekly Newspapers in Laurel, Maryland." PhD diss., University of Maryland, 2011.

Wray, Matt. *Not Quite White: White Trash and the Boundaries of Whiteness.* Durham, NC: Duke University Press, 2006.

Zickuhr, Kathryn, and Aaron Smith. "Home Broadband 2013." Pew Research Center's Internet and American Life Project. http://www.pewinternet. org/2013/08/26/home-broadband-2013.

Index

CPSIA information can be obtained
at www.ICGtesting.com
Printed in the USA
FSHW01n1250250818
51531FS